AMERICA AND THE NEW ETHNICITY

Kennikat Press
National University Publications
Interdisciplinary Urban Series

General Editor
Raymond A. Mohl

AMERICA
AND THE
NEW ETHNICITY

edited and with an introduction by

DAVID R. COLBURN and **GEORGE E. POZZETTA**

National University Publications
KENNIKAT PRESS // 1979
Port Washington, N.Y. // London

Manufactured in the United States of America

Published by
Kennikat Press Corp.
Port Washington, N. Y. / London

Library of Congress Cataloging in Publication Data
Main entry under title:

America and the new ethnicity.

(National university publications)
Bibliography: p.
Includes index.
1. Minorities–United States–Addresses, essays, lectures. 2. United States–Race relations–Addresses, essays, lectures. 3. Ethnicity–Addresses, essays, lectures. I. Colburn, David R. II. Pozzetta, George E.
E184.A1A495   301.45'0973   78-25912
ISBN 0-8046-9222-X (Hardcover)
ISBN 0-8046-9246-7 (Paper)

Dedicated to our parents
Rosemary Colburn and the memory of Earle Colburn, Jr.
and
Attilio and Mary Pozzetta

Contents

Preface

Like so many other anthologies, this volume was born of classroom need. While teaching a variety of courses dealing with the urban and immigrant past in America, we were frequently confronted with the necessity of locating materials to cover the recent resurgence of ethnic awareness in this country. The sources we found were widely scattered and difficult to bring together for student use. After talking with colleagues here and at other universities, we recognized that a wider need existed. Conversations with many friends yielded suggestions for articles to appear in this volume. We would especially like to thank Professor Louis A. Perez, Jr., of the University of South Florida, George E. Mowry of the University of North Carolina at Chapel Hill, and Lester Lamon of the University of Indiana at South Bend for their generous help. Raymond Mohl of Florida Atlantic University proved to be a source of encouragement and aid beyond the usual definition of editor; we are both in his debt. A last vote of thanks goes to our typist, Mrs. Adrienne Turner, who maintained her insistence on perfection despite our best efforts to thwart her designs.

David R. Colburn
George E. Pozzetta

University of Florida
Gainesville
August, 1977

AMERICA AND THE NEW ETHNICITY

Introduction

During the past two decades America's ethnic groups, which for years had confidently been expected to slip quietly into the mainstream of American society, have loudly, and proudly, proclaimed the fact that they have not yet merged. Indeed, many of America's minorities have found renewed relevance and comfort in asserting their separate ethnic identities. As historian Rudolph Vecoli phrased it, "The ethnics have found their voice; they will be heard." This resurgence of ethnic awareness has sent many Americans scrambling for explanations. Where could these impulses have come from? Why have these groups failed to lose completely their age-old customs and values? Has not the much vaunted "melting pot" worked? What is clear is that the ethnic reawakening of the 1960s and 1970s must be understood against the backdrop of America's ethnic past. It is this mosaic which makes the happenings of today comprehensible.

Since 1607, when the English first settled in America, approximately 37 million people from every corner of the earth have freely migrated to the "promised land." An incredible diversity of peoples, languages, cultures, and values found their new homes in America. In these respects, the American experience stands as unique in the world. Most Latin American nations have been populated by people from Portugal, Spain, Italy, and Germany; Australia and Canada were settled largely by Englishmen. Even Russia, with its extremely heterogeneous population, often acquired its people by conquest rather than by voluntary migration. Nothing quite like the American experience has happened in the history of the world.

For many years observers assumed that immigrants came to America simply to find sanctuary from the oppressiveness of European society. Catholics, Jews, and some Protestants migrated, for example, to avoid religious persecution. Others sought to escape wars, political repression, and the poverty of their homeland. It also seems, however, that many immigrants chose America as much because it was seen as a land of opportunity as because it offered refuge. Immigrants perceived it as a place where they could carve out a prosperous life for themselves and their families no matter what their station in life. Some "immigrants," of course, did not come voluntarily. Defeated in battle or captured by bands of slave catchers, millions of black Africans were herded aboard ships to be enslaved in America.

Whatever their reasons for coming to America, almost from the first there has been pressure applied on immigrants to cast off their foreign ways and embrace Anglo-American institutions, culture, and language. John Adams had this imperative clearly in mind when he wrote: "They come to life of labor and, if they cannot accommodate themselves to the character, moral, political, and physical, of this country with all its compensatory balances of good and evil, the Atlantic is always open to them to return to the land of their nativity and their fathers.... They must cast off the European skin, never to resume it." To many it seemed that the American environment possessed an almost magical ability to transform the immigrant just as Adams desired. Writing nearly two hundred years ago, the French nobleman J. Hector St. John de Crèvecoeur graphically described the process of the American melting pot. "Here individuals of all nations are melted into a new race of men," he claimed. "I could point out to you a family whose grandfather was an Englishman, whose wife was Dutch, whose son married a French woman, and whose present four sons have now four wives of different nations." The product of this constant intermingling, he said, was "an American."

Perhaps because many Americans felt that the transforming process was inevitable, there was relatively little external pressure on immigrants to conform until the mid-nineteenth century. Two of the most sizable non-English groups present were Germans and Scandinavians, many of whom had settled on the frontier and engaged in farming. America generally was critically short of all types of labor, and consequently it was happy to receive migrants from Europe and elsewhere. In addition, the presence of a large expanse of unsettled territory led many to believe that this new nation could accommodate hosts of newcomers without disrupting the country's institutions.

Nevertheless, the ability of Americans to embrace an institution like slavery, while at the same time espousing democratic and Judeo-

Christian principles, portended serious problems for non-Anglo-Saxon immigrants. There existed a basic dichotomy in the American psyche—a division between national purpose (the American Dream) and individual attitudes. For subsequent southern and eastern European and Asian immigrants, this meant that America was at once a "land of opportunity," envisioned as such by its natives, and a country where economic, social, and political barriers could be created to block the promised opportunity.

By the 1850s, for the first time, Americans began to question seriously the nation's ability to assimilate all ethnic groups. The focus of this concern was the massive Irish immigration arriving from 1830 to 1860. Frustrated by England's political control which left them landless, stifled by the development of a factory system, and suppressed for their religious beliefs, the Irish were a discontented people. When the potato blight of the late 1840s confronted them with the bleak prospect of starvation, nearly four million decided it was time to leave the homeland.

Apparently tired of farming and the economic suffering that accompanied it and too poor to move inland, they settled in the coastal cities, causing overcrowding and severe social problems. Native Americans feared that their country was becoming overpopulated with these undesirable additions. Poverty, it seemed, was endemic to these immigrants, and the inclusion of such large numbers of them would strain beyond the breaking point the nation's almshouses and charitable institutions. Questions centering on the allegedly low moral character of the Irish also quickened the heartbeat of natives. Could the nation survive such an infusion of people addicted to strong drink, fighting, and general loose living, they asked?

The major nativist criticism of the Irish, however, involved the powerful religious preferences that these immigrants brought with them to the new world. The Irish were devout Roman Catholics who quickly established parishes as they settled principally in urban America. Many Protestant Americans reacted with shock and indignation, convinced that they could not coexist with a vigorous, even aggressive Catholic Church. Some were convinced that the Irish, operating under orders from Rome, would try to subvert Protestantism in America.

Confronted by religious intolerance and stereotyped as intoxicated malcontents, the Irish had difficulty finding their way into the melting pot. Signs declaring "No Irish need apply" were conspicuous in factory windows. Reacting violently to fears of a Catholic invasion, a nativist mob burned the Ursuline Convent near Boston in 1834. On the wider American scene, nativist concerns coalesced into the Know-Nothing movement which denounced Catholicism and the immigrant. Established in the early 1850s, the Know-Nothing party called on the public to recommit itself to the "principle of nationality."

These powerful social forces were overshadowed later in the decade by the even more divisive issues surrounding slavery and the sectional controversy. The Civil War, Reconstruction, and the dramatic postwar industrial expansion did not erase concerns centered on immigrant assimilation, but they did push them temporarily beneath the level of immediate public visibility. Nativism tended to languish as jobs went begging for workers and new lands were opened for settlement in the West. Except for hate campaigns directed against the Chinese in the West, the two decades after the Civil War saw no major challenge to the open immigration policy of America. For a short time America could slip comfortably back into its belief that all diversity would one day disappear as each ethnic group in its turn was digested into the body politic.

This view was not to last long. The industrial revolution overtaking America in the latter part of the 19th century brought with it a massive infusion of so-called "New Immigrants." These newcomers, primarily southern and southeastern Europeans, seemed far removed from the common core of American values, and to many it seemed that they would never assimilate. They prompted a wide range of concerns throughout practically all levels of society. Organized labor, for example, feared that the newly arrived immigrants were undermining their hard-won gains by accepting substandard wages and unsafe working conditions and by refusing to join together in unions. Others worried about the alleged racial inferiority of these aliens and urged that America bar their entry. The heavy migration of European and Russian Jews offended many who viewed this movement as a serious threat to the nation's Protestant heritage. Italian immigrants, like their Irish coreligionists before them, were criticized for their Catholicism. Both groups frequently came under attack for their foreign ways, attachment to radical political philosophies, and involvement in criminal activities.

At the same time that the immigrant community was coming under increasing criticism, a new view of ethnic adjustment was emerging. During the 1880s a group of idealists from the middle and upper classes followed the example set by some young Englishmen in London and settled in the slums of America's major cities to help the poor. While not all these individuals shared her opinions, Jane Addams of Hull House in Chicago and many of her settlement colleagues learned to appreciate the cultural heritages of immigrants and began to defend their uniqueness. This viewpoint received the endorsement of several intellectuals of this period who were proponents of liberalism, internationalism, and tolerance. The so-called cultural pluralists' position received its clearest exposition from Horace Kallen, a Harvard-educated philosopher. Kallen defended the right of each ethnic group to preserve its language, religion, communal institutions, and ancestral culture. He viewed cultural diversity as an important process in a mass democratic society where groups play such an important role. He noted further that these people learned to speak English and participated actively in the economic and political life of the country.

The voices calling for cultural diversity were not influential enough, however, to hold back demands for some sort of immigration restriction. Even settlement house workers occasionally complained that unlimited immigration was making life more difficult for the urban poor. The pressure for a closing of the door began to mount as the 19th century drew to a close.

The first restriction law enacted in 1875 banned prostitutes and alien convicts from entering the United States. An 1885 act also forbade the entrance of contracted laborers. Later laws similarly applied to very specific types of people. As one might suspect, these laws kept out very few people since records were easily forged and proof of these activities was difficult to obtain.

The Chinese Exclusion Act of 1882 was a much more significant piece of legislation. Racially motivated, it was the first statute to block the entry of an entire ethnic group. It was spawned by the intense anti-Chinese feeling present on the West Coast and particularly in California. Ironically, some of the major participants in the drive to pass this law were immigrants who had arrived earlier in the century. White Californians contended that there were vast racial and cultural differences between Orientals and other ethnic groups and that these disparities could not be bridged. The 1882 law made it clear that significant numbers of Americans had serious reservations about certain nationalities assuming residence in the country. Before too long such sentiments would take hold in every section of the nation.

The volume of immigration increased dramatically as the new century began. More than 8.7 million people entered the United States during the prosperous first decade as opposed to a mere 3.7 million during the depression-racked 1890s. The vast majority of these people continued to come from the southern regions of Europe, and thus the trend that had first appeared in the 1880s was accelerated. With the quickening pace of this immigration came a commensurate rise in xenophobia.

Could the United States continue to assimilate these great hordes of people? The answer from nativist America was a resounding "NO." With cities growing at fantastic rates and the frontier officially declared closed, many citizens felt that the melting pot was filled to overflowing. Madison Grant, a lawyer and vice president of the Immigration Restriction League, argued in his widely read book *The Passing of the Great Race* (1916) that the inferior races from southern and eastern Europe could not be assimilated. He warned that America and the superior Anglo-Saxon race would suffer deterioration and ultimate collapse if this immigration trend continued. The Congressional Immigration Commission Report of 1911, in its forty-two volumes, likewise suggested that restrictive legislation was necessary to protect American institutions and values. In response Congress passed a literacy test in 1913 only to have President Wilson veto it. With the outbreak of World War I and its demands for 100 percent Americanism, the tide could no longer be restrained. In 1917, despite another Wilson veto, a literacy test for entry to America became law.

With the end of the first World War, however, the flow of immigration resumed its former vigor. Over 1 million people entered the United States in 1919 and 1920. Coupled with the emergence of communism in Russia and the Red Scare in America, this renewed flood of aliens led many citizens to question again the wisdom of unrestricted immigration. Congress approved in 1921, on a temporary basis, the principle of restriction based on quotas for each nationality. The Johnson-Reed Immigration Act of 1924 recognized the effectiveness of this approach and made it into permanent law. Under its provisions a total of 153,714 immigrants, not including those from the Western Hemisphere, could enter the United States annually. The quota for each nationality was based upon the census of 1890 in order to exclude as many southern and eastern Europeans as possible and computed against the number of those nationals then residing in the country. The public had thus decided that America would no longer be a free and open refuge for people seeking a chance at a better life.

The passage of restrictionist legislation removed many of the more emotional nativist demands. Those that remained were further muted by the Great Depression, a time during which more people actually left the United States than entered. Many Americans nonetheless remained determined to cleanse immigrants of their foreign ways and imbue them with solid American virtues. The pressures of the depression and the World War that followed it generated a drive for uniformity that engulfed the ethnic community. The postwar threat of communism, the Korean War, and McCarthyism produced even greater demands for conformity. "Different" views and values were not only frowned upon, but were also frequently attacked.

These considerations should not overshadow the effects of other pressures on the ethnic community pushing it toward an accommodation with the new homeland. From the earliest colonial times every immigrant group entering America has had forces at work within itself that have sapped its attachments to the old way. Certainly the physical separation that existed from the mother country played its part. For many immigrants there was an emotional separation as well. The inevitable progression of generations also weakened the old traditions, perhaps as effectively as any nativist pressures. Sons and daughters and then their offspring often seemed to drift inexorably from the values of the first generation. Few groups have been able to resist these kinds of forces, and those that have—the Amish, for example—have tended to be small, physically isolated religious sects that can enforce a rigid discipline.

While ethnic and minority concerns may have been temporarily muted in the period after 1930 by these social dynamics, they by no means had disappeared. The fact that older white ethnic groups had retained parts of their cultural heritages often escaped the public eye. They continued to practice their religions, to celebrate special holidays and other ethnic festivities, to intermarry with great frequency, and to vote on the basis of ethnic considerations. Will Herberg has persuasively suggested that during the 1950s religion played an important role in permitting the expression of ethnicity for the third and fourth generations. It was not long, however, before events were to bring many of these ethnic attachments, which for years had simmered just beneath society's surface, to a full boil.

The Supreme Court's decision in *Brown v. Board of Education of Topeka* (1954) which ordered an end to segregated schools, signaled the beginning of a new era in race relations and minority rights. During the next twenty years the Court also decreed the ending of discrimination in housing, public facilities, political representation, and criminal proceedings. The combination of the Supreme Court's landmark decisions and subsequent black civil rights demonstrations led by Martin Luther King, Jr., served as a catalyst for other minority groups who had been dissatisfied with their social and economic condition in America. Embracing the tactics of King and the more militant Black Panther Party, Indians, Puerto Ricans, Mexicans, women and other groups took to the streets to lodge their protests against discrimination.

Some white ethnics, sociologist Peter Rose suggests, supported the black revolution because it challenged "old stereotypes" and racism. Most, however, were angry at being blamed for racial conditions that they had little or no hand in creating. Slavery and racism, ethnic leader Michael Novak has noted, were well established in America long before the arrival of the new immigration. Many ethnics deeply resented the special favors given to blacks through affirmative action programs and quota systems which had been denied to them and their ancestors. "Why can't they work their way up like we did?" became a not untypical ethnic response.

It would be a serious mistake to picture the new ethnicity as solely a racist, anti-black movement, however. There is much that the American people do not know about themselves, and the recent ethnic resurgence can be viewed as a drive toward self-discovery as much as toward protest. It seems clear that ethnics in America desired to learn more about themselves. The popularity of the book *Roots* by Alex Haley can be viewed as only part of a wider search into the backgrounds and heritages of many people. The black pride movement has stimulated and legitimized similar interests in other groups.

Governmental policies have also played a role in encouraging the ethnic resurgence. Unlike years past, an individual often finds today a positive benefit in being identified as a member of a particular group. Various federal and state grant programs, subsidies, tax provisions, and jobs have ethnic stipulations attached to them. Money, power, and influence, therefore, can often stem from having a clear ethnic label. The irony is, of course, that this same attribute was so often a handicap in the past.

This heightened ethnic awareness of the 1950s and 1960s has had additional benefits for minority groups. In particular, it helped spark a movement to abolish the Johnson-Reed Act of 1924. Responding to ethnic pressures, Congress formally terminated the national origin system in 1965. The extremely restrictive quotas of the old law were repealed and replaced with a more flexible system of admissions. Under the Immigration Act of that year 170,000 people (excluding parents, spouses, and children of American citizens) could enter the United States from outside the Western Hemisphere. A limitation of 20,000 people was also placed on any one country. Persons were admitted on a first come, first served basis with relatives, refugees, and those with needed job skills getting preferential consideration.

The question remains as to the long-term impact of this ethnic resurgence. Will it be merely a passing fad with no lasting imprint? There is evidence to suggest that the heightened emotions of the past decade are beginning to cool and perhaps a crest has been reached. Does this necessarily signal a passing away? Some observers feel that interest in ethnicity remains just as strong as ever but in a less dramatic form.

Italian Americans, for example, no longer seem to be interested in taking to the streets in flamboyant demonstrations. Yet, there is a great deal of activity taking place within the group today that relates directly to ethnic issues. The American Italian Historical Association, which was founded in the midst of the ethnic revival, is alive and growing each year. On the political front the Italian American Foundation, with offices in Washington, D.C., is carrying out an effective program of education and lobbying in behalf of issues concerning Italian Americans. Like its more scholarly brother, the Italian American Foundation is less than ten years old. Similar developments have taken place among other ethnic groups.

It thus seems that ethnicity is here to stay; perhaps in a somewhat less emotional, less public stance, but present nonetheless. As the ethnic resurgence continues to develop and become institutionalized, what sort of America will it lead to? No one can be sure, of course, but many people involved with these issues believe that it will create a healthier, more secure America. These observers foresee a country that can more fully benefit from the diversity of human values and lifestyles that are present in this nation. One would surely hope that they are right.

Whatever doubts may remain as to the eventual importance of the ethnic revival, it is clear that ethnic groups are no longer reluctant to make their views known. They have become more confident of their place in American society and are willing to define for themselves and the rest of the nation the precise role that they will play in this country's future. It is the forces which came together to create this new situation which this volume considers.

Four major sections comprise the contents of this book. "The Melting Pot Reexamined" assesses the resurgence of ethnicity as it has developed in America over the past fifteen years. The role of ethnicity is also discussed as a worldwide phenomenon. In "The Emergence of Ethnic Awareness" those groups which formed the vanguard of the ethnic movement in the late 1950s and 1960s are examined. Special attention has been given to the black revolution which served as a catalyst for this entire development. Indians, Puerto Ricans, Mexicans, women, and Cubans all borrowed the programs and tactics of blacks to improve their political, economic, and social status in America. In the process they discovered a sense of ethnic pride and identity that had eluded them for years. "The Resurgence of Ethnicity" analyzes the older ethnic groups such as Italians, Poles, and Japanese, whose ethnic awareness was greatly enhanced by the events of the 1960s. These groups frequently utilized this community awareness to develop new social and cultural institutions and to abolish racial stereotypes. "Criticism of the New Ethnicity" examines the opposition to the ethnic resurgence that has emerged during the past decade. Special attention is given to the impact of ethnic pluralism on schools and society. For additional reading there is a bibliographic essay at the end of the book.

SECTION 1

The Melting Pot Reexamined

MICHAEL NOVAK

The New Ethnicity

Among the many writers analyzing the impact of the new ethnic awareness, Michael Novak is generally recognized as the movement's most perceptive and articulate spokesman. It was his book The Rise of the Unmeltable Ethnics *(1972) that first gave voice to the many concerns and emotions that were spreading throughout ethnic America. A Catholic Slovak American himself, Novak wrote with a rare personal touch that spoke simultaneously to scholars and to the wider population. His article "The New Ethnicity" was written in 1974 and integrates many responses to the criticisms and suggestions that attended the publication of his book.*

Novak claims that the new ethnicity is not a divisive, tribal social force; rather, it aims fundamentally at an increased self-awareness on the part of the millions of Americans of southern and eastern European background. This recognition of historical roots and traditions, however, does have political consequences in America. It is important in this area because of the manner in which ethnicity has historically been approached by the elites of this country. Novak contends that there has been much distortion of the true character and motivations of white ethnic America. Rather than being the stereotyped "hard-hat" racists of popular fancy, Novak argues that white ethnics have tabulated a consistently progressive voting record over the years, especially in America's urban centers where most ethnics reside. To charges that a renewed emphasis on ethnicity will be harmful to the nation in that it will polarize blacks and whites, he counters that

From *The Center Magazine* (July/August, 1974). Reprinted by permission of author.

continued claims of "divisiveness" are only strategies to keep access to the top limited. The "new ethnic politics," in Novak's view, is aimed at practical solutions for urban problems, with blacks and whites working together. In the end, its objective is not a balkanization of America, but rather the structuring of a more flexible cosmopolitan society.

Mr. Novak has written numerous books and articles on religion in America, including Choosing Our King *and* All the Catholic People. *After serving for a time on the staff of the Rockefeller Foundation, he is now director of EMPAC (Ethnic Millions Political Action Committee), which describes itself as "a national civil rights committee, dedicated to a politics of family and neighborhood, to equality and fairness, to a new America."*

The word "ethnic" does not have a pleasing sound. The use of the word makes many people anxious. What sorts of repression account for this anxiety? What pretenses about the world are threatened when one points to the realities denoted and connoted by that ancient word? An internal history lies behind resistance to ethnicity; such resistance is almost always passional, convictional, not at all trivial. Many persons have tried to escape being "ethnic," in the name of a higher moral claim.

There are many meanings to the word itself. I have tried to map some of them elsewhere. There are many reasons for resistance to the word "ethnic" (and what it is taken to represent). Rather than beginning with these directly, I prefer to begin by defining the new ethnicity.

The definition I wish to give is personal; it grows out of personal experience; it is necessitated by an effort to attain an accurate self-knowledge. The hundreds of letters, reviews, comments, invitations, and conversations that followed upon *The Rise of the Unmeltable Ethnics* (1972) indicate that my own gropings to locate my own identity are not isolated. They struck a responsive chord in many others of southern and eastern European (and other) background. My aim was—and is—to open up the field to study. Let later inquiry discern just how broadly and how exactly my first attempts at definition apply. It is good to try to give voice to what has so far been untongued—and then to devise testable hypotheses at a later stage.

The new ethnicity, then, is a movement of self-knowledge on the part of members of the third and fourth generation of southern and eastern European immigrants in the United States. In a broader sense, the new ethnicity includes a renewed self-consciousness on the part of other generations and other ethnic groups: the Irish, the Norwegians and Swedes, the Germans, the Chinese and Japanese, and others. Much that can be said of one of these groups can be said, not univocally but analogously, of others. In this area one must learn to speak with multiple meanings and with a sharp eye for differences in detail. (By "analogous" I mean "having resemblances but also essential differences"; by "univocal" I mean a generalization that applies equally to all cases.) My sentences are to be read, then, analogously, not univocally; they are meant to awaken fresh perception, not to close discussion. They are intended to speak directly of a limited (and yet quite large) range of ethnic groups, while conceding indirectly that much that is said of southern and eastern Europeans may also be said, *mutatis mutandis*, of others.

I stress that, in the main, the "new" ethnicity involves those of the third and fourth generation after immigration. Perhaps two anecdotes will suggest the kind of experience involved. When *Time* magazine referred to me in 1972 as a "Slovak-American," I felt an inner shock; I had never referred to myself or been publicly referred to in that way. I wasn't certain how I felt about it. Then, in 1974, after I had given a lecture on ethnicity to the only class in Slavic American studies in the United States,* at the City College of New York, the dean of the college said on the way to lunch, "Considering how sensitive you are on ethnic matters, the surprising thing to me was how American you are." I wanted to ask him, "What else?" In this area one grows used to symbolic uncertainties.

The new ethnicity does *not* entail: (a) speaking a foreign language; (b) living in a subculture; (c) living in a "tight-knit" ethnic neighborhood; (d) belonging to fraternal organizations; (e) responding to "ethnic" appeals; (f) exalting one's own nationality or culture, narrowly construed. Neither does it entail a university education or the reading of writers on the new ethnicity. Rather, the new ethnicity entails: first, a growing sense of discomfort with the sense of identity one is *supposed* to have—universalist, "melted," "like everyone else"; then a growing appreciation for the potential wisdom of one's own gut reactions (especially on moral matters) and their historical roots; a growing self-confidence and social power; a sense of being discriminated against, condescended to, or carelessly misapprehended; a growing disaffection regarding those to whom one had always been taught to defer; and a sense of injustice regarding the response of liberal spokesmen to conflicts between various ethnic groups, especially between "legitimate" minorities and "illegitimate" ones. There is, in a word, an inner conflict between one's felt personal power and one's ascribed public power: a

---

*This Slavic American course—in a happy symbol of the new ethnicity—is housed in the Program of Puerto Rican Studies, through the generosity of the latter.

sense of outraged truth, justice, and equity.

The new ethnicity does, therefore, have political consequences. Many southern and eastern European Americans have been taught, as I was, not to be "ethnic," or even "hyphenated," but only "American." Yet at critical points it became clear to some of us, then to more of us, that when push comes to shove we are always, in the eyes of others, "ethnics," unless we play completely by their rules, emotional as well as procedural. And in the end, even then, they retain the power and the status. Still, the stakes involved in admitting this reality to oneself are very high. Being "universal" is regarded as being good; being ethnically self-conscious raises anxieties. Since one's whole identity has been based upon being "universal," one is often loathe to change public face too suddenly. Many guard the little power and status they have acquired, although they cock one eye on how the ethnic "movement" is progressing. They are wise. But their talents are also needed.

The new ethnicity, then, is a fledgling movement, not to be confused with the appearance of ethnic themes on television commercials, in television police shows, and in magazines. All these manifestations in the public media would not have occurred unless the ethnic reality of America had begun to be noticed. In states from Massachusetts to Iowa, great concentrations of Catholics and Jews, especially in urban centers, have been some of the main bastions of Democratic Party politics for fifty years. The "new politics," centered in the universities, irritated and angered this constituency (even when, as it sometimes did, it won its votes). Thus there is a relation between the fledgling new ethnicity and this larger ethnic constituency. But what that relationship will finally be has not yet been demonstrated by events.

Those who do not come from southern or eastern backgrounds in the United States may not be aware of how it feels to come from such a tradition; they may not know the internal history. They may note "mass passivity" and "alienation" without sharing the cynicism learned through particular experiences. They may regard the externals of ethnic economic and social success, modest but real, while never noticing the internal ambiguity—and its compound of peace and self-hatred, confidence and insecurity.

To be sure, at first many "white ethnics" of the third generation are not conscious of having any special feelings. The range of feelings about themselves they do have is very broad; more than one stream of feeling is involved. They are right-wingers and left-wingers, chauvinists and universalists, all-Americans and isolationists. Many want nothing more desperately than to be considered "American." Indeed, by now many have so deeply acquired that habit that to ask them point-blank how they are different from others would arouse strong emotional resistance.

For at least three reasons, many white ethnics *are* becoming self-conscious. As usual, great social forces outside the self draw forth from the self new responses. First, a critical mass of scholars, artists, and writers is beginning to emerge—the Italians, for example, are extraordinarily eminent in the cinema. Second, the prevailing image of the model American—the "best and the brightest" of the Ivy League, wealthy, suave, and powerful—has been discredited by the mismanagement of war abroad, by racial injustice at home, and by attitudes, values, and emotional patterns unworthy of emulation internally. The older image of the truly cultured American is no longer compelling. Many, therefore, are thrown back upon their own resources.

Finally, the attitudes of liberal, enlightened commentators on the "crisis of the cities" seem to fall into traditional patterns: guilt vis-à-vis blacks, and disdain for the Archie Bunkers of the land (Bunker is, of course, a classy British American name, but Carroll O'Connor is in appearance undisguisably Irish). The national media present to the public a model for what it is to be a "good American" which makes many people feel unacceptable to their betters, unwashed, and ignored. Richard Hofstadter wrote of "the anti-intellectualism of the people," but another feature of American life is the indifference—even hostility—of many intellectuals to Main Street. In return, then, many people respond with deep contempt for experts, educators, "limousine liberals," "radical chic," "bureaucrats"—a contempt whose sources are partly those of class ("the hidden injuries of class") and partly those of ethnicity ("legitimate" minorities and unacceptable minorities). The national social class that prides itself on being universalist has lost the confidence of many. Votes on school bond issues are an example of popular resistance to professionals.

In my own case, the reporting of voting patterns among white ethnic voters during the Wallace campaigns of 1964 and 1968 first aroused in me ethnic self-consciousness. Descriptions of "white backlash" often put the blame—inaccurately, I came to see—upon Slavs and other Catholic groups. The Slavs of "South Milwaukee" were singled out for comment in the Wallace vote in Wisconsin in 1964. First, South Milwaukee was not distinguished from the south side of Milwaukee. Then, it was not noted that the Slavic vote for Wallace fell *below* his statewide average. Then, the very heavy vote for Wallace in outlying German and British American counties was not pointed out. Finally, the strong vote for Wallace in the wealthy northeastern suburbs of Milwaukee was similarly ignored. It seemed to me that those whom the grandfathers called "hunkies" and "dagos" were now being called "racists," "fascists," and "pigs," with no noticeable gain in affection. Even in 1972, a staff advisory in the Shriver "trip book" for a congressional district in Pittsburgh called the district "Wallace country," though the Wallace vote in that district in 1968 had been 12 percent, and the Humphrey vote had been 58 percent. I obliged the staff member to revise his account and to call the district "Humphrey country." It is one of the most consistently liberal districts in Pennsylvania. Why send this constituency the message that it is the enemy?

Jimmy Breslin was recently asked by an interviewer in *Penthouse* how, coming out of Queens, he could have grown up so liberal. Actually, next to Brooklyn (Kings County), there is no more liberal county in the nation. A similar question was put to a liberal journalist from the Dorchester area, in Boston. The class and ethnic bias hidden in the way the word "liberal" is used in such interviews cries out for attention.

One of the large social generalizations systematically obscured by the traditional anti-Catholicism of American elites is the overwhelming progressive voting record in America's urban centers. The centers of large Catholic population in every northeastern and north central state have been the key to Democratic victories in those states since at least 1916. The hypothesis that Catholics have been, second only to Jews, the central constituency of successful progressive politics in this century is closer to the facts than historians have observed. (Massachusetts, that most Catholic of our states, stayed with McGovern in 1972.) The language of politics in America is, however, mainly Protestant, and Protestant biases color public perception. Protestant leadership is given the halo of morality and legitimacy, Catholic life is described in terms of negatively laden words: Catholic "power," "machine politics," etc.

There are other examples of odd perception on the part of American elites with respect to Catholic and other ethnic populations. The major institutions of American life—government, education, the media—give almost no assistance to those of "white ethnic" background who wish to obey the Socratic maxim: "Know thyself." One of the greatest and most dramatic migrations of human history brought more than 30 million immigrants to this land between 1874 and 1924. Despite the immense dramatic materials involved in this migration, only one major American film records it: Elia Kazan's *America! America!* That film ends with the hero's arrival in America. The tragic and costly experience of Americanization has scarcely yet been touched. How many died; how many were morally and psychologically destroyed; how many still carry the marks of changing their names, of "killing" their mother tongue and renouncing their former identity, in order to become "new men" and "new women"—these are motifs of violence, self-mutilation, joy, and irony. The inner history of this migration must come to be understood, if we are ever to understand the aspirations and fears of some 70 million Americans.

When this part of the population exhibits self-consciousness and begins to exert group claims—whether these are claims made by aggregated individuals or claims that are corporate—they are regularly confronted with the accusation that they are being "divisive." ("Divisive" is a code word for Catholic ethnics and Jews, is it not? It is seldom used of others: white southerners, Appalachians, Chicanos, blacks, native Americans, prep-school British Americans, or others who maintain their own identity and institutions.) Earl Raab writes eloquently of this phenomenon in *Commentary* (May, 1974): "Modern Europe...never really accepted the legitimacy of the corporate Jew—although it was at its best willing to grant full civil rights to the individual Jew. That, for the Jews, was an impossible paradox, a secular version of Christian demands to convert.... [And] it is precisely this willingness to allow the Jews their separate identity as a group which is now coming into question in America." Individual diversity, yes; group identity, not for all.

The Christian white ethnic, like the Jew, actually has few group demands to make: positively, for educational resources to keep values and perceptions alive, articulate, and critical; negatively, for an equal access to power, status, and the definition of the general American purpose and symbolic world. Part of the strategic function of the cry "divisive!" is to limit access to these things. Only those individuals will be advanced who define themselves as individuals and who operate according to the symbols of the established. The emotional meaning is: "*Become like us.*" This is an understandable strategy, but in a nation as pluralistic as the United States, it is short-sighted. The nation's hopes, purposes, and symbols need to be defined inclusively rather than exclusively; *all* must become "new men" and "new women." All the burden ought not to fall upon the newcomers.

There is much that is attractive about the British American, upper-class, northeastern culture that has established for the entire nation a model of behavior and perception. This model is composed of economic power; status; cultural tone; important institutional rituals and procedures; and the acceptable patterns of style, sensibility, and rationality. The terse phrase "Ivy League" suggests all these factors. The nation would be infinitely poorer than it is without the Ivy League. All of us who came to this land—including the many lower-class British Americans, Scotch-Irish, Scandinavians, and Germans—are much in the debt of the Ivy League, deeply, substantially so.

Still, the Ivy League is not the nation. The culture of the Ivy League is not the culture of America (not even of Protestant America).

Who are we, then, we who do not particularly reverberate to the literature of New England, whose interior history is not Puritan, whose social class is not brahmin (either in reality or in pretense), whose ethnicity is not British American, or even Nordic? Where in American institutions, American literature, American education is our identity mirrored, objectified, rendered accessible to intelligent criticism, and confirmed? We are still, I think, persons without a public symbolic world, persons without a publicly verified culture to sustain us and our children.

It is not that we lack culture; it is not that we lack strength of ego and a certain internal peace. As Jean-Paul Sartre remarks in one of his later works, there is a distinction between one's identity in one's own eyes and one's identity in the eyes of others. In the United States, many who have internal dignity cannot avoid noticing that others regard them as less than equals, with a sense that they are different, with uncertainty, and with a lack of commonality. It is entirely possible that the "melting pot" would indeed have melted everyone, if those who were the models into which the molten metal was to be poured had not found the process excessively demanding. A sense of separate identity is, in part, induced from outside in. I am made aware of being Catholic and Slovak by the actions of others. I would be sufficiently content were my identity to be so taken for granted, so utterly normal and real, that it would never have to be self-conscious.

The fact of American cultural power is that a more or less Protestant sensibility sets the tone, and that a fairly aggressive British American ethnocentricity, and even Anglophilia, govern the instruments of education and public life. Moreover, it is somehow emotionally important not to challenge this dominant ethnocentricity. It is quite proper to talk of other sorts of social difference—income, class, sex, even religion. To speak affirmatively of ethnicity, however, makes many uneasy. Some important truth must lie hidden underneath this uneasiness. A Niebuhrian analysis of social power suggests that a critical instrument of social control in the United States is, indeed, the one that dares not be spoken of.

In New York State, for example, the four Democratic candidates for the office of lieutenant governor (not, however, for governor) are named Olivieri, Cuomo, La Falce, and Krupsak. It is the year, the pundits say, for "ethnic balance" on the ticket. But all four candidates insist that their ethnicity is not significant. Two boast of being from *upstate*, one of being a *woman*, one of being for "*the little guy*." It is publicly legitimate to be different on any other account except ethnicity, even where the importance of ethnic diversity is tacitly agreed upon.

If I say, as I sometimes have, that I would love to organize an "ethnic caucus" within both the Democratic Party and the Republican Party, the common reaction is one of anxiety, distaste, and strained silence. But if I say, as I am learning to, that I would love to organize a "caucus of workingmen and women" in both parties, heads quickly nod in approval. Social class is, apparently, rational. Cultural background is, apparently, counterrational.

Yet the odd political reality is that most Americans do not identify themselves in class terms. They respond to cultural symbols intimate to their ethnic history in America. Ethnicity is a "gut issue," even though it cannot be mentioned. A wise political candidate does not, of course, speak to a longshoreman's local by calling its members Italian American and appealing to some supposed cultural solidarity. That would be a mistake. But if he speaks about those themes in the cultural tradition that confirm their own identity—themes like family, children, home, neighborhood, specific social aspirations, and grievances—they know he is with them: he does represent them. In order to be able to represent many constituencies, a representative has to be able to "pass over" into many cultural histories. He may never once make ethnicity explicit as a public theme; but, implicitly, he will be recognizing the daily realities of ethnicity and ethnic experience in the complex fabric of American social power.

According to one social myth, America is a melting pot, and this myth is intended by many to be not merely descriptive but normative: the faster Americans—especially white ethnic Americans—"melt" into the British American pattern, the better. There is even a certain ranking according to the supposed degree of assimilation: Scotch-Irish, Norwegians, Swedes, Germans, Swiss, Dutch, liberal or universalist Jews, the Irish, and on down the line to the less assimilated: Greeks, Yugoslavs, Hungarians, central and east Europeans, Italians, Orthodox Jews, French Canadians, Portuguese, Latins and Spanish-speaking....

Now, it was one thing to be afraid of ethnicity in 1924, in confronting a first and second generation of immigrants. It is another thing to be afraid, in 1974, in confronting a third and fourth generation. Indeed, fears about a revival of ethnicity seem to be incompatible with conviction about how successful the melting pot has been. Fears about a "revival" of ethnicity confirm the fact that ethnicity is still a powerful reality in American life.

What, then, are the advantages and disadvantages in making this dangerous subject, this subterranean subject, explicit?

The disadvantages seem to be three. The first one on everyone's mind is that emphasis on ethnicity may work to the disadvantage of blacks. It may, it is said, become a legitimization of racism. It may "polarize" whites and blacks. Nothing could be further from the truth. Those who are concerned about the new ethnicity—Geno Baroni (Washington), Irving Levine (New York), Barbara Mikulski (Baltimore), Ralph Perrotta (New York), Steve Adubado (Newark), Otto Feinstein (Detroit), Stan Franczyk (Buffalo), Kenneth Kovach (Cleveland), Ivan Dornic (Pittsburgh), Edward Marciniak (Chicago), and others—have given ample proof of their concern for the rights and opportunities for black Americans. Many got their start in the new ethnicity through their work among blacks. The overriding political perception among those concerned with the new ethnicity is that the harshness of life in the cities must be reduced by whites and blacks together, especially in working-class neighborhoods. Present social policies punish neighborhoods that integrate. Such neighborhoods should be rewarded and strengthened and guaranteed a long-range stability.

But fears about ethnicity require a further two-part response. Racism does not need ethnicity in order to be legitimated in America. It was quite well legitimated by Anglo-American culture, well before white ethnics arrived here in significant numbers, well before many white ethnics had ever met blacks. Indeed, there is some reason to believe that, while racism is an international phenomenon and found in all cultures, the British American and other Nordic peoples have a special emotional response to colored races. Not all European peoples respond to intermarriage, for example, with quite the emotional quality of the Anglo-Saxons. The French, the Spanish, the Italians, and the Slavs are not without their own forms of racism. But the felt quality of racism is different in different cultures. (It seems different among the North End Italians and the South Boston Irish of Boston, for example.)

In America, racism did not wait until the immigrants of 1880 and after began to arrive. Indeed, it is in precisely those parts of the country solely populated by British Americans that the conditions of blacks have been legally and institutionally least humane. In those parts of the country most heavily populated by white ethnics, the cultural symbols and the political muscle that have led to civil rights and other legislation have received wide support. Liberal senators and congressmen elected by white ethnics—including the Kennedys—led the way. Even in 1972, both Hamtramck and Buffalo went for George McGovern. Mc-Govern's share of the Slavic vote was 52 percent. Nixon won the white Protestant vote by 68 percent.

It will be objected that white ethnic leaders like Frank Rizzo of Philadelphia, Ralph Perk of Cleveland, and others are signs of a new racism on the part of white ethnics in the northern cities, of a retreat from support for blacks, and of a rising tide of anti-"crime" and anti-busing sentiment. The proponents of the new ethnicity perceive such developments as a product of liberal neglect and liberal divisiveness. The proponents of the new politics talk well of civil rights, equal opportunity, economic justice, and other beautiful themes. But the new politics, in distinguishing "legitimate" minorities (blacks, Chicanos, native Americans) from "less favored" minorities (Italians, Slavs, Orthodox Jews, Irish, etc.), has set up punitive and self-defeating mechanisms. The new politics has needlessly divided working-class blacks from working-class whites, in part by a romance (on television) with militance and flamboyance, in part by racial discrimination in favor of some against others, not because of need but because of color.

The second part of this response is that the politics of "the constituency of conscience" (as Michael Harrington, Eugene Mc-Carthy, and others have called it)—the politics of the liberal, the educated, the enlightened—is less advantageous to blacks than is the politics of the new ethnicity. The new politics is less advantageous to blacks because it is obsessed with racial differences, and approaches these through the ineffectual lenses of guilt and moralism. Second, it is blind to cultural differences among blacks, as well as to cultural differences among whites; and sometimes these are significant. Third, it unconsciously but effectively keeps blacks in the position of a small racial minority outnumbered in the population ten to one.

By contrast, the new ethnicity notes many other significant differences besides those based upon race, and defines political and social problems in ways that unite diverse groups around common objectives. In Chicago, for example, neither Poles nor Italians are represented on the boards or in the executive suites of Chicago's top 105 corporations in a higher proportion than blacks or Latinos—all are of 1 percent or less.* In New York City, "open admissions" benefits white ethnics at least as much as blacks; touting it as a program for blacks made it a needlessly divisive issue. (Nationally, there were proportionately more blacks in college in 1970 than Slavs or Italians.) In Boston,

---

*Cf. "The Representation of Poles, Italians, Latins, and Blacks in the Executive Suites of Chicago's Largest Corporations." The Institute of Urban Life, 820 North Michigan Avenue, Chicago, Illinois 60611.

neither white ethnics nor blacks desire busing, but this highly ideological instrument of social change is supported most by just those affluent liberals—in such suburbs as Brookline and Newton—whose children will not be involved.

The new ethnic politics would propose a strategy of social rewards— better garbage pickup, more heavily financed and orderly schools, long-range guarantees on home mortgages, easier access to federally insured home improvement loans, and other services—for neighborhoods that integrate. As a neighborhood moves from, say, a 10-percent population of blacks to 20 percent or more, integration should be regulated so that long-range community stability is guaranteed. It is better long-range policy to have a large number of neighborhoods integrated up to 20 or 30 percent than to encourage—even by inadvertence—a series of sudden flights and virtually total migrations. Institutional racism is a reality; the massive migration of blacks into a neighborhood does not bring with it social rewards but, almost exclusively, punishments.

There are other supposed disadvantages to emphasis upon ethnicity. Ethnicity, it is said, is a fundamentally counterrational, primordial, uncontrollable social force; it leads to hatred and violence; it is the very enemy of enlightenment, rationality, and liberal politics. But this is to confuse nationalism or tribalism with cultural heritage. Because a man's name is Russell, or Ayer, or Flew, we would not wish to accuse him of tribalism on the ground that he found the Britons a uniquely civilized and clear-headed people, thought the Germans ponderous and mystic, the French philosophically romantic, etc. A little insular, we might conclude, but harmlessly ethnocentric. And if it is not necessarily tribalistic or unenlightened to read English literature in American schools, just possibly it would be even more enlightened and even less tribalistic to make other literatures, germane to the heritage of other Americans, more accessible than they are.

The United States is, potentially, a multiculturally attuned society. The greatest number of immigrants in recent years arrives from Spanish-speaking and Asian nations. But the nation's cultural life, and its institutions of culture, are far from being sensitive to the varieties of the American people. Why should a cultural heritage not their own be imposed unilaterally upon newcomers? Would not genuine multi-cultural adaptation on the part of all be more cosmopolitan and humanistic? It would be quite significant in international affairs. The Americans would truly be a kind of prototype of planetary diversity.

Some claim that cultural institutions will be fragmented if every ethnic group in America clamors for attention. But the experience of the Illinois curriculum in ethnic studies suggests that no one school represents more than four or five ethnic groups (sometimes fewer) in significant density. With even modest adjustments in courses in history, literature, and the social sciences, material can be introduced that illuminates inherited patterns of family life, values, and preferences. The purpose for introducing multicultural materials is neither chauvinistic nor propagandistic but realistic. Education ought to illuminate what is happening in the self of each child.

What about the child of the mixed marriage, the child of *no* ethnic heritage—the child of the melting pot? So much in the present curriculum already supports such a child that the only possible shock to arise from multicultural materials would appear to be a beneficial one: not all others in America are like him (her), and that diversity, as well as homogenization, has a place in America.

The practical agendas that face proponents of the new ethnicity are vast, indeed. At the heights of American economic and social power, there is not yet much of a melting pot. Significant ethnic diversity is manifested in the proportion of each group studying in universities, on faculties, in the professions, on boards of directors, among the creators of public social symbols, and the like. In patterns of home ownership, family income, work patterns, care for the aged, political activism, authoritarianism, individualism, and matters of ultimate concern, group differences are remarkable. About all these things, more information is surely needed. Appropriate social policies need to be hypothesized, tried, and evaluated.

Ethnic diversity in the United States persists in the consciousness of individuals, in their perceptions, preferences, behavior, even while mass production and mass communications homogenize our outward appearances. Some regard such persistence as a personal failure; they would prefer to "transcend" their origins, or perhaps they believe that they have. Here two questions arise. What cultural connection do they have with their brothers and sisters still back in Montgomery, or Wheeling, or Skokie, or Pawtucket? Second, has their personal assimilation introduced into the great American superculture fresh streams of image, myth, symbol, and style or intellectual life? Has anything distinctively their own—formed in them by a history longer than a thousand years—been added to the common wisdom?

The new ethnicity does not stand for the balkanization of America. It stands for a true, real, multicultural cosmopolitanism. It points toward a common culture truly altered by each new infusion of diversity. Until now, the common culture has been relatively resistant to internal transformation; it has not so much arisen from the hearts of all as been imposed; the melting pot has had only a single recipe. That is why at present the common culture seems to have become discredited, shattered, unenforceable. Its cocoon has broken. Struggling to be born is a creature of multicultural beauty, dazzling, free, a higher and richer form of life. It was fashioned in the painful darkness of the melting pot and now, at the appointed time, it awakens.

NATHAN GLAZER AND DANIEL P. MOYNIHAN

Why Ethnicity?

The collaborative work of Nathan Glazer and Daniel Moynihan has yielded several important insights into the nature of ethnic group life in America. It was their important study Beyond the Melting Pot, *first published in 1963, that alerted us to the changed nature of ethnicity in the 1960s. Here they noted that ethnic blocs had, in effect, become interest groups in society. People sought identification with these groups in large part because of the rewards that could accrue to them from this identification.*

In the essay below Glazer and Moynihan place American ethnic developments in a world context. Even in communist and socialist nations, where social and political ideology would seem to render ethnicity unimportant, the authors find a great reliance on ethnic considerations. The reasons underlying this phenomenon are the same as those that hold sway in America. Indeed, in many nations today it is a distinct advantage to be identified as a member of a particular ethnic group because so many societies are distributing their rewards on this basis. Ethnic group attachment, however, is still based in part on affective ties. Overall, the authors conclude that ethnic conflict and identification have become more prevalent in the last two decades, and they surmise that ethnicity will continue to constitute a major trend in modern society.

Both men have had long and distinguished careers in the broad fields

From *Commentary* 58 (October, 1974). Adapted from *Ethnicity: Theory and Experience,* Nathan Glazer & Daniel P. Moynihan, editors, Cambridge, Mass.: Harvard University Press. Copyright © 1974, 1975 by the President and Fellows of Harvard College. Used by permission of Harvard University Press.

of ethnic and minority affairs. Nathan Glazer is professor of education and sociology at Harvard University. He has written numerous articles and books, among them The Lonely Crowd *(1950) with David Riesman, and* American Judaism *(1957). He is presently serving as coeditor of* Public Interest *magazine. Daniel Moynihan taught for many years at Harvard University before embarking on a career of government service. He has served as United States ambassador to India and to the United Nations and is presently United States senator from the state of New York. He has written several books, including* The Politics of a Guaranteed Income *(1973),* On Understanding Poverty *(1969), and* Towards a National Urban Policy *(1970).*

"Ethnicity" seems to be a new term. In the sense in which we use it—the character or quality of an ethnic group—it does not appear in the 1933 edition of the *Oxford English Dictionary,*, and only makes its appearance in the 1972 *Supplement,* where the first usage recorded is that of David Riesman in 1953. It is included in *Webster's Third New International,* 1961, but did not find its way into the *Random House Dictionary of the English Language* of 1966, nor the *American Heritage Dictionary of the English Language,* 1969. It did, however, make the 1973 edition of the *American Heritage Dictionary,* where it is defined as: "1. The condition of belonging to a particular ethnic group; 2. Ethnic pride." One senses a term still on the move. The first of these two definitions fits well with our own: an objective condition. The second, however, is decidedly *subjective:* "pride." Ho v very different from an old meaning, "obs. rare" as the *OED* has it, "heathendom: heathen superstition." At the very least, a change of relative status is going on here, and a shift in the general understanding of ethnic groups. Where they were formerly seen as survivals from an earlier age, to be treated variously with toleration, annoyance, or mild celebration, there is now a growing sense that they may be forms of social life that are capable of renewing and transforming themselves.

Still, one may wonder how useful this new term really is. Does it describe a new reality, or is it simply a new way of describing something old? Is it not a matter of age-old human characteristics and sentiments, finding expression, perhaps, in new settings, but in themselves nothing new? We think not. In our judgment, something new *has* appeared. A reader of the early 19th century, encountering the assertion that industrialization was shaping distinctive social classes, could well have shrugged it off with the thought that there had always been social ranks, always different ways of earning a living. Yet to have done so would have been to miss a big event of that age. Similarly, we feel that to see only what is familiar in the ethnicity of our time is to miss the emergence of a new social category as significant for the understanding of the present-day world as that of social class itself.

Perhaps the best way to getting at what is new here is by reference to the prevailing ideas of most contemporary social scientists regarding the course of modern social development. One such idea has been called by Milton Gordon the "liberal expectancy"—the expectation that the kinds of features which distinguish one group from another would inevitably lose their weight and sharpness in modern and modernizing societies, that there would be increasing emphasis on achievement rather than ascription, that common systems of education and communication would wipe out group differences, that nationally uniform economic and political systems would have the same effect. Under these circumstances, the "primordial" (or in any case antecedent) differences between groups would become less and less significant. This "liberal expectancy" flowed into the "radical expectancy"—that class would become the main line of division between people, erasing the earlier lines of tribe, language, religion, national origin, and that these class divisions would themselves, after the Revolution, disappear. Thus Karl Marx and his followers reacted with impatience to the heritage of the past, as they saw it, in the form of ethnic attachments. *Interest* should guide rational men in social action; and interest was determined by economic position.

Yet one of the striking characteristics of the present situation is the extent to which the ethnic group itself is now behaving as an interest group. Interest is pursued effectively by ethnic groups today as well as by interest-defined groups: indeed, perhaps it can be pursued even more effectively. As against class-based forms of social identification and conflict—which of course continue to exist—we have been surprised by the persistence and salience of ethnic-based forms of social identification and conflict.

Thus, whereas in the past religious conflicts were based on such issues as the free and public practice of a religion, today they are based—like the one which is tearing Northern Ireland apart—on the issue of which group shall gain benefits or hold power. Language conflicts—as in India—today have little to do with the right to the public use of the language, as they did in the 19th century when, for example, there were efforts to Russify the Russian empire and Magyarize the Hungarian kingdom. They have more to do with which linguistic group shall have the best opportunity to get which job. It would be wrong to insist on too sharp a distinction: certainly the prestige of one's religion and language is involved in both kinds of conflict. Nevertheless the weight has shifted from an emphasis on culture, language, religion, *as such,* to an emphasis on the economic and social interests of the members of the linguistic or religious group.

There are two related explanations which may account for this development. The first is the evolution of the welfare state in the more advanced economies of the world and the advent of the socialist state in the underdeveloped economies. In either circumstance, the *state* becomes a crucial and direct influence on economic well-being, as well as on political status and everything flowing from that. In such a situation it is usually not enough, or not enough for long enough, to assert claims on behalf of large but loosely aggregated groups such as "workers," "peasants," "white-collar employees." Claims of this order are too broad to elicit a very satisfactory response, and even when they do, the benefits are necessarily diffuse and often evanescent, having the quality of an across-the-board wage increase which produces an inflation that leaves everyone about as he was. As a matter of strategic efficacy, it becomes necessary to disaggregate, to assert claims for a group small enough to make significant concessions possible and, equally, small enough to produce some gain from the concessions made. A British prime minister who does "something for the workers" probably doesn't do much and almost certainly does even less for his party. Doing something for the Scots, however, becomes an increasingly attractive and real option for Westminster. *That* much in the way of resources can be found, and the Scots are likely both to know about it and to consider it a positive gain, at least past the point of the next general election.

The welfare state and the socialist state appear to be especially responsive to ethnic claims. This is everywhere to be encountered: an Indian minister assuring his parliament that "Muslims, Christians, and other minorities" will receive their "due and proper share" of railroad jobs; a Czech government choosing a Slovak leader; a Chinese prime minister in Singapore choosing an Indian foreign minister; and so on. Leaders of groups are aware that political skills in pressing such claims vary, and occasionally voice their concern, as reported in a recent Associated Press dispatch from Los Angeles:

> The Asian-American community leaders have accused the U.S. Department of Labor of exploiting their inexperience in "the political game" to exclude them when allocating federal funds.
>
> "We Asians have always been a quiet minority. We've always been taken for granted, and we always get the crumbs,"

Miss —, a leader of the Chinese Community Council, told newsmen.

Miss — was referring to the distribution of $314,000 in federal funds for career counseling projects. The council leaders accused the U.S. manpower area planning council of doing "a tremendous wrong" in giving the funds away entirely to black and Chicano groups, whose project proposals were more professionally drafted.

The strategic efficacy of ethnicity as a basis for asserting claims against government has its counterpart in the seeming ease whereby government employs ethnic categories as a basis for distributing its rewards. Nothing was more dramatic than the rise of this practice on the part of the American government in the 1960s, *at the very moment it was being declared abhorrent and illegal.* The Civil Rights Act of 1964 was the very embodiment of "the liberal expectancy." "Race, color, religion, sex, national origin": all such ascriptive categories were abolished. No one was to be classified by such primitive terms. In particular, government was to become color blind. Within hours of the enactment of the statute, in order to enforce it, the federal government, for the first time, began to require ever more detailed accountings of subgroups of every description, job trainees, kindergarten children, kindergarten teachers, university faculties, front-office secretaries in terms of—race, color, sex. (We have not yet proceeded to religion and national origin.) The expectancy that such characteristics would be ignored—in the immediate postwar years governments were busy eliminating all references to race and religion from official forms, even forbidding universities to request photographs of applicants for admission—was instantly replaced by the requirement that they not only be known but the facts as to distribution justified. Random distributions would not do: quotas appeared in American society, the instrument of national social policy designed ostensibly to prevent discrimination by going—inevitably, perhaps—beyond that to positive efforts on behalf of those presumptively discriminated against, a list which in short order commenced to lengthen.

Statutes began to reflect this new strategy. A small example: the Drug Abuse Education Act of 1970 provides "for the use of adequate personnel from similar social, cultural, age, ethnic, and racial backgrounds as those of the individuals served under any such program." In other words, the federal government was not only to know the peculiar ethnic patterns of various kinds of drug abuse, but was to match the therapists with patients: Azerbaijani junkie, Azerbaijani counselor.

In a variation of folk medicine, it was judged that wherever a malady was found, there too would a remedy reside. Which may or may not be nonsense: what is not to be denied is that the statute appropriated many millions of dollars for social services which were going to end up in the pockets of those who would dispense them, and these could be concentrated in specific ethnic groups. If government was doing a group a favor by providing special therapeutic services, it could compound the favor by concentrating the patronage involved within the very same group.

In addition to the strategic efficacy of ethnicity in making claims on the resources of the modern state, another reason for the shift to ethnicity as the organizing principle of interest conflicts concerns the issue of equality. Men are not equal; neither are ethnic groups. Whether they should be, or shouldn't be, is, of course, a wholly different question. If one is to describe the way the world is, one describes people everywhere ranked in systems of social stratification in which one person is better or worse off than another. This is the empirical fact. As with individuals, so with groups of individuals, with social groups defined by ethnic identity. We follow Ralf Dahrendorf in holding that inequalities among groups arise in the same way as he says they do among individuals: from differential success in achieving norms. Dahrendorf's thesis is that every society establishes norms selected from a universe of possible values. There seems no end to human ingenuity in thinking of characteristics that can be described as desirable or undesirable. It can be thought a good thing to be wealthy, or to be poor; to be dark or to be light; to be skinny or fat; generous or mean; religious or atheistic; fun-loving or dour; promiscuous or chaste. However, once a selection is made as to what is good and what is bad, individuals—and, we add, ethnic groups—have different levels of success in attaining the desired condition. Woe to blacks in Rhodesia; pity the white in Uganda. Pity the Nepalese in Bhutan who labors on construction gangs before the eyes of a landowning peasantry which despises such servility; woe to the Malay facing the onslaught of Chinese industriousness.

In Dahrendorf's account the individual encounters the norms of his society *and* the "sanctions designed to enforce these principles." Some do better than others and reap the rewards; some suffer the punishments. But as between different ethnic groups, which have made quite different selections from the universe of possibilities, the norms of one are likely to be quite different from those of another, such that individuals who are successful by the standards of their own groups will be failures by those of the others. In a situation where one group is dominant—which is to say that its norms are seen as normal not just for them, but for everyone—there follows an almost automatic consignment of other groups to inferior status. This is not an entirely automatic consequence, since some groups will discover that they are good at achieving the norms of the dominant group, and may even be better than the group that laid down those "laws." In Kenya the Indians were evidently better at trading than the Africans, and so the Indians are being expelled. Jews have known the experience, Japanese, Chinese: who has not? (There are, of course, situations in which no one group is dominant, and where differing norms compete with one another, but this makes if anything for less social peace, as no one is ever quite certain what constitutes success or failure.)

Herein lies the dynamic element in the system. Dahrendorf writes that "inequality always implies the gain of one group at the expense of others; thus every system of social stratification generates protest against its principles and bears the seeds of its own suppression." It is not perhaps necessary to assert that *every* system of social stratification generates protest against its principles. Some may not. But most that we run into in the 20th century seem to do so. This is to say that a *different* set of norms is set forth as desirable. Struggle ensues. Changes occur, not infrequently changes that favor those previously unsuccessful. Things *they* are good at come to be labeled good.

At this point we come back to the strategic efficacy of ethnicity as an organizing principle. In the most natural way the unsuccessful group has the best chance of changing the system if it behaves *as a group*. It is as a group that its struggle becomes not merely negative, but positive also, not merely against the norms of some other group, but in favor of the already existing norms of its own. One of the difficulties of social class as an organizing principle surely is that there just isn't that much conflict of norm between most social classes. In the West intellectuals and others at the top of the social stratification will fantasize about the differences between the values of those at the bottom and those in the middle—always to the advantage of the former—but it usually turns out that those at the bottom pretty much share notions of desirable and undesirable with those in the middle. Ethnic groups, however, often do differ as to what is desirable and what is undesirable.

Marxists thought ethnic groups would disappear. Why on earth would one wish to be a Pole when one could be a Worker. One reason, we are suggesting, is that being a Pole—or a Sikh, or a Mestizo— frequently involves a distinctive advantage or disadvantage, and that remaining a Pole, or a Sikh, or a Mestizo is just as frequently a highly effective way either to defend the advantage or to overcome the disadvantage.

Some individuals opt otherwise. They "pass" out of their own ethnic group into another, typically one that offers greater advantages. This process of absorption is extremely powerful: in the United States, at least, it is probably still quite the most important social process. Americans become more "American" and less ethnic all the time. But they may also—and simultaneously—become more ethnic. This was most dramatically the experience of Negro Americans during the 1960s—they even changed their name to "blacks" to establish that new assertion of distinctiveness—and other groups followed suit, or accompanied them on parallel tracks. As with student activism, this was a phenomenon whole parts of the world were experiencing, and any explanation that depends solely on local elements is not likely to remain satisfactory for long. Something larger was going on: something so large that Ralf Dahrendorf has recently referred to the "refeudalization" of society, the return of ascribed rather than achieved characteristics as determinants of social stratification. It may be that ethnicity is merely part of this larger development.

In a most tentative way one further suggestion may be advanced concerning the new saliency of ethnicity. Dahrendorf notes that for almost two centuries—"from Locke to Lenin"—"property dominated social and political thought: as a source of everything good or evil, as a principle to be retained or abolished." Yet, he continues, in societies such as those of the Soviet Union, Yugoslavia, and Israel, where private property has been reduced to "virtual insignificance," social stratification—class—persists, even flourishes. Further, we would add, the new stratification is to a considerable extent correlated with ethnicity. It probably always was, but the preoccupation with property relations obscured ethnic ones, which, typically, were seen either as derivative of the former, or survivals from a precontractual age. Now—as Yugoslav Communists struggle hopelessly (or so it would seem) to achieve some equity of development and living standard as between Bosnia-Herzegovina, Croatia, Macedonia, Montenegro, Serbia, and Slovenia; as Israeli Socialists look with alarm at the persisting differences in the "social class status" of "European" Jews as against "Oriental" Jews in their homeland; as Great Russians prattle on about the equality of ethnic groups in the Soviet Union, while Ukrainians in Washington rally in protest at the *Russian* embassy, and Jews in Moscow demand to be allowed to emigrate to Israel—it is property that begins to seem derivative, and ethnicity a more fundamental source of stratification.

This phenomenon is likely to be as much in evidence in an advanced capitalistic society where property relations are attenuated, as in a communist or socialist society where they are abolished. But it is the communist nations which have shown the more pronounced concern with ethnic matters, possibly because ethnic reality is so at odds with

Marxist-Leninist theory. (Otto Bauer, one of the few communist theorists to attempt to incorporate "nationalities" into communist theory was, perhaps significantly, a product of the Austro-Hungarian world at a time when Croatia was governed from Vienna.) There are scores of official nationalities in the Soviet Union, and every citizen, at age sixteen, must opt for one such identity, which he retains for life. Similarly, the Chinese, with their great, central Han culture, find themselves paying considerable heed to "minority nationalities." According to a recent news dispatch from Peking:

> More than 143,000 people of minority nationalities in the autonomous regions of Sinkiang, Tibet, Inner Mongolia, Kwangsi and Ningsia, and the Province of Yunnan have been admitted into the Communist Party of China since the Ninth Party Congress in 1969. They include Tibetans, Mongolians, Uighurs, Chuangs, Huis, Koreans, Kazakhs, Yaos, and Miaos.
>
> Most of the new party members are workers and former poor and lower-middle peasants or herdsmen. There is a certain number of revolutionary intellectuals. The new members are both men and women and range in age from young to old.
>
> Many of the new party members from national minorities are emancipated slaves or serfs, or children of former slaves or serfs. They warmly love Chairman Mao, the Party, and the New Society, and hate the old society.*

In short, while religion, language, and concrete cultural differences did decline, at least in the West, as specific foci of attachment and

---

*Compare the following item taken from a recent issue of *GOP Nationalities News*, a publication of the Republican National Committee:

"*Martin E. Seneca, Jr.,* a Seneca Indian, has been appointed to the important position of Director of Trust Responsibilities, Bureau of Indian Affairs, by BIA Commissioner Morris Thompson. Seneca, with a doctorate of law degree from Harvard, is an Associate Professor of Law at the University of Utah....

"At the April 21 meeting in New York of the newly-formed *Albanian-American Republican Club,* the following slate of officers were elected: *Hamdi H. Oruci,* Chairman; Mrs. *Nejmie Zaimi* and Dr. *Ligoz Buzi,* Vice Chairmen; *Lumo M. Tsungu,* Secretary; and *Mick Kajtazi,* Treasurer.

"Present at the 11th Annual Hungarian Ball of the *Hungarian Freedom Fighters Federation of the U.S.* held in Washington, D.C., on April 20, were Republican Congressman *Larry Hogan* of Maryland; the Director of the RNC Heritage Division and Mrs. *Julian Niemczyk;* and Mr. and Mrs. *Laszlo Pasztor* and Dr. and Mrs. *John B. Genys,* Chairman and Treasurer respectively of the NRHG(N) Council.

"Mrs. *Angela Miller,* of *Colombian* origin, who is vice president of the *Latin American Nationalities* Council, 3rd vice chairman of the Republican Business Women of New York, and president of All Nations Women's Club, Inc., was elected co-chairman of Activities and Planning Committee of the NRHG(N) Council.

"Mrs. *Inese Stokes,* of *Latvian* heritage, recording secretary of the Illinois Republican State Nationalities Council, was elected co-chairman of the NRHG(N) Awards Committee."

concern (to the extent the "liberal expectancy" was fulfilled), the groups defined by these cultural characteristics were differentially distributed through the social structure. Hence, even as their cultural characteristics were modified by modern social trends and became increasingly "symbolic," they were nevertheless able to serve as a basis for mobilization. Class was once expected to become the focus in the modern world for mobilizing group interests—it related directly to the rational character of society, and the way society generated different interests. Nation was the other great pole around which group interests could be mobilized. We do not in any way suggest that these are not the central categories for understanding modern societies; what we do propose is that ethnicity must now be added as a new major focus for the mobilization of interests, troublesome both to those who wish to emphasize the primacy of class, and those who wish to emphasize the primacy of nation.

But in order to understand why ethnicity has become stronger as a basis of group mobilization, it is necessary to modify the bald assertion that ethnicity serves as a means of advancing group interests—which it does—by insisting that it is not *only* a means of advancing interests. Indeed, one reason that ethnicity has become so effective a means of advancing interests is that it involves more than interests. As Daniel Bell puts it: "Ethnicity has become more salient [than class] because it can combine an interest with an affective tie," while, on the other hand, in the case of class, "what had once been an *ideology* has now become almost exclusively an *interest*."

Illuminating as they are, however, such observations do not answer the questions: Why ethnicity? and Why now? Harold Isaacs, describing the making of a basic group identity, begins his analysis with something so immediate as body image. Clearly that, as well as language and intimately transmitted culture, all play a role in the affective component of ethnicity. But in a world of rapid change and shifting identity, any fixed notion of the "primordial" as the basis of group formation is bound to run into trouble. One problem with the primordial is that nowadays we know how recently many "primordial" groups were created. It is also clear that circumstances have much to do with degrees of ethnic attachment, mobilization, and conflict. In some circumstances, there is much; in others, very little.

These are two poles of analysis—the "primordialist" and the "circumstantialist"—between which explanations for the persistence or revival or creation of ethnic identities tend to waver—ours included. We do not celebrate ethnicity as a basic attribute of men which, when suppressed, will always rise again; nor do we dismiss it as an aberration on the road to a rational society in which all such heritages of the past will become irrelevant to social and political action. For as a political idea, as a mobilizing principle, ethnicity in our time has manifested itself under widely disparate conditions with luxuriantly varied results.

Thus, in the United States the rising demands among blacks first for civil rights, then for equality of opportunity, finally for some equality of participation in the social, economic, and political institutions of the country, can be understood in terms of the distinctive history of blacks in the United States. But it is striking that the black movement found an echo among other ethnic groups in the United States—Latin American, American Indian, Oriental, and eventually whites of various kinds. The circumstances of each of these groups were different. Some had been conquered, some had emigrated from colonies, some from free countries, some had met substantial prejudice and discrimination, others nothing much more than the inconvenience of a new country. Yet the form of the mobilized ethnic group seemed, in some degree, to satisfy individuals in each. (Indeed, many had been involved in vigorous ethnic politics for half a century or more. What changed was that such activity was legitimated: previously it had been disapproved and to some degree disavowed.) We do not assert that some common need, some common distress, existed in everybody ready to be evoked. We do not say that ethnicity is something like the identity of parents in Victorian novels which must be discovered lest some nameless distress follow. But on the other hand we do not believe that the new intensity of ethnic identification among a number of groups was merely a matter of imitation, or even of protective mimicry. Some combination of need and imitation seems to have been at work.

The black revolution had as surprising a resonance abroad as at home. A "black power" movement developed in the West Indies, a "civil-rights" movement in Northern Ireland, and "Black Panthers" formed in Israel. Once again, as we consider the relative weight of primordial and circumstantial factors, we find a complex interplay. The Catholics of Northern Ireland did not need the black example to teach them that they were aggrieved—their miseries go back farther in history than those of American blacks—nor did the Oriental Jews of Israel need the American blacks to remind them that something was amiss with their position. Nevertheless through the ever more universally pervasive mass media, the black example exerted its influence to some indeterminate extent, just as on their side American blacks were influenced by certain developments abroad.

The American civil-rights movement, for example, avowedly and explicitly adopted techniques developed in 20th-century India during the struggle against British rule. The more recent (and, it is hoped, marginal) incidents of urban terrorism followed, albeit without any evident awareness of the fact, a model of resistance developed by the Irish in the 19th century, and still dominant there. Underground "commandants" in San Francisco issuing "execution" orders against deviant revolutionaries were acting out the drama of Dublin in 1920. North Africans picked up the technique, or else invented it on their own; and an Italian made a movie, *The Battle of Algiers,* which American revolutionaries were soon trying to imitate. And so exchanges proceeded, with, in our time, ever mounting violence. Hijacking was invented, we believe, by the Palestinians—but Croatian workers resident in Sweden and Moslem dissidents in Ethiopia (to refer only to some of those who have acted out of some ethnic interest) have both made use of it.

What of the future? In the 18th and 19th centuries, international economic developments led to great migrations of labor, which in turn led to the creation of a good number of multi-ethnic states. This process is still going on. Never in history did western Europe import as much labor as in the years after the second World War. A new colored population of West Indians, Indians, and Pakistanis was added to England. One-third of the labor force of Switzerland, one-eighth of the labor force of Germany, and substantial parts of the labor forces of France, Belgium, the Netherlands, and Sweden came to be made up of foreign workers. The legal circumstances of each of these waves of new immigrants varied. Some, like the new colored groups of England, were permanent, and had all the rights of citizenship. Some were from neighboring members of the European Commonwealth, and had claims to full social benefits in any other state of the Commonwealth. Some—like the Algerians in France—came from former colonies and had special rights. Others—Turks and Yugoslavs in Germany—came under permits and, theoretically at least, had no right to any permanent settlement. In other cases, such as Sweden, an egalitarian philosophy of government treated all newcomers, whether Italian or Finnish, generously, both as to social benefits and political rights.

Varied though the patterns are, however, we see everywhere two different approaches in conflict. On the one hand, the common philosophy of egalitarianism asserts that *all* should be treated alike: not only natives and older citizens of a nation, but those who come to work and settle there. On the other hand, western Europeans have learned that new and permanent settlements of other ethnic groups mean ethnic conflict, and they intend to avoid it if they can. For Great Britain it is too late: although only 2 percent of the population, the new colored groups already form an issue in British politics that far outweighs their minuscule numbers, and further immigration has virtually been halted. The North Africans, Spanish, and Portuguese in France, and the Italians, Yugoslavs, and Turks in Germany have lesser rights than the West Indians, Pakistanis, and Indians in England, but one wonders whether they will actually be any less permanent a part of those countries. Will the problems arising from the new heterogeneity of France and Germany—the familiar conflicts over housing, schooling, jobs—really be settled by simple mass expulsions, legal as that may be?

Alone of the major nations in the world, the United States continues to accept large numbers of permanent immigrants. Moreover, these immigrants are of quite different "stock" from those of the past. Most notably, they are Asians, and most notable of all, they are to an unprecedented degree professional, upper-middle-class persons. What this means is that the process which took even the most successful of earlier groups two generations at least—is likely to be rapid for these most recent newcomers. Thus, however much western Europeans and others may succeed in protecting themselves from the ethnic storms of the 20th century, we may be sure they will continue to buffet the Great Republic.

Nor, of course, can the remaining nation-states easily succeed in avoiding their share of such difficulties. Since the second World War almost every new nation—and they far outnumber the older nations— has come into existence with a number of serious ethnic conflicts waiting, as it were, their turn to be the focus of post-independence political life. The old European states, while becoming somewhat more diverse with the addition of new groups, are still in the process of finding out just how diverse they had already become. Add to this the fact—still given surprisingly little attention—that in a world in which each society becomes ethnically more diverse, we have had, since the second World War, a strong prejudice against the formation of new states organized along ethnic lines. As Samuel Huntington has written, "The 20th-century bias against political divorce, that is, secession, is just about as strong as the 19th-century bias against marital divorce." Bangladesh is an exception, but the general rule remains in force. Certainly these political realities alone seem to provide a good number of the ingredients for a greater degree of ethnic conflict than was experienced, for example, in the world of the Great Depression.

Indeed, there is already evident an increase in both the number and intensity of ethnic conflicts. Walker Conner has undertaken the invaluable task of recording the rise and extent since the French Revolution of what he calls "ethnonationalism." He reports that nearly half of the independent countries of the world have been troubled in recent years by some degree of "ethnically inspired dissonance." We do not have benchmarks for earlier periods, but it seems clear that ethnic conflicts have shown a rise, too, in intensity in the last decade or so. As some examples, consider the Anglophone-Francophone conflict in Canada, Catholic and Protestant in Northern Ireland, Walloon and Fleming in Belgium, Jews and other minority groups versus Great Russians in the Soviet Union, Ibo versus Hausa and Yoruba in Nigeria, Bengali versus non-Bengali in Pakistan, Chinese versus Malay in Malaysia, Greek versus Turk in Cyprus. If we had measurements of intensity we would not necessarily find that every one of these conflicts has become uniformly more intense. Some of them seem happily to have peaked (sometimes in war and violent conflict), and measures of harmonization and accommodation seem to have had some effect since these peaks were reached (Nigeria, the United States). In at least one other case—Pakistan—conflict has reached the point of separation, and has subsequently declined in intensity, to be succeeded perhaps by a rise in ethnic discord within each one of the two successor states.

There are those who say that ethnic conflict is simply the form that class conflict has been taking on certain occasions in recent decades, and that without the motor of class exploitation nothing else would follow. Others say that ethnic conflicts must be decomposed into a variety of elements: colonial conflicts; the uprising of the "internally" colonized; the ambition of self-appointed leaders; fashions and fads. To us, however, it seems clear that ethnic identity *has* become more salient, ethnic self-assertion stronger, ethnic conflict more marked everywhere in the last twenty years, and that the reasons include the rise of the welfare state, the clash between egalitarianism and the differential achievement of norms, the growing heterogeneity of states, and the international system of communication. This set of reasons scarcely amounts to a theory, but it does, we believe, suggest that there is a phenomenon here that is, in ways not yet explicated, no mere survival but intimately and organically bound up with major trends of modern societies.

SECTION 2

The Emergence of Ethnic Awareness

WILLIAM J. WILSON

Power, Racism, and Privilege

The black protest movement of the 1950s and 1960s, which so many authors have recognized as being a catalyst for the ethnic resurgence, has itself evolved significantly during the past twenty years. In the following essay William Wilson of the University of Chicago analyzes the changes in strategy and goals that have occurred.

He notes that the early black protest was confined mainly to the activities of the National Association for the Advancement of Colored People's Legal Defense Fund. Despite overwhelming success in the courts culminating with the Brown *decision in 1954, the black leadership realized that southerners were able to block, ignore, or seriously delay the implementation of many of these decisions. As a consequence, litigation was gradually replaced by the rise of passive or nonviolent resistance under the leadership of Martin Luther King, Jr., and the Southern Christian Leadership Conference. Beginning with the bus boycott in Montgomery in 1957 and culminating with the march on Selma in 1965, nonviolent demonstrations helped bring about the adoption of the Civil Rights Acts of 1957, 1960, 1964, and 1965. Wilson views sit-in demonstrations, begun in North Carolina in 1960, as the most important development in the period of massive resistance. It was this action, he contends, that marked a decisive break with the legalistic actions of the past.*

Despite the gains achieved through the nonviolent demonstrations of the early 1960s, black leaders could not stop the growing militancy of

From William J. Wilson, *Power, Racism, and Privilege: Race Relations in Theoretical and Sociohistorical Perspectives* (1973), pp. 129–40. Reprinted with permission of Macmillan Publishing Co., Inc. Copyright © 1973, William J. Wilson.

northern blacks, particularly those living in the ghettos. Spurred by the rhetoric of Stokely Carmichael and Malcolm X, blacks in the northern cities took to the streets to find answers to their economic difficulties. From 1964 to 1968 the civil rights movement shifted from the South to the North and from passive resistance to violence as the country was wracked by the ghetto riots in Newark, Detroit, Los Angeles, and elsewhere. The Black Panther Party now became the leading spokesman for civil rights protest. The militancy of those years did not last, however, and Wilson argues that the position which enjoys majority support in the black community today is one of cultural nationalism. It is based upon a positive race identity and an emphasis on culture building.

William Wilson is a political science professor at the University of Chicago. His specialty is black politics.

Throughout the discussion of black social thought and protest in the United States, one pattern of behavior seems to emerge: *the changing goals of black advancement tend to be associated with the changing definition of black despair, and both the defined problem and the conceived goal are ultimately associated with the choice of possible pressure or constraint resources that blacks can mobilize in pressing for the desired solution.* However, it should be noted that despite the definition of the problem and the conception of the goal, the choice of pressure resources is influenced or determined by the extent to which blacks find themselves in competitive relations with whites. The now more conservative black protest movements, such as the NAACP and the National Urban League, developed and gained momentum when racial accommodations were undergoing change but when the dominant-group controls were so strong that the pressure tactics of the mid-20th century activist movements would not have been tolerated.[1]

Before the emergence of the activist black protest movements, the drive for civil rights was therefore in the hands of a few professionals competent to work through controlling legal and educational channels.[2] The NAACP tended to define the racial problem as legal segregation in the South, and its major goal, popularized by the slogan "Free by 1963," was the elimination of all state-enforced segregation. Although the officials of the NAACP have lacked a power orientation, the mobilization of their legal machinery has represented a display of power—the power of litigation—in this instance, a power resource of high liquidity. Working through prevailing institutional channels, the NAACP was able to win an overwhelming number of cases in the

Supreme Court and thus helped to produce laws designed to improve racial conditions in America, although white southerners ingeniously circumvented the new laws and thus usually prevented their implementation. Lewis M. Killian has discussed this matter:

> It is ironic that the white South was extremely successful in minimizing the impact of the desegregation decision of the federal court without arousing the indignation of the rest of the nation. As much as the White Citizens Council and the Ku Klux Klan are invoked as symbols of the southern resistance, they and their extra-legal tactics did not make this possible. Far more effective were the legal stratagems, evasions, and delays that led Negroes to realize that although they had won a new statement of principle they had not won the power to cause this principle to be implemented.[3]

White procrastination made it apparent to many black leaders that both the goal and the problem had been too narrowly defined. A new definition of the problem thus emerged—token compliance with the newly created laws—and a corresponding new goal—the elimination of both de facto and de jure segregation. Litigation, no longer an effective pressure resource in the face of white procrastination, was replaced by passive or nonviolent resistance. The fact that the power balance between blacks and whites had undergone some alteration also helped bring about the shift to nonviolent direct-action protest. As blacks increased their political and economic resources, as the Supreme Court rendered decisions in favor of desegregation, and as the United States government became increasingly sensitive to world opinion of its racial situation, black expectations were heightened, continued white resistance became more frustrating, and consequently support for direct-action (albeit nonviolent) protests quickly mushroomed. Although some writers have identified the successful Montgomery bus boycott of 1955–56 as the beginning of the black revolt,[4] Meier and Rudwick have maintained that "the really decisive break with the pre-eminence of legalistic techniques came with the college student sit-ins that swept the South in the spring of 1960."[5] These demonstrations set a chain of nonviolent resistance movements...into motion that subsequently swept the country from 1960 to 1965. Even though the initial emphasis was on persuasion resources rather than constraint resources, the technique of nonviolence was in reality an aggressive manifestation of pressure. Its twofold goal was to create and to implement civil rights laws. Even though many of the nonviolent protests were not specifically directed at the federal government, they were in many cases intended to apply indirect pressure on it. Black leaders recognized that because of their political and pressure resources and because of the United States' concern for world opinion, the government was not in a position to ignore their stepped-up drive for civil rights.

For a brief period of time, the nonviolent resistance strategy proved to be highly effective. In addition to forcing local governments and private agencies to integrate facilities in numerous southern cities and towns, the nonviolent demonstrations pressed the federal government into passage of civil rights legislation in 1964 and voting rights legislation in 1965—acts that satisfied many of the black demands of the early 1960s. There are several reasons why the federal government responded favorably to many of the demands emanating from the nonviolent protest movement: (1) the demands that accompanied the protests tended to be fairly specific, e.g., "End discrimination in voting," and hence the government was able to provide "remedies" that clearly approximated the specifications in the demands; (2) the attempt to satisfy these demands did not call for major sacrifices on the part of whites, and hence there was little likelihood that a significant political backlash against the government would occur in sections of the country other than the South; (3) the demands were consistent with prevailing ideals of democracy and freedom of choice, and hence they could not be easily labeled "extreme" either by the white citizens or by governmental authorities; (4) the more blacks pressed their demands and carried out their protests, the more violent was the southern response, and because these developments were receiving international attention, the government became increasingly concerned; (5) the government was sensitive to the political resources blacks had developed and became cognizant of the growing army of northern whites sympathetic to the black cause; (6) blacks' political strength seemed to be magnified by the united front they presented, as groups ranging from the relatively conservative NAACP to the radical Student Nonviolent Coordinating Committee all joined in nonviolent protests to effect change.

To understand why many blacks shifted away from nonviolence both as a philosophy of life and as a technique to achieve racial equality, it is necessary to understand the dynamics of minority protest: if an extended period of increased expectations and gratification is followed by a brief period in which the gap between expectations and gratifications suddenly widens and becomes intolerable, the possibility of violent protests is greatly increased. Davis applies this analysis to the black rebellion of the 1960s:

> In short—starting in the mid-1950s and increasing more or less steadily into the early 1960s—white violence grew against the now lawful and protected efforts of Negroes to gain integra-

tion. And so did direct action and later violence undertaken by blacks, in a reciprocal process that moved into the substantial violence of 1963–67. That three-year period may be considered a peak, possibly the peak of the violence that constituted the black rebellion. It merits reemphasis that during this era of increased hostility progress intensified both the white reaction to it and the black counteraction to the reaction, because everytime a reaction impeded the progress, the apparent gap widened between expectations and gratification.[6]

Even though there was no sudden or sharp increase in black unemployment and no sudden reversal in the material gains blacks had accumulated during the prosperous 1960s, "there was, starting notably in 1963, not the first instance of violence against blacks but a sudden increase in it. This resurgence of violence came after, and interrupted, the slow but steady progress since 1940. It quickly frustrated rising expectations."[7] For the first time, there was a real sense of apprehension among blacks that, not only would conditions stop improving, but gains already achieved could very well be lost unless steps were taken to counteract mounting white violence.

Birmingham, Alabama, in 1963 was the scene of this initial wave of white violence and black counterreaction. In April, Birmingham police used high-pressure water hoses and dogs to attack civil rights marchers, and blacks retaliated by throwing rocks and bottles at the police; in May, segregationists bombed the homes of black leaders, and blacks retaliated by rioting, setting two white-owned stores on fire, and stoning police and firemen; on September 15, whites enraged by school desegregation bombed a black church, killing four small girls and injuring twenty-three other adults and children, and blacks angrily responded by stoning police.[8]

However, racial violence was not restricted to Birmingham, Alabama, in 1963. Medgar Evers, an NAACP official in Jackson, Mississippi, was shot to death in front of his home on May 28, 1963. Whites and blacks in Cambridge, Maryland, engaged in a gun battle after blacks had stormed a restaurant to rescue sit-in demonstrators beaten by whites; the black quarter in Lexington, North Carolina, was attacked by a white mob after blacks had attempted to obtain service at white restaurants, and in the ensuing gun battle a white man was killed; mounted police at Plaquemine, Louisiana, galloped into a group of civil rights demonstrators and dispersed them with electric cattle prods—fifteen demonstrators were injured; police used tear gas, shotguns, and high-pressure water hoses in Savannah, Georgia, to break up a protest demonstration that turned into a riot—at least ten whites and thirteen blacks were injured; and mass arrests of civil rights activists took place in Athens, Georgia; Selma, Alabama; Greensboro, North Carolina; Orangeburg, South Carolina; and several other southern towns.[9]

The gap between expectations and emotional gratifications[10] increased black support for violent protest and was reflected, not only in the way blacks responded to white attacks beginning with the Birmingham incident in 1963, but also in the changing philosophy of younger civil rights activists. In the early months of 1964, members of the Student Nonviolent Coordinating Committee (SNCC) and the Congress of Racial Equality (CORE) openly challenged the philosophy of nonviolence and called for more belligerent forms of protest.[11] It was during this same period that Malcolm X, shortly after he resigned from the Nation of Islam, called for blacks to arm themselves and abandon nonviolence and that the Brooklyn chapter of CORE attempted to tie up New York traffic (on April 22, the opening of the World's Fair) by emptying the fuel tanks of two thousand automobiles and abandoning them on the freeways leading to the fairgrounds (lacking support, the strategy failed).[12] Continued white violent acts such as the murder of civil rights workers by white terrorists in Mississippi in 1964, Ku Klux Klan terrorism in Mississippi and Alabama in 1965, attacks against CORE organizers in Bogalusa, Louisiana, in 1965, the beating and murder of civil rights activists in Selma, Alabama, in 1965, and police brutality that precipitated rioting in northern ghettoes in 1964 deepened the militant mood in the black community and widened the gap between expectations and emotional gratification.

In the face of these developments, the call by some black leaders for greater militancy was based on the optimistic belief that the larger society was more likely to respond properly to black demands backed by belligerent and violent protests than to those reinforced by nonviolent resistance. Theoretical analysis suggests either that blacks believed they possessed sufficient resources not only to disrupt the larger society but also to prevent an all-out repressive reaction by whites, or that they felt that by the mid-1960s the system had developed a high tolerance for minority protests.[13] However, it was lower-class urban blacks who dramatically demonstrated that a more belligerent mood had gripped the black community when they rocked the nation with a proliferation of ghetto revolts from 1964 to 1968. In the early 1960s, nonviolent protests were heavily populated by middle-class or higher-educated blacks, who were far more likely at this period to participate in a drive for social justice that was disciplined and sustained.[14] Ghetto blacks for the most part were not directly involved in the nonviolent resistance movement of the early 1960s, and many of the gains achieved did not materially benefit them (the civil rights movement up to 1965 produced laws primarily relevant to privileged blacks with competitive resources such as special talents or steady income);[15] nevertheless, the victories of the nonviolent movement increased expectations among all segments of the black population.[16] In the age of mass communication, northern ghetto blacks, like blacks throughout the country, were very much aware of and identified with the efforts of Martin Luther King, Jr., and other civil rights activists. By the same token, they were also cognizant of the white violence that threatened to halt the gradual but steady progress toward racial equality.

Accordingly, ghetto rebellions cannot be fully explained in isolation or independently of the increasingly militant mood of the black community. However, what made the situation of ghetto blacks unique was the fact that the gap between expectations and emotional gratification was combined with concrete grievances over police brutality, inferior education, unemployment, underemployment, and inadequate housing. It is true that these conditions have always existed in ghetto life and did not suddenly emerge during the 1960s, but the important point is that increased expectations and greater awareness of racial oppression made these conditions all the more intolerable.[17] Charles Silberman was essentially correct when he stated that "it is only when men sense the possibility of improvement, in fact, that they become dissatisfied with their situation and rebel against it. And 'with rebelling' as Albert Camus put it 'awareness is born,' and with awareness, an impatience 'which can extend to everything that [men] had previously accepted, and which is almost always retroactive.'"[18] Likewise, as the number and intensity of ghetto revolts increased, black complaints about human suffering became more explicit and focused.

The Harlem revolt in 1964 actually marked the beginning of ghetto uprisings of the 1960s (where groups of blacks looted stores, burned buildings, and attacked firemen and police in the black community), but the most serious revolts occurred in 1965 in Watts (resulting in 34 deaths, 900 injuries, 4,000 arrests, and an estimated property damage of $100 million), in 1967 in Detroit (43 deaths, 1,500 injuries, 5,000 arrests, and $200 million in property damage), and Newark (26 deaths, 1,200 injuries, 160 arrests, and $47 million in property damage). The assassination of Dr. Martin Luther King, Jr., precipitated the final series of ghetto rebellions in the spring of 1968. During that four-year period (1964–68) of intense racial violence, thousands of persons, mostly black, were killed or injured, and the property damage was estimated in the billions of dollars.

In addition to these manifestations of greater black militancy, the emergence of the Black Power movement in 1966, with its shift in emphasis to racial solidarity and its explicit repudiation of nonviolence as a strategy of protest and way of life, can also be associated with the sudden gap between rising expectations and emotional gratification. In a fundamental sense, however, the Black Power movement represented a return to the self-help philosophy and emphasis on black solidarity that usually occurs "when the Negroes' status has declined or when they experienced intense disillusionment following a period of heightened but unfulfilled expectations."[19]

Unlike the self-help nationalistic philosophies that developed in the 1850s following increased repression in the free states, in the Booker T. Washington era as a response to the growth of biological racism and resurgence of white supremacy, and in the post–World War I period as a reaction to white violence perpetrated against black urban immigrants in the North, the Black Power movement developed during a period when blacks had achieved a real sense of power.

> Killian has commented on this new feeling of power: The nonviolent demonstrations of SCLC, CORE, and SNCC... had not solved the bitter problems of the Negro masses, but they had shown that the Negro minority could strike terror into the hearts of the white majority. They had produced concessions from white people, even though the triumph of winning these concessions had soon turned to despair because they were never enough. Watts and other riots reflected no clearly formulated demand for new concessions. They did reflect the basic truth that Negroes, mobilized in ghettoes to an extent never before experienced and made confident by earlier victories, were no longer afraid of white power. Within a few months after Watts, they would begin to proclaim their faith in Black Power.[20]

This new sense of power was reflected not so much in the programs actually introduced under the banner of Black Power as in the revolutionary rhetoric used to articulate Black Power philosophy. That certain black radicals dared, through national media, to call openly for the use of violence to overthrow racial oppression was a clear indication that blacks felt secure enough to threaten the very stability of the larger society. In actual fact, however, although Black Power advocates often disagreed about the aims and purposes of the movement, their various demands and programs were more reformist in nature than revolutionary[21] (e.g., programs emphasizing black capitalism, the running of black candidates for political office, self-help in the area of jobs and housing, black studies in high schools and colleges, and black culture and identity). Some of the programs introduced by Black Power spokesmen were an extension of the conservative separatism advocated by the Nation of Islam (Black Muslims) under the leadership of Elijah Muhammad. From the 1950s to the first half of the 1960s, when black social thought continued to be overwhelmingly supportive of integration,[22] the Nation of Islam served as the major medium for a black nationalist philosophy.[23] Commenting on Muslim philosophy, Cruse wrote that the

> Nation of Islam was nothing but a form of Booker T. Washington economic self-help, black unity, bourgeois hard work, law abiding, vocational training, stay-out-of-the-civil-rights-struggle agitation, separate-from-the-white-man, etc., etc., morality. The only difference was that Elijah Muhammad added the potent factor of the Muslim religion to race, economic, and social philosophy of which the first prophet was none other than Booker T. Washington. Elijah Muhammad also added an element of "hate Whitey" ideology which Washington, of course, would never have accepted.[24]

The most significant influence on the radical flank of the Black Power movement was ex–Muslim minister Malcolm X. Because of differences with Elijah Muhammad, Malcolm X resigned from the Muslim organization and moved beyond its program of territorial separation and bourgeois economic nationalism. Shortly before he was assassinated in 1965, he had begun to formulate a philosophy of revolutionary nationalism (that "views the overthrow of existing political and economic institutions as a prerequisite for the liberation of black Americans, and does not exclude the use of violence"[25]) subsequently adopted by militant Black Power leaders such as Stokely Carmichael and H. Rap Brown and incorporated into the philosophy of the newly emerging Black Panther Party in the late 1960s.

Yet, of all the philosophies of nationalism or racial solidarity that emerged under the banner of Black Power, none has received as much support from black citizens as has cultural nationalism.[26] Cultural nationalism is concerned mainly with positive race identity, including the development and/or elaboration of black culture and history. One of the most illustrative statements of this theme has come from Blauner:

> In their communities across the nation, Afro-Americans are discussing "black culture." The mystique of "soul" is only the most focused example of this trend in consciousness. What is and what should be the black man's attitude toward American society and American culture has become a central division in

the Negro protest movement. The spokesmen for black power celebrate black culture and Negro distinctiveness; the integrationists base their strategy and their appeal on the fundamental "American-ness" of the black man. There are nationalist leaders who see culture building today as equal or more important than political organization. From Harlem to Watts there has been a proliferation of black theater, art, and literary groups; the recent ghetto riots (or revolts, as they are viewed from the nationalistic perspective) are the favored materials of these cultural endeavors.[27]

But certainly we must not lose sight of the fact that cultural nationalism, like other forms of nationalism, has become popular during certain periods in history—periods when black disillusionment follows a brief interval of black optimism and commitment to integration. It is not so important that structural assimilation,[28] especially for middle-class blacks, is occurring at a greater rate than ever before; what is important is the black perception of the racial changes that are occurring. Black awareness has been heightened by the efforts of both the civil rights and the Black Power activists, and impatience and frustration with the pace of racial equality have become more intense. Whereas the cultural nationalism of the 1850s and of the Harlem Renaissance period was largely confined to segments of the black intelligentsia,[29] the cultural nationalism of the late 1960s and early 1970s has transcended class lines. Awareness of the evils of racial oppression and of white resistance to racial equality is characteristic of all segments of the black population; support for racial solidarity with emphasis on black culture and racial identity has reached unprecedented heights.

MARLENE DIXON

Why Women's Liberation—2?

As with other women's reform movements of the past, the women's liberation movement of the 1960s was heavily influenced by the societal changes that preceded and surrounded it. In the case of women's liberation, many college women had been actively involved in the civil rights movement of the 1950s and 1960s. In their effort to end discrimination against black Americans, many women came to the realization that their status in some respects was equally low. Gradually they shifted their attention away from the male-dominated civil rights effort to a reform movement which sought to end discrimination against women in America. In doing so they adopted many of the methods and goals that have characterized ethnic group behavior of the last two decades.

In a militant feminist statement Marlene Dixon describes the conditions of the past fifty years that necessitated such a reform movement. In particular, she castigates the economic exploitation of women. Dixon believes male chauvinism can be understood only when it is viewed as a form of racism, "based on stereotypes drawn from a deep belief in the biological inferiority of women." The women's movement should then seek to destroy the ideology of male supremacy. But Dixon goes beyond this goal to alleviate the plight of women. She argues that women need to understand the context in which this exploitation is found. For Dixon the brutalization of women is only part of an inhumane economic and political society in the United States. Reflecting upon her own radicalization, she contends that the condition of women can be improved only through a commitment to oppose oppression throughout the world and by the termination of female chauvinism. In concluding she issues a call to arms—for a worldwide revolution.

Marlene Dixon is a professor of sociology at McGill University in Canada. This article is a sequel to her "Why Women's Liberation?" which was published by Ramparts *magazine in December, 1969.*

The old women's movement burned itself out in the frantic decade of the 1920s. After a hundred years of struggle, women won a battle, only to lose the campaign: the vote was obtained, but the new millennium did not arrive. Women got the vote and achieved a measure of legal emancipation, but the real social and cultural barriers to full equality for women remained untouched.

For over thirty years the movement remained buried in its own ashes. Women were born and grew to maturity virtually ignorant of their own history of rebellion, aware only of a caricature of blue stockings and suffragettes. Even as increasing numbers of women were being driven into the labor force by the brutal conditions of the 1930s and by the massive drain of men into the military in the 1940s, the old ideal remained: a woman's place was in the home and behind her man. As the war ended and men returned to resume their jobs in factories and offices, women were forced back to the kitchen and nursery with a vengeance. This story has been repeated after each war and the reason is clear: women form a flexible, cheap labor pool that is essential to a capitalist system. When labor is scarce, they are forced onto the labor market. When labor is plentiful, they are forced out. Women and blacks have provided a reserve army of unemployed workers, benefiting capitalists and the stable male white working class alike. Yet the system imposes untold suffering on the victims—blacks and women—through w wages and chronic unemployment.

With the end of the war, the average age at marriage declined; the average size of families went up; and the suburban migration began in earnest. The political conservatism of the fifties was echoed in a social conservatism that stressed a Victorian ideal of the woman's life: a full womb and selfless devotion to husband and children.

As the bleak decade played itself out, however, three important social developments emerged that were to make a rebirth of the women's struggle inevitable. First, women came to make up more than a third of the labor force, the number of working women being twice the prewar figure. Yet the marked increase in female employment did nothing to better the position of women, who were more occupationally disadvantaged in the 1960s than they had been twenty-five years earlier. Rather than moving equally into all sectors of the occupational structure, they were being forced into the low-paying service, clerical, and semi-skilled categories. In 1940, women had held 45 percent of all professional and technical positions; in 1967, they held only 37 percent. The proportion of women in service jobs meanwhile rose from 50 to 55 percent.

Second, the intoxicating wine of marriage and suburban life was turning sour; a generation of women woke up to find their children grown and a life (roughly thirty more productive years) of housework and bridge parties stretching out before them like a wasteland. For many younger women, the empty drudgery they saw in the suburban life was a sobering contradiction to adolescent dreams of romantic love and the fulfilling role of woman as wife and mother.

Third, a growing civil rights movement was sweeping thousands of young men and women into a moral crusade—a crusade that harsh political experience was to transmute into the New Left. The American Dream was riven and tattered in Mississippi and finally napalmed in Vietnam. Young Americans were drawn not to Levittown, but to Berkeley, Haight-Ashbury, and the East Village. Traditional political ideologies and cultural myths, sexual mores and sex roles with them, began to disintegrate in an explosion of rebellion and protest.

The three major groups that make up the new women's movement—working women, middle-class married women, and students—bring very different kinds of interests and objectives to women's liberation. Working women are most concerned with the economic issues of guaranteed employment, fair wages, job discrimination, and child care. Their most immediate oppression is rooted in industrial capitalism and felt directly through the vicissitudes of an exploitative labor market.

Middle-class women, oppressed by the psychological mutilation and injustice of institutionalized segregation, discrimination, and imposed inferiority, are most sensitive to the dehumanizing consequences of severely limited lives. Usually well educated and capable, these women are rebelling against being forced to trivialize their lives, to live vicariously through husbands and children.

Students, as unmarried, middle-class girls, have been most sensitized to the sexual exploitation of women. They have experienced the frustration of one-way relationships in which the girl is forced into a "wife" and companion role with none of the supposed benefits of marriage. Young women have increasingly rebelled not only against passivity and dependency in their relationships, but also against the notion that they must function as sexual objects, being defined in purely sexual rather than human terms, and being forced to package and sell themselves as commodities on the sex market.

Each group represents an independent aspect of the total institutionalized oppression of women. Yet, in varying degrees all women suffer from economic exploitation, from psychological deprivation, and from exploitative sexuality. Within women's liberation there is a growing understanding that the common oppression of women provides the basis for uniting to form a powerful and radical movement.

Clearly, for the liberation of women to become a reality, it is necessary to destroy the ideology of male supremacy that asserts the biological and social inferiority of women in order to justify massive institutionalized oppression.

The ideology of male chauvinism can only be understood when it is perceived as a form of racism, based on stereotypes drawn from a deep belief in the biological inferiority of women. The very stereotypes that express the society's belief in the biological inferiority of women are images used to justify oppression. The nature of women is depicted as dependent, incapable of reasoned thought, childlike in its simplicity and warmth, martyred in the role of mother, and mystical in the role of sexual partner.

It has taken over fifty years to discredit the scientific and social "proof" that once gave legitimacy to the myths of black racial inferiority. Today most people can see that the theory of the genetic inferiority of blacks is absurd. Yet few are shocked by the fact that scientists are still busy "proving" the biological inferiority of women.

Yet one of the obstacles to organizing women remains women's belief in their own inferiority. This dilemma is not a fortuitous one, for the entire society is geared to socialize women to believe in and adopt as immutable necessity their traditional and inferior role. From earliest training to the grave, women are constrained and propagandized. Spend an evening at the movies or watching television and you will see a grotesque figure called woman presented in a hundred variations upon the themes of "children, church, kitchen" or "the chick sex-pot." Such contradictions as these show how pervasive and deep-rooted is the cultural contempt for women, how difficult it is to imagine a woman as a serious human being, or conversely, how empty and degrading is the image of woman that floods the culture.

Countless studies have shown that black acceptance of white stereotypes leads to mutilated identity, to alienation, to rage and self-hatred. Human beings cannot bear in their own hearts the contradictions of those who hold them in contempt. The ideology of male supremacy creates self-contempt and psychic mutilation in women; it creates trained incapacities that put women at a disadvantage in all social relationships.

It is customary to shame those who would draw the parallel between women and blacks by a great show of concern over the suffering of black people. Yet this response itself reveals a refined combination of white middle-class guilt and male chauvinism, for it overlooks several essential facts. For example, the most oppressed group within the feminine population is made up of black women, many of whom take a dim view of the black male intellectual's adoption of white male attitudes of sexual superiority. Neither are those who make this pious objection to the racial parallel addressing themselves very adequately to the millions of white working-class women living at the poverty level, who are not likely to be moved by this middle-class, guilt-ridden one-upmanship while having to deal with the boss, the factory, or the welfare worker day after day. They are already dangerously resentful of the gains made by blacks, and much of their "racist backlash" stems from the fact that they have been forgotten in the push for social change. Emphasis on the real mechanisms of oppression—on the commonality of the process—is essential lest groups such as these, which should work in alliance, become divided against one another.

White middle-class males already struggling with the acknowledgment of their own racism do not relish an added burden of recognition: that to white guilt must soon be added "male." It is therefore understandable that they should refuse to see the harshness of the lives of most women—to face honestly the facts of massive institutionalized discrimination against women.

We must never forget that the root of the ideology of male superiority, female inferiority, and white racism is a system of white male supremacy. White male supremacy is part of the ideology of imperialism, first European, then American. The European powers stripped India, China, Africa, and the New World of their wealth in raw materials—in gold, slaves, in cheap labor. Such brutal forms of exploitation required justification, and that justification was found in the doctrines of white racial superiority and the supremacy of European and American "civilization" over the "heathen" civilizations of Africa, Asia, and Latin America. Even more, we must never forget that the doctrine of white supremacy included the *supremacy of white women* as well as of white men.

The rise of capitalism in the West was based upon the wealth looted from other civilizations at the point of a gun: imperialism was the root and branch of racism and genocide then as it is now. It is at the root of mass prostitution in Saigon, of the torture and murder of innocent Vietnamese and Indochinese women and children, of all the sufferings of war inflicted upon the innocent at home and in Indochina. White American women must understand their oppression in its true context, and that context *is* a brutal, antihuman system of total exploitation having its corporate headquarters in New York and its political headquarters in Washington, D.C. And white women must understand that they are part of the system, benefiting from the loot secured through genocide.

This is why we must clearly understand that male chauvinism and racism *are not the same thing.* They are alike in that they oppress people and justify systems of exploitation, but in no way does a white woman suffer the exploitation and brutalization of women who are marked by both stigmata: being female *and* nonwhite. It is only the racism of privileged white women, self-serving in their petty, personal interests, who can claim that they must serve their own interests first, that they suffer *as much* as black women or Indochinese women or any women who experience the cruelty of white racism or the ruthless genocide of American militarism.

The contradiction of racism distorts and contaminates every sector of American life, creeps into every white insurgent movement. Understanding their own oppression can and must help white women to confront and to repudiate their own racism, for otherwise there will be no freedom, there will be no liberation.

The institution of marriage is the chief vehic' for the perpetuation of the oppression of women; it is through the role of wife that the subjugation of women is maintained. In a very real way the role of wife has been the genesis of women's rebellion throughout history.

Looking at marriage from a detached point of view, one may well ask why anyone gets married, much less women. One answer lies in the economics of women's position, for women are so occupationally limited that drudgery in the home is considered to be infinitely superior to drudgery in the factory. Secondly, women themselves have no independent social status. Indeed, there is no clearer index of the social worth of a woman in this society than the fact that she has none in her own right. A woman is first defined by the man to whom she is attached, but more particularly by the man she marries, and secondly by the children she bears and rears—hence the anxiety over sexual attractiveness, the frantic scramble for boyfriends and husbands. Once she has obtained and married a man, the race is then on to have children, in order that their attractiveness and accomplishments may add more social worth. In a woman, not having children is seen as an incapacity somewhat akin to impotence in a man.

Beneath all of the pressures of the sexual marketplace and the marital status game, however, there is a far more sinister organization of economic exploitation and psychological mutilation. The housewife role, usually defined in terms of the biological duty of a woman to reproduce and her "innate" suitability for a nurturant and companionship role, is actually crucial to industrial capitalism in an advanced state of technological development. In fact, the housewife (some 44 million women of all classes, ethnic groups, and races) provides, unpaid, absolutely essential services and labor. In turn, her assumption of all household duties makes it possible for the man to spend the majority of his time at his work place.

It is important to understand the social and economic exploitation of the married woman, since the real productivity of her labor is denied by the commonly held assumption that she is dependent on her husband, exchanging her keep for emotional and nurturant services. Household labor, including child care, constitutes a huge amount of socially necessary labor. Nevertheless, in a society based on commodity production, it is not usually considered even as "real work" since it is outside of trade and the marketplace. In a society in which money determines value, women are a group who work outside the money economy. Their work is not worth money, is therefore valueless, is therefore not even real work. And women themselves, who do this valueless work, can hardly be expected to be worth as much as men, who work for money.

Women are essential to the economy not only as free labor, but also as consumers. The American system of capitalism depends for its survival on the consumption of vast amounts of socially wasteful goods, and a prime target for the unloading of this waste is the housewife. She is the purchasing agent for the family, but beyond that she is eager to buy because her own identity depends on her accomplishments as a consumer and her ability to satisfy the wants of her husband and children. This is not, of course, to say that she has any power in the economy. Although she spends the wealth, she does not own or control it—it simply passes through her hands.

In addition to their role as housewives and consumers, increasing numbers of women are taking outside employment. These women leave the home to join an exploited labor force, only to return at night to assume the double burden of housework on top of wage work—that is, they are forced to work at two full-time jobs. No man is required or expected to take on such a burden. The result: two workers from one household in the labor force with no cutback in essential female functions—three for the price of two, quite a bargain. Regardless of her status in the larger society, within the context of the family, the woman's relationship to the man is one of proletariat to bourgeoisie. One consequence of this class division in the family is to weaken the capacity of oppressed men and women to struggle together against it.

For third-world people within the United States, the oppressive nature of marriage is reflected negatively—for example, motherhood out of wedlock is punished, either through discriminatory welfare legislation or through thinly disguised and genocidal programs of enforced sterilization. This society punishes unmarried women even more than it punishes married women. As a result, many third-world and poor white women want help with their families and need a husband in the home. The destruction of families among poor people, as a result of economic exploitation and social oppression, results in the deprivation of every facet of life for poor women and children. White middle-class women, bound up with the psychological oppression of marriage, have often been blind to the extent of suffering—and the extent of the needs—that the deliberate destruction of the families of the poor has created. Unemployment and pauperization through welfare programs creates very different problems than does the experience of boredom in the suburbs.

In all classes and groups, the institution of marriage nonetheless functions to a greater or lesser degree to oppress women; the unity of women of different classes hinges upon our understanding of that common oppression. The 19th-century wome i's movement refused to deal with marriage and sexuality and chose instead to fight for the vote and to elevate the feminine mystique to a political ideology. That decision retarded the movement for decades. But 1969 is not 1889. For one thing, there now exist alternatives to marriage. The cultural revolution—experimentation with lifestyles, communal living, collective child rearing—have all come from the rebellion against dehumanized sexual relationships, against the notion of women as sexual commodities, against the hardship, alienation, and loneliness of American life.

Lessons must be learned from the failures of the earlier movement. The feminine mystique must not be mistaken for politics or legislative reform for winning human rights. Women are now at the bottom of their respective worlds and the basis exists for a common focus of struggle for women in American society. It remains for the movement to understand this, to avoid the mistakes of the past, to respond creatively to the possibilities of the present.

Women's oppression, although rooted in the institution of marriage, does not stop at the kitchen or the bedroom door. Indeed, the economic exploitation of women in the work place is the most commonly recognized aspect of the oppression of women.

The rise of new agitation for the occupational equality of women also coincided with the reentry of the "lost generation"—the housewives of the 1950s—into the job market. Women from middle-class backgrounds, faced with an "empty nest" (children grown or in school) and a widowed or divorced rate of one-fourth of all marriages, returned to the work place in large numbers. But once there, they discovered that women, middle-class or otherwise, are the last hired, the lowest paid, the least often promoted, and the first fired. Furthermore, women are more likely to suffer job discrimination on the basis of age, so the widowed and divorced suffer particularly, even though their economic need to work is often urgent. Age discrimination also means that the option of work after child rearing is limited. Even highly qualified older women find themselves forced into low-paid, unskilled, or semi-skilled work—if they are lucky enough to find a job in the first place.

Most women who enter the labor force do not work for "pin money" or "self-fulfillment." Sixty-two percent of all women working in 1967 were doing so out of economic need (that is, were either alone or with husbands earning less than $5,000 a year). In 1963, 36 percent of American families had an income of less than $5,000 a year. Women from these families work because they must; they contribute 35 to 40 percent of the family's total income when working full time and 15 to 20 percent when working part time.

Despite their need, however, women have always represented the most exploited sector of the industrial labor force. Child and female labor were introduced during the early stages of industrial capitalism, at a time when most men were gainfully employed in crafts. As industrialization developed and craft jobs were eliminated, men entered the industrial labor force, driving women and children into the lowest categories of work and pay. Indeed, the position of women and children industrial workers was so pitiful and their wages were so small that the craft unions refused to organize them. Even when women organized themselves and engaged in militant strikes and labor agitation—from the shoemakers of Lynn, Massachusetts, to the International Ladies' Garment Workers and their great strike of 1909—male unionists continued to ignore their needs. As a result of this male supremacy in the unions, women remain essentially unorganized, despite the fact that they are becoming an ever larger part of the labor force.

The trend is clearly toward increasing numbers of women entering the work force: women represented 55 percent of the growth of the total labor force in 1962, and the number of working women rose from 16.9 million in 1957 to 24 million in 1962. There is every indication that the number of women in the labor force will continue to grow as rapidly in the future.

Job discrimination against women exists in all sectors of work, even in occupations that are predominantly made up of women. This discrimination is reinforced in the field of education, where women are being short-changed at a time when the job market demands higher educational levels. In 1962, for example, while women constituted 53 percent of the graduating high school class, only 42 percent of the entering college class were women. Only one in three people who received a B.A. or M.A. in that year was a woman, and only one in ten who received a Ph.D. was a woman. These figures represent a decline in educational achievement for women since the 1930s, when women received two out of five of the B.A. and M.A. degrees given, and one out of seven of the Ph.Ds. While there has been a dramatic increase in the number of people, including women, who go to college, women have not kept pace with men in terms of educational achievement. Furthermore, women have lost ground in professional employment. In 1960 only 22 percent of the faculty and other professional staff at colleges and universities were women—down from 28 percent in 1949, 27 percent in 1930, 26 percent in 1920. 1960 does beat the 20 percent of 1919: "You've come a long way, baby"—right back to where you started! In other professional categories, 10 percent of all scientists are women, 7 percent of all physicians, 3 percent of all lawyers, and 1 percent of all engineers.

Even when women do obtain an education, in many cases it does them little good. Women, whatever their educational levels, are concentrated in the lower-paying occupations. The figures tell a story that most women know and few men will admit: most women are forced to work at clerical jobs, for which they are paid, on the average, $1,600 less per year than men doing the same work. Working-class women in the service and operative (semi-skilled) categories, making up 30 percent of working women, are paid $1,900 less per year on the average than are men. Of all working women, only 13 percent are professionals (including low-pay and low-status work such as teaching, nursing, and social work), and they earn $2,600 less per year than do professional men. Household workers, the lowest category of all, are predominantly women (over 2 million) and predominantly black and third world, earning for their labor barely over $1,000 per year.

Not only are women forced onto the lowest rungs of the occupational ladder, they are in the lowest income levels as well. The most constant and bitter injustice experienced by all women is the income differential. While women might passively accept low-status jobs, limited opportunities for advancement, and discrimination in the factory, office, and university, they choke finally on the daily fact that the male worker next to them earns more and usually does less. In 1965, the median wage or salary income of year-round, full-time women workers was only 60 percent that of men, a 4 percent loss since 1955. Twenty-nine percent of working women earned less than $3,000 a year as compared with 11 percent of the men; 43 percent of the women earned from $3,000 to $5,000 a year as compared with 19 percent of the men; and 9 percent of the women earned $7,000 or more as compared with 43 percent of the men.

What most people do not know is that in certain respects all women suffer more than do nonwhite men and that black and third-world women suffer most of all.

Women, regardless of race, are more disadvantaged than are men, including nonwhite men. White women earn $2,600 less than white men and $1,500 less than nonwhite men. The brunt of the inequality is carried by 2.5 million nonwhite women, 94 percent of whom are black. They earn $3,800 less than white men, $1,900 less than nonwhite men, and $1,200 less than white women.

There is no more bitter paradox in the racism of this country than that the white man, articulating the male supremacy of the white male middle class, should provide the rationale for the oppression of black women by black men. Black women constitute the largest minority in the United States, and they are the most disadvantaged group in the labor force. The further oppression of black women will not liberate black men, for black women were never the oppressors of their men— that is a myth of the liberal white man. The oppression of black men comes from institutionalized racism and economic exploitation, from the world of the white man.

Consider the following facts and figures. The percentage of black working women has always been proportionately greater than that of white women. In 1900, 41 percent of black women were employed, as compared to 17 percent for white women. In 1963, the proportion of black women employed was still a fourth greater than that of whites. In 1960, 44 percent of black married women with children under six years were in the labor force, in contrast to 29 percent for white women. While job competition requires ever higher levels of education, the bulk of illiterate women are black. On the whole, black women—who often have the greatest need for employment—are the most discriminated against in terms of opportunity. Forced by an oppressive and racist society to carry unbelievably heavy economic and social burdens, black women stand at the bottom of that society, doubly marked by the caste signs of color and sex.

Faced with discrimination on the job—after being forced into the lower levels of the occupational structure—millions of women are inescapably presented with the fundamental contradictions in their unequal treatment and their massive exploitation. The rapid growth of women's liberation as a movement is related in part to the exploitation of working women in all occupational categories.

Male supremacy, marriage, and the structure of wage labor—each of these aspects of women's oppression and exploitation has been crucial to the resurgence of the women's struggle. It must be abundantly clear that revolutionary social change must occur before there can be significant improvement in the social position of *all* women.

The heart of the movement, as in all freedom movements, rests in women's knowledge, whether articulated or still only an illness without a name, that they are not inferior—not chicks or bunnies or quail or cows or bitches or ass or meat. Women hear the litany of their own dehumanization each day. Yet all the same, women know that they are not animals or sexual objects or commodities. They know their lives are mutilated, because they see within themselves a promise of creativity and personal integration. Feeling the contradiction between the essentially creative and self-actualizing human being within her and the cruel and degrading less-than-human role she is compelled to play, a woman begins to experience the internal violence that liberates the human spirit, to experience the justice of her own rebellion. This is the rage that impels women into a total commitment to women's liberation, a ferocity that stems from a denial of mutilation. It is a cry for life, a cry for the liberation of the spirit.

Yet, we must never forget that we women are not unique in our oppression, in our exploitation. Understanding ourselves should help us understand all others like us and not divide us from them. We must also remember that in one way white American women are unique, for they suffer least of all: their experience cannot approach the abysmal suffering of the third-world women or of third-world men, subject to American racism and imperialism. How does one understand rape; forced prostitution; torture; and mutilation; twisted, crippled children; deformed babies; a homeland laid waste; memories of perpetual war; perpetual oppression? It is not a question of guilt; it is a question of revolutionary struggle.

1969 was a year of explosive growth and measureless optimism for women's liberation. It was the year of sisterhood: "Sisterhood is powerful!" "Sisterhood is beautiful!" "Sisterhood is unity!" The turning point for the women's struggle was 1969, the year in which the movement came up from underground by gaining recognition and legitimacy—recognition from the male-dominated white left and legitimacy as a protest "issue" in the larger society. The slogans of sisterhood reflected a joyful optimism, an overwhelming intuitive belief that *all* women could identify with each other, all women could struggle together—even lead—a vast movement or social transformation.

By 1971, the joyful optimism was increasingly being replaced by a sense of dismay and conflict in many women: "Women's liberation is a nonstruggle movement"; "Women's liberation is a racist movement"; "Women's liberation is an apolitical movement"; "Women's liberation is a liberal, middle-class movement." What did all of this mean? What had happened to the women's movement?

The United States of America had "happened" to women's liberation: all of the contradictions of a society torn by class and racial conflict, all of the contradictions of a society that is in fact based upon militarized state capitalism and institutionalized racism and class exploitation began to tear the women's movement apart. The apolitical simplicity of "Sisterhood is unity" and "Understand your own psychological oppression" was powerless to contend with or understand the internal, disruptive forces of the most exploitative, brutal, and complex oppressor nation in the history of Western imperialism—the United States of America.

The women's movement is no longer a struggling, tender shoot; it has become a mass movement; and women remain, often despite the movement, potentially a powerful, radical force. In the beginning, women were attacked from every quarter, most destructively from the left, for left politics became identified with male chauvinism. Originally, the attack from the left was corrupt, a ploy by radical men to keep women down. Now, however, the criticism does not come from the men, but from women within women's liberation. A movement that cannot learn from its past, that is too insecure and fearful to engage in self-criticism, that is too self-interested to be able to change its direction, too blind to see that all women are *not* sisters—that class exploitation and racism are fundamental to American society and exist *within* the women's movement—becomes a trap, not a means to liberation. In the brief critique that follows, I am correcting some of my own mistakes, for I too believed in sisterhood, I too believed that "common oppression provides the basis for uniting across class and race lines." In that belief I was wrong; this is what I have learned from the past year of the movement. There are many women and many groups within the women's struggle to which the following criticism does not apply, but there are still more who were, and still are, wrong.

The mysticism of *sisterhood* disguised the reality that most women in women's liberation were white, young, and middle class, so that under all the radical rhetoric the movement's goals were reformist and its ideology was almost exclusively of middle-class female psychological oppression. The women's movement did not talk about *exploitation,* but about *oppression*—always in subjective terms. The women's movement did not talk about class struggle, nationalization of medicine, abolition of welfare, or the ultimate destruction of American imperialism. The needs of poor women, of working women, of black women were nowhere central to the demands of the rhetoric of women's liberation. The middle-class, reformist nature of the movement was not clearly and objectively revealed until the struggle over the equal rights amendment—an amendment that would have made *discrimination* unconstitutional but would not have included a single reference to exploitation, an amendment that would have benefited professional women at the expense of working-class women.

Fighting against *discrimination* is a middle-class, reformist goal—it says: let us *in* so that the privileges of our middle-class men can be extended to us middle-class women. Fighting against *exploitation* is revolutionary. To end exploitation, it is necessary to end "militarized state capitalism." To end class exploitation, it is necessary to abolish classes. To end racism, it is necessary to abolish white male supremacy, to abolish imperialism. White middle-class America, male and female, enjoys an affluence that is looted from half the world, that is stolen by means of poor white and black soldiers, that is turned into new cars and washing machines by workers, black and white, male and female. White middle-class America, *male and female,* enjoys incomes protected from inflation by means of the deliberate unemployment of workers, black and white, male and female, who suffer enforced pauperization so that the young girls of the middle class can go to the university and struggle for a women's center to give them a better education, the better to enjoy their class privileges, the better to explore the meaning of life and the adventures of a new, untrammeled sexuality. Genocide is committed against the people of Vietnam; war spreads to all the peoples of Indochina. So who cares? It's only a "penis war." It is of no concern to the young women of the middle class, who will never be soldiers, never be workers, never be on welfare, never suffer racism. The problem is *discrimination.* Women can only earn $10,000 a year teaching college while men earn $15,000 a year—that is the problem! "Sisterhood is unity! Don't criticize the movement! Don't make us feel guilty! Don't show us the blood on *our* hands—after all, we are oppressed too!"

The "black analogy" was originally used in women's liberation to help women through their understanding of their own oppression, to understand the oppression of others. By 1971 the "black analogy" had become a tool of white racism. The cries "We are oppressed too" and even more terrible "We are equally oppressed" permitted white middle-class women to dismiss the black struggle, to dismiss their complicity in a racist system, to dismiss criticisms of the movement from black women as motivated by the influence "the male chauvinism of black men" has upon them—ultimately to complete the cycle of white middle-class racism by reducing black and third-world people within the United States to invisibility. White middle-class women, bloated with their own pious claims to oppression, blind within their own racism, refused to see that black women were trying to teach them something when they spoke at conferences saying: "I am black and a woman, but am I first black or first a woman? First I am black." Or "We fear the abortion program, it may be used against us." Or, "We must destroy exploitation and racism *before* black women can be liberated—for what does it mean to us, black women, if you white women end discrimination? We are still black; we are still exploited; we are still destroyed and our children with us." All the white women could answer was "black male chauvinism!" They remained completely blind to the fact that third-world people are a colony and a minority within the heart of the monster, that their survival depends upon a resolution to the contradiction of male chauvinism and male supremacy that *does not* divide black women and black men into antagonistic factions.

The purest expression of self-serving middle-class ideology is reflected in the blind hatred of men that makes no distinction between the system of white male supremacy and male chauvinism. Only very privileged women can in the security of their class status and class earning power create a little "manless Utopia" for themselves. They need only withdraw from the psychological discomfort of male chauvinism to create a new and different life for themselves—they are not faced, as a class, with the necessity to struggle against another class; they are not driven by exploitation and repression to understand that male chauvinism is reactionary but that it can also be defeated, so that men and women can resolve the contradiction between them, emerge stronger, and unite in mutual opposition to their real enemies—the generals, the corporate bosses, the corrupt politicians.

Liberal guilt is worthless. Appealing to women who are completely devoted to their own self-serving class interests is equally useless. There is no mass movement in the United States that can avoid the contradictions of racism and class conflict, thus moralistic pleas are a waste of time. Nonetheless, women in the United States—and everywhere outside of the revolutionary world—are oppressed and exploited, suffer and die in silence. For the thousands and thousands of women who are poor, who are working class, who were born into the middle class but have turned away from it in disgust and revulsion, the women's movement, as a revolutionary struggle, remains their chief commitment and their only hope. Our challenge is to correct past mistakes, to learn what we must know to avoid future mistakes, to teach and to learn from each other. We *must* learn how to build, within the very heart of the monster, a revolutionary movement devoted to the liberation of all people *in practice*. Such a movement will not be self-serving, cannot be merely reformist. It must be political, must know history and economics, must understand that all revolutionary movements in the world today are interdependent. We can no longer be an island of affluence, blind to the lesson that what happens to a black woman happens to us. The United States is not an empire that will stand for a thousand years, but is an oppressive monster that the peoples of the world will dismember and destroy before the world is all finished. We must choose which side we will be on—the path of revolution or the path of exploitation and genocide.

The women's movement is turning and twisting within its contradictions. Some women speed off into mysticism, claiming, but not explaining, how women by rejecting "male" politics and finding "female" politics effect world revolution—a world revolution in which the people's war in Vietnam plays no part, in which all previous world revolutions—Russian, Chinese, North Vietnamese, North Korean, Cuban—play no part. Still others seek escape in "sexual liberation," hoping to find, as does the youth movement, a personalized, individual salvation in a "lifestyle revolution" in which racism is dismissed as a problem of "black male chauvinism" and Vietnam is dismissed as a "penis war" of no concern to women. To be in the "vanguard," it is only necessary to love a woman sexually. Still others cling to the worn-out slogans of the early days, continuing with "consciousness raising" as weekly therapy and engaging in endless discussions of anti-elitism (an elite being anyone who does anything at all threatening to any woman in a small group) and "anti-elitist structure" in the organizing of the women's center.

These tendencies reflect the other face of women's oppression, not anger or strength, but fearfulness, turning inward to avoid challenge, to avoid thinking, to avoid struggle, to avoid the large and frightening world of conflict and revolution, which cannot be contained within a small group or understood through the subjective oppression of a privileged woman. Women *are* mutilated, especially passive, nurturant middle-class women. They are made manipulative, dishonest, fearful, conservative, hypocritical, and self-serving. Celebrating women's weakness—elevating mutilation to a holy state of female grace—corrupts the movement into a reactionary and self-serving force.

Women are seen as absurd, and they blame the media. Women are criticized for being reactionary and racist. They howl "male-defined," "male-identified." Women are isolated from the liberation struggles of other people, and they scream that those movements are *male-dominated!* How many more excuses will be found until women have the strength to confront their mistakes and their failures? How many revolutions are we going to be called upon to make to assure rich and comforting interpersonal relationships and unhampered fucking for the people whose privilege is so great that they can afford to worry about their spirits instead of their bellies? How many more people are we going to help die in Indochina by howling that fighting against imperialism is "antiwoman" or a "penis war" or "dominated by men"? How long are we going to remain absurd because, in the eyes of the vast majority of peoples in the world, *we are absurd, self-seeking, blind,* and *ignorant!*

It is time, past time, to get our heads together, to listen to and learn from women who have made and are making revolutions, to study to fight, to fight to win, with strength and dignity and a proper respect for the suffering of others and a complete devotion to ending all oppression practiced against the majority of the peoples of the world, male and female, in the colonies of the monster and in the heart of the monster. Then, and only then, shall we know something of liberation.

JOAN W. MOORE

Mexican Americans

In many ways the growth of Mexican American, or Chicano, militancy has mirrored that of blacks. At first Chicano groups lobbied for a greater integration into American society. Gradually these goals shifted to broader themes: the development of group identity, the revival of old land claims against the United States government, and the formation of separate political parties. Young militants, espousing "La Raza," saw a much different place in American society for Mexican Americans from that perceived by the older generation. It was a view that envisioned a full equality for all Chicanos.

In the following essay Joan Moore analyzes the dynamics behind the Chicano movement. She indicates the importance of the black revolution to the politicization of the Mexican community. Beginning in the middle 1960s, a new militancy took hold under the leadership of several gifted individuals. César Chávez, perhaps the nation's best known Mexican American, generated national publicity with his strike efforts on behalf of Mexican agricultural laborers, beginning in 1965.

Though militants have captured the majority of headlines, the Chicano movement has exhibited a full range of ideologies and tactics. These have included advocates of the old-style politics, street demonstrations, and the more radical tactics of the Brown Berets. Though to this date direct political methods have not yielded major benefits to the group, Moore believes that ethnicity has played an important role in creating the more informed and involved Mexican community of today.

From Joan W. Moore, with Harry Pachon, *Mexican Americans,* 2nd edition, 1976, pp. 149–55. Reprinted by permission of Prentice-Hall, Inc., Englewood Cliffs, New Jersey.

Joan Moore is presently a professor at the University of Wisconsin, Milwaukee. She has worked with the Mexican American Study Project at the University of California, Los Angeles.

From the vantage point of the 1970s it appears that various events accelerated the realization among Mexican Americans that the traditional styles of ethnic politics would not accomplish the needed changes. Among the most significant of these events were the black civil rights movement and the Black Power movement of the 1960s. The impact of the black movement was threefold. First, the movement revealed that civil equality was not sufficient in itself to achieve meaningful social change. Second, the Black Power movement legitimized an ideology that rejected assimilation and fixed blame on the larger society for the deprivation of black Americans. Mexican Americans were occupying a similar socio-economic position and they could see the relevance of such terms as "institutional racism." Third, and most important, was the effect of the black riots on the Mexican American community's view of government. Federal, state, and local governments responded to the black riots with pledges of massive amounts of aid. This reaction jolted and politicized all elements of the Mexican community. One question epitomizes Mexican feelings during this time: "Do we have to riot in order to receive attention?" Many Mexican Americans felt that problems facing Mexican Americans in the Southwest were as severe (if not worse) than those of the black community. Consequently, when the federal antipoverty programs of the War on Poverty and Model Cities were started, Mexican Americans began demanding a "fair share" of these.

In addition to the black movement, such events as the Vietnam antiwar effort and the whole "counterculture" movement provided alternative ideologies and models of political action to which Mexican Americans and especially young Mexicans could adapt. Inside the community itself, the emergence of ethnic leaders into national prominence gave further legitimacy to unconventional ethnic political efforts.

It is the emergence of ethnic political leaders like César Chávez, Reis Tijerina, and Rodolfo (Corky) González that brings full realization of the multiple factors behind the variegated nature of the Mexican American movement today. Each of these three individuals represents to some extent a different factor in the history of the struggle behind the Mexican American emergence into a nationally recognized ethnic minority. All three individuals were active in Mexican American community affairs prior to the middle 1960s. César Chávez was a community organizer for Community Service Organization during the 1950s and moved to Delano, California in 1962 to begin organizational efforts for the Mexican and Filipino farm workers. Reis Tijerina was active in New Mexico attempting to regain the lands lost during the Anglo-American conquest. In 1963, for example, Tijerina journeyed to Mexico City to seek support from the Mexican national government in attempting to regain these lands. González was active in the Viva Kennedy movement during the early 1960s and in the antipoverty programs in Denver. All three individuals emerged at different times as leaders. But all three leaders contributed to the new ethnic militancy that captured national attention.

This new militancy began sometime in the mid-1960s. César Chávez began the strike effort of *"La Huelga"* in 1965. Also in 1965 Corky González resigned from the Denver poverty program boards and founded La Crusada para la Justicia, which later was to support high school strikes, demonstrate against police brutality, and advocate mass actions against the Vietnam War. In 1966, the National Farm Workers Association began a highly publicized march in California and Texas to dramatize the conditions of the Mexican farm workers. And in 1966 Mexican American leaders began demanding that Mexicans be included as target populations for federal antipoverty programs. In March, 1966, Mexican Americans walked out of an Equal Employment Opportunity Commission conference in Albuquerque, New Mexico. This group petitioned the Johnson administration for a special conference, demanded more federal jobs, and threatened to picket a White House conference if their demands were not met. But the actions of this group were quickly eclipsed by Reis Tijerina and his supporters who occupied the Kit Carson National Forest to publicize claims of the Alianza Federal de Mercedes to these New Mexican lands. The next year the lieutenant governor of New Mexico was forced to call out the National Guard and the state police (with two tanks and a helicopter) after a spectacular "raid" on the courthouse at Tierra Amarilla. These events almost immediately held the sympathy of a significant segment of the Mexican American community. In particular, it excited and attracted young people.

Many young Chicanos (it was now possible to identify throughout the Southwest as part of a regional "movimiento") met at a "La Raza" conference held in October 1967.* This meeting provided an opportunity and a forum for the young to articulate their frustrations and

---

*Literally translated "La Raza" means race, but when the term is employed by Chicanos it refers to certain cultural elements that all Mexican Americans share.

anger at the traditional style of politics. Armando Rendon captures this anger when he quotes one participant saying, "The young Chicanos see this conference as the last chance you older Chicanos have to come through. If nothing happens from this you'll have to step aside—or we'll walk over you."[1] The United Mexican American Students (UMAS), the Mexican American Youth Organization (MAYO), and the Brown Berets were all organized in the same year (1967). Common to all three organizations was an active rejection of traditional styles of political action.

These specific events and their conjunction with the Black Power movement (and the antiwar effort) provided the genesis of the Chicano movement. Today the word "Chicano" is synonymous with Mexican American, perhaps as "black" means black American, but the term in the mid-1960s was something new for the Mexican American community. Originally the word "Chicano" was used almost exclusively by poor, lower-class Mexicans but now began to represent an ethnic viewpoint. Chicano ideology or *Chicanismo* was most actively (but not exclusively) promulgated by Mexican American student and youth organizations. These included UMAS, the Mexican American Student Association (MASA), the Mexican American Student Confederation (MASC), the Movimiento Estudiantil Chicano de Aztlan (MECHA), and MAYO.

In its essence, *Chicanismo* is an eclectic ideology that at times has drawn inspiration from the black experience, the Latin American revolutionary experience, and the Mexican revolutionary tradition.[2] A full range of possible political actions is encompassed by different factions of the Chicano movement. Many Chicanos feel that the traditional forms of political participation are the least effective, especially participation in the two party system. Others favor confrontation-type tactics of mass demonstrations and "walk-outs." A minority endorses the active self-defense tactics of the Brown Berets, and a smaller number sympathized with the revolutionary activities of the Chicano Liberation Front.

Chicanismo sees Chicanos as basically a conquered people—a people who were stripped of their land, their history, and their culture as the result of Anglo exploitation. The Chicanos in the American economy are victims of an exploitative relationship. Chicanos have been used as a source of cheap labor for the economy of the Southwest but they have received little economic reward. Deculturization means that Chicanos are ashamed of their Mexican Indian heritage. Chicanos should have pride in their cultural heritage and in their unique adaptation to Anglo-American society. Meanwhile, the process of deculturization continues in schools that fail to teach Chicano children their bilingual-bicultural heritage. *Chicanismo* emphasizes the concept of *la raza*—and it rejects materialistic standards of individualistic self-achievement. Rather, collective orientations based on *la raza* are more valuable standards.

The new ideology profoundly affected the Mexican American community, particularly the youth and the college students. The impact may have been greatest in the politics of education. Here increased demands for ethnic studies programs, ethnic heritage classes, and ethnic personnel reflected the ideological precepts of *Chicanismo*. The high school "blow-outs" (walk-outs) that swept throughout the Southwest indicate the strong appeal of *Chicanismo* in the community.

But the general course of ethnic militancy after 1968 followed old issues that had long been important to everyone. Many of the issues that were important rallying points in the Chicano movement—protests against police brutality, protests against miseducation, demands for more political voice—were always active issues in the community. But young Chicanos articulated these issues in ways that both were unconventional and grasped the attention of all American society. Consider, as an example, activism in school reform. Efforts by Mexican Americans to reform southwestern school systems reach back into the 1930s. The new Chicano approaches were marked by blow-outs and protest demonstrations. These appeared in California (1968), Texas (1969), and Colorado (1969). They were watched with interest by the general community, bringing as they did the inevitable police reprisals and reviving old tensions.[3] Colleges and universities felt Chicano protests for the first time, reflecting the greater number of Mexican Americans entering these institutions.

But there were some issues peculiar to the 1960s that emerged from the Chicano movement. The National Chicano Moratorium Committee organized demonstrations against the Vietnam War in 1969 and 1970. The protest in August, 1970, in East Los Angeles resulted in large-scale violence between the police and the demonstrators. In a terrifying manner it brought to national consciousness the anger and the frustration always latent in the *barrios*. (A noted Mexican American journalist was shot to death by the police, and a great deal of property damage done.) The antiwar issue rapidly lost momentum, but the question of police behavior continued to be a problem that Chicano activists used to generate community support.

In addition to this articulation of long-standing grievances and certain new issues, the most highly publicized aspect of ethnic militancy in the Mexican American community was the formation and development of a separatist third party effort—La Raza Unida Party

(LRU). LRU may be seen as a response by Chicanos to the insensitivity of the American political system. Thus just as MAPA was an ethnic response in the 1950s, the new party was an ethnic militant separatist reaction in the late 1960s and early 1970s. The concept of the third party was developed by José Angel Gutiérrez, a cofounder of MAYO and the leading spirit of the LRU in Texas. It was actively supported by Corky González, who once described the two major parties as "an animal with two heads eating out of the same trough." The rationales for an ethnic party are numerous: third party organizations have access to media during elections; third party campaigns need not compromise with either of the established parties and thus can allow clear articulation of Chicano goals. Tactically, Chicano third party efforts in areas where Chicanos are a majority present opportunities for Mexicans to gain control of their own communities. An additional advantage is that by running candidates in general elections (even where there is little, if any, chance to win) the potential for a Chicano bloc vote is further developed.

Since its birth in 1970 in Texas, La Raza Unida has had some noteworthy successes. The most notable of these was in Crystal City, Texas. Here LRU candidates gained control of the city council and board of education in the 1970 elections. Since then "el partido" has been successful in such other Texas towns as Cotulla and Carriza Springs. Even in its defeats, La Raza Unida has made its presence felt. In the Texas state elections of 1972, the LRU candidate for governor, Ramsey Muñiz, captured close to 6 percent of the vote. At present the LRU has official party standing in Texas and is seeking official status in California and Colorado. In New Mexico, La Raza Unida has not made significant inroads because of the ethnic representation that has existed historically in the major parties.[4] La Raza Unida is perhaps the most representative vehicle of the new militancy. It is comprised mostly of younger community people and has adopted radical or left-of-center positions on most issues—even to the point of splitting with César Chávez for his endorsement of George McGovern in 1972. At the present time there appears to be a schism in the party between the Colorado faction (Corky González) and the Texas faction (José Angel Gutiérrez) on whether the right priorities are local level organizational efforts and the winning of elections (the Texas position) or building a vanguard type of party designed to politicize the Mexican American community (the Colorado position).[5]

Yet for all the excitement, its electoral showing in states other than Texas has not been strong. In California and Colorado no LRU candidates have been elected. In 1974 only twenty thousand LRU voters were registered in California. In addition to its poor electoral showing in states other than Texas, there are several obstacles on the way to a viable political organization for Chicano interests. Mexican Americans are a minority in all five southwestern states. Mexicans do not reach a majority in most urban centers of the Southwest. Chicano control of cities or counties is not possible outside towns and counties in southern Texas or possibly New Mexico. (The victory in Crystal City heartened many Mexican Americans but the total population of Zavala County around Crystal City is 74.4 percent Spanish surname. Thus the uniqueness of Crystal City indicates certain limitations on LRU strategy.)

The second obstacle appears when the major parties run Mexican American candidates. La Raza Unida candidates splinter the Chicano vote and defeat both the Mexican candidates. Thus LRU candidacies resulted in the defeats of Joe Bernal in Texas and Richard Alatorre in California. It is not possible to assume (considering the diversity of political outlook among Mexican Americans) that Democratic or Republican candidates are not "true" representatives. Quite possibly "ethnic solidarity" may not be present in the Mexican American community now or ever, any more than it is present in black communities. In the case of Crystal City, the new party was able to capture political power through a unique set of circumstances: the socio-economic characteristics of the community included a large number of migrant workers who were more easily mobilized and the disproportionate number of Chicano voters in the community.[6] In the long run, therefore, appeals based solely on ethnicity may be of limited usefulness. La Raza Unida now has existed for more than four years and the pressure to win elections and to get candidates into offices appears to be building slowly but strongly. The 1976 elections (especially in Texas) may be crucial in determining the continued growth and viability of this ethnic third party.

It may appear at first glance that the impact and the actual gains of the Chicano movement are minimal. To say the least, La Raza Unida has not made extensive gains. Many militant organizations such as the Brown Berets have come and gone; ethnic militancy, in fact, appears to be on the wane. Yet in retrospect, Chicano militancy has had tremendous impact on the Mexican community. In the American political system protest activity must always be considered a potential political resource.[7] The protest activities and the new awarenesses brought by the Chicano movement have served at the very least as political resources that have benefited other political groups in the Mexican community.

JOHN KIFNER

At Wounded Knee, Two Worlds Collide

American Indians, this nation's oldest "minority," have also become increasingly restless with their position in society, and, like other groups in America, have been attempting to forge a new identity. It is generally recognized that the dramatic takeover of Wounded Knee, South Dakota, in 1973 represented the full emergence of this new awareness. The incident generated national headlines, not just for a brief period of hours, but for days, and it provided a forum for the expression of Indian demands. It dramatized the goals of the militant Indian leadership of the American Indian Movement (AIM) and revealed clearly the gap that separated these Indians from those in the traditional tribal structure. Indeed, at times it seemed that the divisions that existed within the Indian camp were as wide and potentially unbridgeable as those which existed between Indians and whites.

The causes that the new militants espoused—separatism, political activism, rejection of white values, and the abandonment of existing tribal organizations—impelled a reconsideration of the entire Indian question. Many scholars, such as Wilcomb E. Washburn, believe that the AIM and its programs represent an extreme minority viewpoint among Indians and that the AIM's radical outlook stands little chance of implementation or acceptance from either side. Though this assessment may be proved correct, it is undeniable that increased activism has opened the eyes of the nation to the plight of the Indian.

Anyone reasonably familiar with the lot of contemporary Indians can find ample reason for their dissatisfaction. John Kifner, reporter for the New York Times, *details in his perceptive article that poverty, dependence, unemployment, high suicide rates, and all the other indices of social disruption fully characterize the Indian community. In their search for remedies Indian militants have begun a search for Indian pride and, like other ethnic groups, have looked back into their origins and traditions. This quest has progressed on several levels. Indian tribes are increasingly pressing their claims for lost lands and privileges in the courts, and they are not infrequently successful. The Oneida Indians, for example, recently won a legal fight to regain possession of lands they once occupied in central New York State, and several tribes are making similar claims against the state of Maine. Dramatic publicity events also seem to have a place in the Indian movement. The occupation of Alcatraz Island in San Francisco harbor and the burning of the Custer, South Dakota, Chamber of Commerce building generated national publicity. Whatever the eventual outcome of these efforts, the central place of Wounded Knee, as a symbol for a new Indian, seems assured.*

WOUNDED KNEE, S.D., March 21—In a scrubby valley here in this empty, wind-swept plains country, a band of young Indians and their allies are dug in, armed and painted for war, while on the hillsides around them a federal force of armor and automatic weapons stands nervously.

The impasse at Wounded Knee has already lasted more than three weeks. But behind it lies a century-long clash of values between a defeated Indian culture and a dominant white culture.

It is a tragic and twisted history, and it takes in both the tribal officials in nearby Pine Ridge, with their closely cropped hair and triplicate Government forms, and the long lines of Indian men who sit at the crossroads in the early spring sun blankly watching the dust as white Justice Department officials, marshals, lawyers, and newsmen rush by.

To the occupiers of this tiny hamlet, led by members of the militant American Indian Movement, it is a struggle to overthrow the elected government headed by Richard Wilson, which they contend is dictatorial and corrupt. Mixed in is a deeply felt will to return to a tribal purity that they never really knew.

To the Interior Department, the Bureau of Indian Affairs, and the elected tribal officials, it is a struggle to preserve a duly constituted government. They fear that if the Government is successfully challenged by the rebels, dissent will spread to other reservations throughout the country and imperil policies of forty years' standing.

The militants have chosen to mount their challenge here for symbolic reasons. This settlement is sacred ground to the Sioux nation, for it was here that Big Foot's band was wiped out by the Army's Hotchkiss guns in 1890 in the last clash of the Indian wars. Among families here, the history is only two or three generations old and the sense of it is deep, divisive, and frequently filled with troubling contradictions.

An old man came by the sandbagged Bureau of Indian Affairs office the other day to press his plea on the superintendent that the United States Army be called in to rout the dissidents. But he opened the conversation by recalling the 1890 clash, in which he said his father, as a child, had been shot in the leg. "They was ghost dancing with horns and everything," he said, and he spoke of the bugles and described the gunfire.

"Now that wasn't a battle, was it?" he said. "That was a massacree."

The Oglala Sioux fought some of the fiercest stands against the cavalry as the whites pushed west, closing the Bozeman Trail and attacking Fort Phil Kearny eighty-one times until, under the Treaty of 1868, they were guaranteed all land west of the Missouri River.

But gold was discovered near here, there was a new push of northern European immigrants, and although Crazy Horse defeated the troopers at the Little Big Horn that same year, 1876, the Black Hills were ceded to the whites. In 1889, the Sioux reservations were set up, and in 1910 Bennett County, an area in the eastern portion of the reservation, with a murky legal status, was opened to homesteading by whites.

The last chapter of the Indian wars was written here on December 29, 1890. Ghost dancing, a religious fever with odd Christian overtones, swept the plains that fall. Wovoka, the Paiute messiah, who claimed to be the returned Christ, held that after new floods had come, drowning the white man, the dead would return, as would game, and protection would be granted those who wore painted shirts and partook in a special dance.

Alarmed, the Indian Bureau told its agents to telegraph the names of all "fomenters of disturbances." Among the names was Sitting Bull, one of the last of the great leaders who remained recalcitrant. He was killed in a fight with Indian police sent to arrest him at Fort Robinson. His followers fled, and one band, under Big Foot, moved toward Pine Ridge to seek the protection of Red Cloud, a leader of the Oglala Sioux.

They were stopped by a cavalry troop near Porcupine Butte and taken to camp at Wounded Knee Creek for the night. Another Army unit, part of the Seventh Cavalry, arrived, and four Hotchkiss guns were mounted on the hills, positioned to sweep the Indian encampment. The next morning, the Indians were ordered to pile their arms.

As they did so, a shot was fired—accounts vary as to how—and gunfire swept the plains. Some 153 men, women, and children were known to have been killed, although some accounts run upwards of 200, along with about 30 soldiers, mainly from their own cross-fire.

The Indians are buried in a mass grave, marked by a single gravestone, behind the Sacred Heart Catholic Church here. The Army awarded eighteen Congressional Medals of Honor.

"We once owned all of this great country," Red Cloud told the United States Army toward the close of the frontier. "We have sold it to you. We will live well by its selling."

For the seven tribes of the Teton Sioux, it was the end of a proud history as a hunting, warring, nomadic people and the beginning of a fenced-in existence as wards of a Government whose policies, though usually well-meaning, were constantly shifting and contradictory, and sometimes treacherous.

Today, the Pine Ridge Reservation is a bleak picture of some of the worst poverty in America. Abandoned, rusted cars cluster around tumble-down shacks and litter the prairie hills, the best acres of which are grazed by white men's cattle. The unemployment rate stands at 54 percent and goes up to 70 percent in the winter months. More than half the families are on welfare, and every index of social disorder and decay is higher than among the nation's black population. Hopeless, drunken men lurch about the streets at mid-morning.

At the heart of the situation lies the concept that the white man's Government, in exchange for the land, will be the provider for the Indians. In the early days, rations were used as a kind of bribe to keep the Indians in line, and the tradition continues today, with a limited Government largesse that seems only to induce a resentful dependency. Both dissident Indians and those allied with the authorities say that treaty promises have not been kept.

The thrust of federal Indian policy has been toward acculturation— the integration of Indians into white society—and B.I.A. officials here say that at times this has included deliberate, conscious attempts to destroy Indian culture. Older men, for instance, remember being beaten in school for wearing Indian garb and being forced to chew pieces of soap if they spoke in Lakota, the Sioux language. And, in a traditionally masculine culture, men no longer have their roles as hunters, warriors, and providers.

Over all, according to a study of the Pine Ridge Reservation made by the Community Health Program of the U.S. Public Health Service, the psychic damage has been severe. The study noted an alarmingly high rate of suicide attempts, chronic alcoholism, an 81 percent school dropout rate by the 12th grade, disintegrating family structures, and feelings of inferiority and futility.

"Eyeska" is the Sioux word for mixed-blood or half-breed. Literally translated, it means "those who speak white."

The conflict between mixed-bloods and full-bloods is the deepest and most symbolic division on the reservation. The division is more a matter of cultural affiliation than actual blood count, for there are few pure Indians left, but there is little doubt where anyone stands. The mixed-bloods control the government and what there is of the economy. The full-bloods live on the land, but are largely unable to use it.

The mixing of blood began with the French explorers and trappers here, but the implications of the division have their roots in the early reservation days when white men came to Pine Ridge with the Bureau of Indian Affairs and other Government installations. The whites took Indian women, and their offspring became acculturated to the white ways. Because they were deemed competent, and they were nearby, they began to move into the Government jobs. Thus, today, most of the mixed-blood population lives in Pine Ridge, the scraggly village that is the reservation capital, and dominates the B.I.A. and tribal bureaucracies that provide most of the reservation's jobs.

Here, as on other reservations, there are charges that the mixed-bloods are turncoats who are profiteering off the misery of other Indians. But many of the mixed-bloods regard themselves as a sturdy middle class that has adapted to necessity and that has held the tribe and its lands together.

Many of the mixed-bloods appear to be undergoing somewhat of an identity crisis, perhaps similar to that felt by successful middle-class Negroes under the pressure of black militancy, and there are constant assertions of Indian-ness and Sioux nationalism.

Indeed, aside from allegations of communism by Wilson supporters (there is a strong political overlay of rural midwestern conservatism here), the most common attack on the Wounded Knee occupiers is that they are "outsiders" interfering with the sovereignty of the Sioux tribe.

Tribal Councilman Leo Wilcox, a strong supporter of the regime, who was named by Mr. Wilson about eight months ago to run the federally funded food program, was saying in a conversation the other day, for instance, . . . "That Russell Means [the A.I.M. leader], he's only fifteen-thirty-seconds Sioux. He didn't grow up on the reservation. What does he know?"

The constitution of the Oglala Sioux was written by Felix Cohen, a white attorney for the Department of Interior who was widely known as "the Father of Indian Law." It is a standardized document, accepted by many tribes under the terms of the Indian Reorganization Act of 1934. The law was an attempt by the federal authorities to establish Indian self-government and strengthen the tribes. Previously, the Government had dealt with each Indian on an individual basis, either through the reservation superintendent or the "boss farmer," a Government official, usually white, who supervised smaller districts within the reservation.

The traditional political structure of the Sioux was a government of mutual consent. Clans and tribes were led by a man of influence, called a Vicasa Itancan, who held his position on the basis of respect, and there were councils and special structures for war and the hunt. Decisions were made by general agreement, and sharp conflicts were to be avoided. Those who disagreed with a policy could move out of the circle and were not bound by it, or could start a new band with their own followers.

There was also a tradition of factionalism and rivalry, which became heightened during the reservation period as superintendents played leaders off against one another and which became institutionalized along family and blood lines in the current electoral politics.

There was no Indian equivalent of a "chief." The concept was the imposition of the white men who sought a single, powerful leader to make treaties with and serve as head man of the reservation. Similarly, the tribal constitution was an imposition of a white system of order, with rather indifferent results.

The constitution sets up a president, a five-member executive committee, and a twenty-member Tribal Council, apportioned among the eight old "boss-farmer" districts. Elections are held every two years.

No president has ever succeeded himself, and there have been impeachment attempts, frequently for misuse of tribal funds, against every president. "We are a jealous people," explained Lloyd W. Eaglebull, the long-time tribal secretary and somewhat of an elder statesman. "When one rises up, the others try to bring him down."

The actual lawmaking powers of the council are practically nonexistent. Any ordinance the council passes must be approved by the superintendent of the reservation before becoming law, and may be vetoed anywhere along the line up to the Secretary of Interior. The powers of the council are limited, too, elected leaders and B.I.A. officials complain, by the indifference of the federal Government, which they say has provided little money for roads, schools, or other necessary services.

What the council does is function like a ward heeler system. It controls jobs and the distribution of services and, traditionally, each president appoints his friends, supporters, and relatives to the Government payroll. Since the Government supplies most of the jobs here, every appointment is highly political.

The current superintendent, Stanley Lyman, a tall, tired-looking white man, is fond of saying that it is he who is "a puppet" in the face of Mr. Wilson's domineering personality. But the Government structure is essentially colonial. There is a white Government administrator, regarded in the end as "the boss" of the reservation, a native government of dubious power, a thirteen-man native police force, and a tribal court, with untrained judges and attorneys, empowered only to hear misdemeanors. White men may be tried in the court only if they give their assent, and felonies, under the Ten Major Crimes Act of 1886, are the province of the white authorities.

It is in the countryside, "out in the districts," as the phrase goes here, that the opposition to the tribal government is strongest. This is where the full-bloods live, in clusters around the crossroads and in isolated log cabins, clinging, as much as possible, to the traditional ways. By every measure, they are poorer than the mixed-bloods. While a recent study found that 61 percent of the mixed-blood households had electricity, for example, the figure was only 40 percent among full-bloods.

Many of the necessary social services are centered in Pine Ridge, a long distance from many full-bloods. It is a hundred miles, for instance, from the outlying village of Wanbloe, and the going fee for a car ride is about $20. Some people must still walk miles for water. The high school in Pine Ridge, because of distance and lack of money, is a boarding school during the week.

Many of the full-bloods reject the official government and look instead to the leadership of what is known here as the "traditionalist" organizations. The principal groups are the Landowners, an association of older, full-blooded men who hold land on the reservation, and the Treaty Council (sometimes known as the "Old Dealers"), again, a group of older, full-blooded men.

Three councilmen from the traditionalist, full-blood districts failed last month in impeachment proceedings against Mr. Wilson on charges of nepotism and misuse of funds. Afterward, the two traditionalist organizations and a newer group, the Civil Rights Organization, which also opposes Mr. Wilson, invited in the young A.I.M. militants. Two nights later, Wounded Knee was seized.

Since then, many of the most visible traditionalist political leaders have been sympathetic to the Wounded Knee takeover, but have stood slightly apart. Largely under the direction of Gerald One Feather, the immediate past tribal chairman, the traditionalists have been seeking signatures out in the districts on a petition for a referendum to overthrow the tribal constitution. This week they reported getting more than the required number—one-third of registered voters—and federal officials accepted the petition and began checking the validity of the signatures.

The land on this reservation once totaled more than 4 million acres, but has been nibbled back to about 3 million, still twice the size of the state of Delaware. Of this, about 1 million acres within the reservation is now owned by whites, mainly in the lusher southeastern portion, about half a million is owned jointly by the tribe, and about a million and a half is owned by individual Indians but held and managed "in trust" for them by the Bureau of Indian Affairs. Nearly all of the land is leased out for cattle grazing, much of it to white ranchers.

The complicated land ownership and use situation stems from the shifting policies of the federal Government. The original thrust of Indian policy was an attempt to turn the Indians into farmers or ranchers. To this end, under the Allotment Act of 1888, parcels of land varying from 40 to 320 acres were allotted to individual Indian families. The land was to be theirs, but held in trust by the B.I.A. for twenty-five years—later extended indefinitely—in hopes that this would protect it from going out of Indian hands.

But, in 1906, under pressure from South Dakota officials, a system under which Indians could be given the actual deed—or patent—to their lands was devised. Competency commissions went about passing judgment on the ability of the Indians, and numerous deeds, known as "forced patents," were issued.

What this meant was that the land was now privately held and subject to state taxation. Many Indians lost their land because of their inability to pay taxes, some mortgaged their land and had it foreclosed, and others were simply cheated or bilked out of it by whites.

Around 1910, the Sioux here had a promising cattle raising industry under way. But, in another shift of federal policy, the Government decided in the period before and during World War I that it desperately needed wheat.

The plains Indians could adapt to the cowboy mode, but had little interest in farming and, under Government encouragement, leased their land to wheat growers. The Indians moved to the towns, losing touch with their lands, most of which were eventually taken over by whites. Under this process, which was given impetus by the opening of Bennett County in the eastern area of the reservation to homesteading, much of the best farmland was lost.

During the nineteen-twenties, Government policy actively encouraged the sale of Indian land. In the last few years, officials here assert they have tried to keep the land in Indian hands.

The lands still owned by the Indians have been greatly subdivided through inheritance so that today, in extreme cases, some Indians own as little as a third of an acre. Much of the individually owned land is thus too small for a herd of cattle and, in any case, ranching requires a large initial capital investment that the Indians do not have. There are about twenty-five successful Indian ranchers here, mainly mixed-bloods, federal officials say.

Under the trust arrangement, the land is leased out under the direction of the B.I.A. It is leased in large grazing units, overlapping many individual tracts. About 83 percent of the landowners lease out their land and receive payments, known as "allotment money," once a year, around Christmas time. The price for leasing grazing land on the reservation runs up to about $1 an acre per year, although a substantial number of families get less than a dollar.

There are about 3,000 employable people on the reservation, federal officals estimate, but less than 1,500 jobs. Of these, most are with the Government and its social welfare agencies. The tribal government has 340 jobs, the Bureau of Indian Affairs has 250, and the Public Health Service 50. Some of the jobs with higher educational requirements are held by whites—this includes 70 percent of the teachers—but some established mixed-blood families count members of several generations in Government jobs and also live in Government housing. About $10 million in federal money comes into the reservation each year.

There is a moccasin factory in Pine Ridge, run by the Sunbell Corporation of Albuquerque, N.M., which employs 180 people and also sends out piece-work to Indian homes. About 250 Indians find employment in agriculture or in other seasonal jobs such as construction.

A few years back, there was a fishhook factory here, which employed several hundred Indians in four locations at the tedious work of tying on nylon leaders. While the factory was operating, social workers say, there was a noticeable increase in the pride and stability of families, and children went to school better clothed. But the operation was partly supported by a federal job-training grant and when it ran out, the factory could not compete with Japanese imports and moved to Mexico in search of cheap labor.

There is little in the way of Indian-owned business. A large supermarket, the Sioux Nation Store, stands in Pine Ridge, but is operated by whites on leased tribal land. It extends credit, but its prices are markedly higher than those outside the reservation.

In the tiny outlying towns, a dominant institution is the local trading post, again run by whites. Many Indians resent the white traders, who, they charge, get higher rates of interest for loans and credit, abuse their positions as postmasters by opening Indian mail in search of money, and pay Indians small sums for such work as beading and sewing porcupine quills on moccasins, which they then sell to tourists at a huge profit. The traders are supposed to operate under a license issued by the tribe.

The per capita income on the reservation from all sources, including welfare, is $846. State welfare statistics give some idea of the extent of poverty and dependency. While only 7.1 percent of the under-eighteen population in South Dakota is Indian, for instance, Indians account for 46.4 percent of those receiving state aid to dependent children.

In addition to the state categories, in November, the last month for which figures are available, some 2,446 people on the reservation were receiving federal general assistance relief. It was a relatively light month.

But there are more than physical implications to the drab economic picture. A major social problem here is that, in a traditionally masculine society, the male role has been destroyed. In the moccasin factory, the reservation's single industry, 60 percent of the employees are women, whites hold the business positions, and the male employees are largely old men and young boys who perform such tasks as making tiny bundles of twigs for the dolls to carry. Even welfare, under the categorical grant system, goes primarily to women, thus further undermining the men and weakening the family structure.

In the traditional culture, emotions were not expressed and release was found for men in physical exploits. Now, release is sought largely in drink, and alcoholism is an enormous problem.

"It's killing us," one high-ranking Indian official said of the drinking problem, "it's the bane of everything we do."

The Indian sentries at their checkpoint of two burned-out pick-up trucks by the entrance to Wounded Knee confiscated a big grocery bag filled with six-packs of Budweiser the other day. They tore off the tops and poured the beer down a gully, in accordance with the rule that no alcohol or drugs are to be permitted.

Inside the encampment, surrounded by great black swatches of prairie where the flares from the federal lines have started grass fires, the young men brandished guns, sometimes with an alarming casualness, and wore Indian jewelry looted from the trading post. The women are formally relegated to such traditional tasks as cooking and washing.

A round lodge for purifying sweat baths stands by the teepee where meetings are held and Crow Dog, the medicine man, prepares religious ceremonies. Some of the negotiating sessions have been held in the

teepee, with old men of the tribe sitting cross-legged around a smoldering fire poetically telling Government officials in city suits of the promises Washington has made and broken.

Some of the two-hundred-odd people here are from the reservation, including a scattering of older full-blooded men and women. Others have come in from Canada, Montana, Oklahoma, California. They are angry at white society, responding to the stirring of Indian pride, and trying to find their origins. But many are urban Indians a long way from their roots.

When the Indians first began rustling cattle in the nearby fields for food, for instance, a group selected the largest cow for slaughter. Being with calf, she proved to have little meat. The Indians shot the cow twice, but were unable to kill it. Finally, a television technician took a gun and shot the beast between the eyes. Then he took a knife from one of the Indians and showed them how to skin and butcher it.

The American Indian Movement, the spearhead of the takeover, began in a meeting of a small group of young Indians living in Minneapolis in 1968. It is supported largely by money from the Lutheran Church. In the early days it focused on urban Indians. But in the last year it has been involved in a series of demonstrations that have seen a courthouse damaged, a chamber of commerce building burned down, and the National Guard called out.

The group's first appearance in this area—and its first major victory—came after Raymond Yellow Thunder, a reservation Indian, was beaten up by white toughs while drunk, thrown half-naked into an American Legion dance, and found dead in a car the next morning. A.I.M. demonstrations forced concessions from white officials, and convictions were obtained.

Some of the A.I.M. leadership comes out of tough backgrounds with early criminal records, but others are college-educated. While some Indians are wary of them because of their wild reputations, their assertions, pride, and masculinity are appealing to others.

The militants appear to be trying to break away from their urban past and seek their identity in tribal culture. There is a good deal of talk here about returning to traditional ways and "reverence for Mother Earth," but for many the traditions are fuzzy or unknown, and the goals seem vague.

And even the rebels are enmeshed in the white man's idea of order and structure. After the "new nation" was proclaimed, the provisional government's first act was a plea for more typists and secretaries to create a bureaucracy and make records and keep lists.

Richard Wilson, the former plumber who is president of the Oglala

Sioux Tribal Council, is a stocky man who wears dark glasses, a blue wind breaker, and a crewcut. He denounced A.I.M. after the Washington building [Bureau of Indian Affairs] seizure, and the tribal courts banned militant leaders from attending tribal gatherings. Federal funds were found in the reservation's tight budget to hire a force of about forty-five loyalist Indian guards, armed with clubs and Mace, to protect against "A.I.M. incursions." Mr. Wilson later called in the federal marshals.

He dismisses the militants as "vagrants" and suggests the best way to get rid of them would be "to offer them a job." In the early days of the occupation, he vowed to "take eight hundred or nine hundred guns up there and clean them out," but this was regarded as an idle threat.

Even two of Mr. Wilson's stranded supporters conceded in conversation that "despotic" and "dictatorial" were apt descriptions of his political style. But Mr. Wilcox, the tribal councilman, said such exercises of power were "residual rights, which go back to time immemorial."

Mr. Wilson's opponents accuse him of nepotism, misuse of tribal funds, and other forms of corruption. They charge, too, that he enforces his power through what is widely known as "the goon squad."

But, while Mr. Wilson may be a strong man in the small world of the reservation, he has been simply pushed aside by the wave of white federal officials from the Interior and Justice departments who have rushed out here to deal with the crisis.

JOSÉ YGLESIAS

Right On With The Young Lords

The efforts of the Black Panther Party in the 1960s to politicize and radicalize black ghettos in the North and West strongly affected the attitudes and actions of other ethnic groups. Negatively, it led to indignation and hostility among white ethnic groups who rejected the revolutionary plans and the societal demands made by the Panthers. Leaders like Huey Newton and Eldridge Cleaver, however, were greatly admired for their actions by other nonwhite ethnic groups, particularly by the Puerto Rican youth.

In 1968 the Young Lords Organization of Chicago, a Puerto Rican street gang, became a political action group modeled after the Black Panther Party. The New York chapter of the Young Lords, described very favorably by writer José Yglesias in the following essay, organized numerous activities to aid the Puerto Rican community, including a breakfast program, health clinic, and day care center. The Lords portrayed themselves as a party "fighting for the liberation of all oppressed people." Specifically, they wanted independence for their homeland, community control of their economic, social, educational, and political institutions, and freedom for all political prisoners. Their hero is Ché Guevara.

In spite of their closeness to the Panthers, they are, according to Yglesias, "very Latin." They honor the mores and traditions of Puerto Rico and the attitudes of their parents. They are in Yglesias's eyes a distinctly ethnic welfare organization.

José Yglesias is a novelist and a magazine writer. He has written several books, including A Wake *in Ybor City (1963),* An Orderly

Life *(1968)*, Down There *(1970)*, The Truth about Them *(1971)*, *and* Chile's Days of Terror: Eyewitness Accounts of the Military Coup *(1974)*.

Suddenly in East Harlem last summer people began throwing garbage and wrecked furniture into the middle of the streets. Traffic was stopped frequently; mid-town businessmen avoiding the clog of the East River Drive found themselves stalled inside stifling cars in an area whose residents looked upon their discomfiture with little sympathy. The police and sanitation workers would clear one intersection and find that two blocks away—east or west, downtown or up—another one was blocked with the kind of debris that in middle-class sections of the city is not allowed to languish on the sidewalks. The Mayor's office got the message and a twenty-four-hour pickup of garbage was begun. For a while El Barrio, that part of Harlem where the first Puerto Rican migrants settled, was cleaner than anyone remembered. With this "garbage riot," the Young Lords first made their presence felt in New York.

Indeed, it was then that they earned the name. Afterward, the Young Lords Organization of Chicago, a Puerto Rican street gang that by late 1968 had evolved into a political-action group, gave the El Barrio youths a license to start a New York chapter, and by last September the new affiliate had signed a lease for a storefront on Madison Avenue between 111th Street and 112th, and set up shop.

The Barrio got to know them right away. The rest of New York did not pay attention until in December they occupied a Methodist church in the area. They had negotiated for weeks with the minister for use of the church to conduct a breakfast program, health clinic, and day-center. It was not a confrontation that the Lords disingenuously sought: the church was conveniently located in the heart of the Barrio, it was in use only on Sundays, there was no other space that they could afford— "and, anyway, churches are tax-exempt because they are supposed to serve the community," any Lord will tell you.

The minister was adamantly opposed. He was a Cuban exile, and he must have felt that the revolution he had fled was dogging him. The Lords held the church for ten days and for that period turned it into a center of service for the community. The Cuban minister obtained an injunction that required the Lords to vacate the church or face contempt proceedings. There was much sympathy for the Lords—there were even indications from the Methodist hierarchy that it was not pleased with the unbending position of the local minister—but when they did not leave, the police forcibly removed them.

Felipe Luciano, the chairman of the New York Lords, came out of it with a broken arm, and trials for the group arrested are pending. During late March, when I spent two weeks visiting the Lords, there were still two cops on duty in front of the church every day; it was still open only on Sundays, despite an announcement by the minister in December that it was going to be used for community programs; and the congregation was still small, most of its members Cuban exiles and most of them outside the Barrio.

But the rush thereafter by young Puerto Ricans to join the Lords—who will also accept non–Puerto Rican blacks from the Barrio—was so great that the organization has had to close its rolls temporarily, and take steps to make certain that each applicant understands the kind of commitment that is required of him and to prevent police and F.B.I. agents from infiltrating. (How many Young Lords there are is kept secret.) Membership is not confined to the Barrio; members also come from the Puerto Rican ghettos in the South Bronx, Brooklyn, and the Lower East Side. One such, a girl from Brooklyn, getting a rundown from Felipe Luciano in my presence, asked, "Are the pigs still in the church?" Felipe smiled. "They're still there but they're going to have to go away someday," he said. "When the enemy advances you get out of the way. When he withdraws you move in. I didn't say that—Giap did!"

The first "rule of discipline" of the organization reads: "You are a Young Lord 25 hours a day," and after one sees the Lords sign in and out of their headquarters, getting their daily assignment from the Officer of the Day who sits at the front desk, the statement seems no exaggeration. Those who don't support themselves with part-time or full-time jobs are carried by the organization. Each day the O.D. doles out stipends for breakfast, lunch, and dinner; and, as the organization grows, the central committee decides which Lords to put on this supported basis.

Since the church bust, as the Lords refer to the evacuation of the Methodist Church, the Tactical Police Force has several times held mock raids on Madison Avenue between 111th and 112th Street. Traffic into the area is stopped, and police take stances on street corners and tops of buildings. So at least the Lords describe these rehearsals. The Lords have a rule that no one in uniform is allowed to walk into their office without a warrant, and to date the police have not attempted that.

Last Maundy Thursday, one of the two or three days when I wasn't in the Barrio, the Lords responded to a report that narcotics agents were arresting two young men on 111th Street; as is usual in such cases, the agents had taken the two into the hallway of a tenement to search them. The people on the street came to the Lords because the young men, they said, were being beaten, an accusation that when made against the police no one in Harlem ever doubts. When the Lords got there the street was crowded with angry residents and the two agents were being attacked; a passing fire engine had called for police reinforcements and when they arrived the Lords gave the order to "split."

The police headed for the Lords, caught one, and issued a warrant for a second three days later. The charges brought against them ranged from felonious assault to incitement to riot—and lend credence to the Lords' contention that the police are out to get them.

On Good Friday, Madison Avenue between 111th and 112th Street was full of people, all of them keeping their cool but all on the lookout. While waiting for a press conference the Lords had called, I saw an unmarked car with five plainclothesmen circling the block; during the course of an hour it came to a halt regularly across from the Lords' headquarters, and its occupants would give us all lingering looks. A bad move. One of the first newspaper people to arrive was a tough grandmotherly reporter from a Spanish-language daily, and Yoruba Guzmán, the Lords' minister of information, gave her a hug and a kiss and told her what was happening. She listened to him skeptically, but a few moments later got an opportunity to see the car and the occupants who looked so out of place that far uptown on Madison Avenue. She went away, called the police precinct, and returned with the message that the plainclothesmen were there because an anonymous phone caller had said that a cop was in trouble.

"So you should figure," she concluded, "that you have an informer in the neighborhood."

David Pérez, the Lords' minister of defense, a tough, bright twenty-year-old, tried to tell her that the police don't need any anonymous calls to do what they were doing and, while he was at it, did his best to "politicalize" her. She was an archetypal reporter, impatient with generalizations. At first she only demurred. When David persisted, she scolded him like a loving Puerto Rican mother. *"No seas tan cabezón que te doy un cocotazo*—don't be so hard-headed or I'll rap you on the noggin!" David liked that, and for a moment politics was forgotten.

It's the Lords' politics, however, that the authorities cannot forget. The Lords are revolutionary nationalists, and the one-sentence preamble to their thirteen-point program reads, "The Young Lords Organization is a revolutionary political party fighting for the liberation of all oppressed people." When the phone rings in the tiny front office—beyond it are two improvised rooms only Lords may enter—the O.D. always answers, "Free Puerto Rico now!" That is the first point in their program, and there is almost no other that is not an affront to the defenders of the status quo.

On the first point not much more is said than that the Lords "want liberation and the power in the hands of the people, not Puerto Rican exploiters." Like the nationalist groups in Puerto Rico, they do not believe in plebiscites, such as the one held in 1967 in Puerto Rico in which only 1 percent of those voting (the total was less than 50 percent of those qualified to vote) indicated that they preferred national independence over statehood or commonwealth status. Indeed, the Lords are in accord with the nationalists who called for a boycott of the referendum, if only because any three-month resident on the island, including Americans, can vote, and the results have to be approved by the U.S. Congress. More than that, they believe that national independence can only be gained by a combined program of education and direct struggle by Puerto Ricans, and that the political aims must be accompanied by economic ones which would break American domination of the island.

In a sense, their position on Puerto Rican independence is an academic one—at least for the moment. The Chicago and New York chapters of the Lords are the only ones in existence, and they view their job as that of organizing the 1 million Puerto Ricans in the United States, while leaving the main job to the nationalist groups on the island. If you ask individual Lords whether they would stay in New York or go to Puerto Rico if the kind of independence they want is achieved, you will get answers that are both personal and an extension of their total political position. Some would go to Puerto Rico simply because they prefer it there. Others say, in effect, that when such a day comes it would mean that the United States itself is free of a government that exploits them—or any minority group—either here or on the island. That is why they preface the first point on their program with the general statement that they fight "for the liberation of all oppressed people." Subsumed in all this is their conviction that they cannot go it alone, and their hope that white and black revolutionaries will help them liberate the United States. The Black Panthers are the group to whom they are closest.

Some of the Lords' other points call for "self-determination for all Latinos," "liberation of all third-world people," "community control of our institutions and land." (Their programmatic point on community control certainly extends the meaning that phrase has had in local New York City politics: "We want control of our communities by the people and programs to guarantee that all institutions serve the needs of the people. People's control of police, health services, churches, schools, housing, transportation, and welfare are needed. We want an end to attacks on our land by urban removal, highway destruction, universities, and corporations.")

The Lords also demand "freedom for all political prisoners"; they oppose "capitalists and alliances with traitors" and "the American military." They state: "We believe armed self-defense and armed struggle are the only ways to liberation"; and "We want a socialist society." The final salutation of the written program is, *"Hasta la victoria siempre*—always until victory," the phrase Ché Guevara used in his farewell letter to Fidel Castro.

Mid-March, Sanford Garelik, president of the City Council, declared at a press conference after the offices of three large corporations were bombed, that New York City was now a battleground for urban guerrilla groups, and he included the Lords among them. He explained them as "the outgrowth of an era of disrespect for law and the acceptance of a Maoist philosophy of guerrilla warfare," a statement that would not seem to qualify him as an analyst of the social origins of political movements or as historian of the Chinese Red Army; he was for years chief inspector of the Police Department, and for two was head of the section dealing with subversives.

Yoruba Guzmán replied, when questioned by the press, that the Lords had no weapons but did not blink their position on armed struggle. He referred newsmen to the point in the Lords' program mentioned above; in full it reads:

> We are opposed to violence—the violence of hungry children, illiterate adults, diseased old people, the violence of poverty and profits. We have asked, petitioned, gone to courts, demonstrated peacefully, and voted for politicians full of empty promises. But we still ain't free. The time has come to defend the lives of our people against aggression, for revolutionary war against the businessman, politician, and police. When a government oppresses the people, they have the right to abolish it and create a new one.

The language is their own, but the content is not much different from Jefferson's on the right of the people to revolution. Jefferson, in fact, was much bloodier.

This exchange between Garelik and Guzmán was more formal than another I heard one Saturday afternoon on the same subject between a young black Puerto Rican and one of the Lords. The young Puerto Rican was tall, handsome, mod-dressed—a slick brother, in the language of the Barrio—and he was one of a steady stream of people coming into the office on various errands. He had to wait his turn to talk to the O.D. The latter was, that afternoon, one of the young cadres, a sixteen-year-old in an organization whose oldest leader is twenty-three-year-old Juan González.

"Listen, I was here, you know, to get some information about your organization," the slick brother said, with a self-conscious smile, "but I was high that day and you said I should come back another time."

The young cadre nodded encouragingly; he was glad the brother had learned the organization was strict about dope. (Any stranger who walks in is watched closely to see he does not plant dope in the office.) A moment earlier I had seen the O.D. deal equably with a happy junkie who'd rolled in the door hoping to get money for a beer. He had said, "Brother, you know the Lords ain't got money for that...and you can't stay here now, you know, 'cause you're high." The junkie couldn't seem to aim for the door, and another Lord came over to him, took his arm and said with the special compassion they have for anyone who is blood, "Here, we talk out on the street," and went out with him.

"What I want to know is, how you going to take power?" said the mod-dressed brother right off. "'Cause I'm glad to see an organization out to help my people. About time."

"The people will seize power," the O.D. said.

"Seize power?"

"They get a lot of harassment, you know, from the man. You too. They keep tapping you on the back saying everything is going to be all right. But things getting worse. This organization is explaining to Puerto Ricans where it's at."

"This is whitey's land," said the brother, shaking his head. "They got the shackles."

"We got to take it back."

"Only way you going to do it, man, is war, blood and killing, 'cause whitey don't give up nothing."

The young cadre smiled. The Lords are always telling one another the people know their oppression better than they do.

"Why you let the opposition know you're aggressive?" the brother continued, his voice taking on a worried tone. "You let them know that and they burn you. You shouldn't let them know where you're at."

The O.D. explained. "This is an aboveground organization. We got to educate the people about the contradictions, point them up. We got to lead them...."

The other nodded and nodded while the O.D. spoke. "You got any literature?"

The O.D. pointed him to the shelves where their leaflets, newspapers, policy statements are stacked. He began to help himself from them, and I noticed that on the back wall of the shelves a quote from Che Guevara was painted: "Every day we must fight that this great love for humanity translate itself into concrete acts." The young man insisted on paying for the leaflets and newspapers and said, "I'm going to study these." When he turned to face the door, he added, "You out here right on the street. They can burn you."

The thought preys on the Lords' minds. But it heartens them that people in the Barrio, like the mod-dressed brother, are continually giving them advice on this score. On Good Friday evening, the Lords held a membership meeting to assess Maundy Thursday's action with the narcotic agents, and Juan González reported how an old Puerto Rican woman had cornered him on the street. "Any Lords they get warrants out for," the old woman had said, "I shall swear were with me all the time." The woman had been helped by the Lords to get on relief, Juan reported, and then added, "But that wasn't all. She gave me a political-education class right there. She said that we can't go on fighting the pigs with our bare hands—they are armed, you got to be armed. And I'm standing there saying yeah, yeah, yeah!"

I had seen one of those women in the front office soon after the mod-dressed brother left. An old American black woman with a southern accent. She was toothless and her face was black leather deeply creased. Someone helped her take the step from the sidewalk into the office. In one hand she grasped two envelopes just arrived in the mail and she was looking for Felipe Luciano; he had helped her apply for welfare benefits, and, since she was illiterate, she hoped he would tell her that the mail she had received had something to do with that.

"I want him to tell me what this is," she said, and let everyone see the envelopes. "Now this one, looks like a check to me. Yessir, I think it is. You tell Felipe—God bless him—the relief check arrived. I think." Then she held out the other letter, the large census folder everyone in the city was receiving those days. "Now this one—what you suppose it is?"

David Pérez looked up and said, "The census."

The old lady looked puzzled. "The census?"

"They're counting heads," David explained. "They want to know how many of *us* there are."

The old lady shook her head. "Oh no, we got to keep them wondering," she said and broke out in a superb, toothless grin. "No sir."

Obviously she was pleased to have received mail and she kept showing the two letters to everyone in the office and speculating about what she should do about them. Each time she got the census envelope she said, "Census! Why, they's just me and my old dog—starving together!" Finally, she handed the O.D. both envelopes. "I tell you what I'm gonna do. You keep them there until Felipe comes and you remind him, now."

When she turned to leave, she caught my eye and began to speak in a wailing voice. "My grandchild got shot in Vietnam. He dead. Black boy shedding his blood—for what? It's a bitter pill to swallow. But I'm going to swallow it, I am. Muriel Snead is my name. My grandchild dead!" Everyone became very quiet and the O.D. asked a Lord standing security in the office to walk her home.

On the question of the wisdom of the people, the Lords—or in any case, their leaders—talk like classical revolutionaries. I heard Yoruba Guzmán several times say, no use our talking about being the vanguard, man, the people are much more radical. Most times he used the example of the garbage riots: the Lords were first to throw the garbage into the streets and the people went much further, going to the avenue intersections and piling on furniture.

The first week in April, Yoruba acquired another story to bolster his thesis. I had gone back to Madison Avenue to find out what happened to the Lords at the Central Park demonstration for the Panthers. A citywide committee to defend the Panthers held the rally and then some ten thousand people marched across the 59th Street bridge to Queens where the Panthers awaiting trial were held. The Lords turned out in a group, and were set upon in the subways after the demonstration and beaten by the police. Yoruba told me this and his new story about a people's action. A day earlier, on 111th Street, two police made some obligatory arrests (Harlem residents believe they have a daily quota to fill) and the people on the street didn't call for the Lords this time; they chased the police and freed the men arrested.

"The people on the street," a phrase the Lords often use, is their equivalent of the liberals' "common man," the Marxists' "working class." A former drug addict, a twenty-year-old who had kicked the habit cold only three weeks earlier, sat with me at La Cabaña, a Puerto Rican restaurant across from their offices, explaining how he had gone to the Lords for help and how proud he felt to be a Lord now. I asked him what specific political ideas he had gained from the organization in the short time he was with them. He smiled modestly and then spoke gently so as not to seem to be criticizing me for my short-sightedness. "The people in the street know everything about oppression. We know where it's at. I was just cynical. Defeated. When we get over that. . . ." And still smiling he looked over my head as if he could see that day come.

He had watched the Lords' actions in the neighborhood, admired them, hoped if he could kick the habit that they might accept him. On his own he had tried going off dope a couple of times and found that he had no friends except junkies. It was very lonely sitting in his mother's apartment enduring the disapproving presence of his stepfather. Late this February he went to the Lords' office, full of determination, and talked to Felipe Luciano. "I told him I wanted to kick and become a Lord and he rapped to me for a while and then said right on I could stay with two brothers and they would help me." He went home to pack a bag and he could have shot up then and there. Should he put off kicking? He went upstairs and packed and returned to the Lords.

He has never been alone since. During the worst of it there were always two Lords in the apartment to help hold him down. Next to him at the restaurant sat Jim, assigned never to leave him by himself. On Maundy Thursday, when the order came to split, they were separated for a while, and at the membership meeting the following night Yoruba publicly criticized Jim.

Without any self-consciousness the former addict spoke of the onerousness of always having to make sure Jim was with him when he stepped out of the office or the apartment, and hoped that there would soon be some trust in him. Yoruba told him that it should be some six months before this could happen, and reminded everyone of the case of one brother who backslid.

But at the restaurant the new Lord had no complaints. "I got a family now," he said, and Jim confirmed it. "We're three of us in the apartment and it's together, man."

"I see my street partner every once in a while," the new Lord said. "He passes me by and he thinks it's beautiful what I'm doing now and hopes he can do it too someday." For two and a half years the new Lord had never worked; he and his partner got all the money they needed for their habit with holdups and muggings. "I feel a little guilty about it still, you know, 'cause sometimes we stole from brothers. That was bad. It was an escape from reality into a worse reality."

I asked him what he meant by that and he gave me an example of something that happened to him which is not an uncommon occurrence with dope addicts. He was almost killed last summer because some of the other junkies told stories to his pusher. The pusher got mad with him because they made him believe that he (the new Lord) would never pay him off. "I always had, but he comes on me in the street when I had no money. I told him and he stepped back and took out his gun. He shot four times but the gun only went click, click. So I walked toward him and he shot again and this time a bullet came out. I was almost killed. The bullet went through my groin and got to my spine and so they never took it out. It bothers me when the weather changes. A reminder."

One of the most popular cadres in the Lords is a sixteen-year-old they call Cake. He is light-skinned, small, lithe, with black curling hair and enormous black eyes. In the Lords' purple beret he looks like a young Ché Guevara. I had spent a couple of hours outside the Barrio with him on my first day, when he acted as guard for the minister of finance at a speaking engagement at Finch College, and learned that for all his happy, light manner he was shrewd and politically fluent. "You don't know the half about Cake," Juan González said about him a few days later. When Cake came to the Lords last fall, he was a street cat with only one interest—fighting; and one political commitment—hatred of whites.

That reputation stayed with Cake and one day in a self-criticism session Yoruba Guzmán said to Cake: Sometimes it seems to me you think fighting is all the Lords is about. "You know how we criticize each other," Juan explained to me. "Well, Yoruba got an answer from Cake that almost brought tears to his eyes. No, man, Cake says, I've done so many things since I'm a Lord—I've given free breakfasts to the kids, free clothes to the people, and rapped about politics with the cats in the street. I've done so many things I don't care if I die now."

Juan continued, "Cake said another thing that goes for a lot of us. If the pigs vamped on us and wiped out the organization—'cause that's all we got, that storefront—I don't know what I'd do with myself. My life would be over."

When you interview a Lord, he is more likely to talk about another than about himself. Always appreciatively. It is also a rule of discipline that a Lord may not criticize another when not in his presence. Membership meetings on Wednesday nights and political education classes on Mondays are occasions for that. In their daily dealings with one another they are also strict, calling each other down for attitudes, opinions, and actions not consistent with being a Lord. Women Lords don't let what they consider male chauvinist remarks by a brother pass. The Officer of the Day is one guardian of such behavior; he hands out disciplinary correction for infractions of all kinds and often the O.D. is a woman. A Lord signs in late in the morning and you may find him in the back doing twenty-five push-ups or, if a girl, running a number of times up and down the block.

The Lords run a breakfast program at Emmaus House (a nonsectarian religious institution on 116th Street devoted to social work), which lends them its kitchen from 7 to 8:30 every school day morning; the Lords not only prepare and serve the breakfasts but also escort the children from their area of Madison Avenue to Emmaus

House and then to their school.

For a few months now the Lords have devoted Saturdays to giving tuberculin tests in the Barrio. They are also prodding the health authorities by testing children for lead poisoning in the old tenements that despite new housing projects still dominate the landscape of East Harlem.

They collect clothes and distribute them free to the people of the neighborhood, and word of that has got out of the community—the only non–Puerto Rican whites you see on 111th Street these days are elderly ladies from as far away as Washington Heights bringing bundles of clothes. The Lords have also been getting ready to distribute, also free, several hundred pots, factory seconds donated by a sympathizer. They have also taken the first steps toward establishing, away from their crowded offices, what they call a Guerrilla Clinic to rehabilitate dope addicts, and also an information center on Puerto Rico and Latin America; to find locations for them they sent out searching parties for apartments and storefronts.

Every Monday the Lords tape a half-hour show for WBAI, and every day of the week they are out with leaflets or with Y.L.O., the organization's newspaper (published in the Chicago headquarters), or responding to appeals for help from Barrio residents with medical and welfare difficulties. Besides the newspaper sales and donations, the Lords' only source of income is from selling buttons showing an upraised brown arm holding a rifle against a green outline of an island and above them the statement in Spanish, "I Carry Puerto Rico in My Heart."

Although some of the unmarried Lords of the same sex live together, there are no communes. "We don't relate to that," is the way Yoruba puts it, "and we don't get involved in people's private lives unless it interferes with the organization." One top leader was busted from his post in February because of complications in his love life, and it takes very little time for an observer to confirm that for a full-time Lord the organization is his whole life. It *is* one big family.

Not that the Lords encourage members to leave their homes. On the contrary, they like to organize along family lines, to get a whole family involved in one activity or another of the organization. Political education classes are not to be interrupted, but one night when I sat with the section that met in the back of the storefront, two telephone interruptions were allowed because in each case it was a mother calling a Lord. One call was for Yoruba, the minister of information who is nineteen, and when he finished, he announced, "That's my mother for you. One day she throws me out of the house because of my politics and now she calls up to find out when I'm going to be on radio!" He is very proud of his father, who lost a job last fall when he swung at another worker who called his son a Commie.

Benny, a fifteen-year-old who every morning shows up at Emmaus House to cook and serve breakfast before he goes off to junior high school, told me his mother works in the free-clothing drive. "She's for the Lords, too," he said. When he had a moment to relax after all the children had been fed, he lit up a cigarette and the older Lord in charge called him down for it. "I got permission from my mother," Benny said, "but I don't smoke in front of her because I lose respect." The older Lord enjoyed his response as much as I had, but he insisted, "You can't do anything in front of me that you wouldn't do in front of your mother, so put it out." Benny did.

In all this they are very Latin. If they agree with white revolutionaries on the nature of American imperialism and racism, they do not insist on the generation gap. They honor the mores and traditions of Puerto Ricans. Even about so unequalitarian a tradition as *machismo* they take an unexpected stand; they say it "must be revolutionary, not oppressive." For them, being a *macho,* a real male, means standing up to the Man, a statement they make in the context of arguing for full equality for women. "I don't care if they call us liberals and everything else," said Juan González. "We're going to be with our people. Like Felipe says, we are going to be the sons and daughters of our fathers and mothers. Except that we're political."

The Lords' ministers and cadres and active sympathizers go out together to distribute leaflets or move through the tenements with the tuberculin tests; their leaders are available to anyone. Felipe Luciano, the chairman, seemed surprised when I commented on it. "Listen, if any Puerto Rican mother on the street doesn't feel free to grab my Afro and say, *Oye, eortate ese mono*—Hey, why don't you cut down that bush—then there's something wrong with the way I'm acting." They are not going to pick up guns until the Barrio is ready to do the same.

However thought-out this strategy is, its origins, it seems to me, spring from the belated realization by these young people that they are Puerto Ricans. I say belated, although so many are not yet out of their teens that it could be argued that this is properly the time for their ideological coming-of-age. In any case, their identification with Puerto Rico is relatively recent. Most are first-generation mainlanders—and had turned away when they were children from their parents' language and ways, as happens with the children of most minority groups. Thus, some of their leaders first became politically conscious through their association with American blacks, and little by little, over the last two years, came to sense their own special cultural and political identity.

Many of them are trying now to become fluent in Spanish. At a membership meeting in March the members forced Felipe Luciano to speak entirely in Spanish. "It was beautiful," he said. "The brothers and sisters helped me along, but it was tough going." David Pérez, the minister of defense, can go the longest in Spanish because he came from Puerto Rico at age ten. "That's oppression, man," said Yoruba to a Latin American who had asked him what language they should converse in. "We can understand Spanish but . . . ." None, however, are trying to practice a pure Castilian or a standard Latin American Spanish. They know that the Spanish of the Barrio has undergone its Norman conquest; it does not bother them that *la carpeta* comes from carpet, *friscar* from freeze. Latin Americans with whom it is a custom to bemoan the corruption of the language in Puerto Rico are going to be surprised by the linguistic liberality of these revolutionary Puerto Rican nationalists.

One of the Lords mulling over this subject pointed out to me that at a street demonstration this year commemorating a nationalist anniversary it was a younger-generation speaker frequently lapsing into American phrases who most aroused the audience. The older nationalist speakers in full command of traditional Spanish rhetoric received only respectful attention. The experience led the Lord to believe that one of the reasons that Pedro Albizu Campos, the nationalist leader responsible for the postwar uprising in Puerto Rico, failed was that he spoke an unreconstructed Spanish. "Don Pedro wasn't talking the language of the people," the Lord concluded. "In the Barrio the language is something we call Spinglish."

The Lords' attitude toward left-wing political jargon is similar. The first time I talked to Felipe Luciano he described to me the personal background of the members of the Lords' central committee. I said, "Then all of you are of working-class background?" He smiled and replied, "Working-class? No, man, we're talking about welfare people." Returning to the Barrio from taping a radio show at WBAI, Yoruba was reading a story on the Lords in *Workers World,* a Marxist newspaper, and quoted a phrase describing them that amused him— "young workers." He likes to tell what would happen to a Communist using the word *lumpenproletariat* with people in the Barrio—"They'd give him a lump in the face!" In an interview last summer, Cha-Cha Jiménez, head of the Young Lords in Chicago, is quoted as saying: "We're not so politically educated, from books or anything, but we're educated from the streets, from being Puerto Ricans, from being different shades of skin."

They speak, then, the language of the streets, a language in which obscenity plays its part but is seldom nasty. In a political education class they will go from a discussion about a street action (extracting from it tactical lessons) to the Declaration of Independence (drawing a parallel between the thirteen colonies and the black colonies in the mother country) without any self-conscious modulation of speech. In this, as in many other things, they are like the Black Panthers, but they have not had much exposure outside the Puerto Rican communities and consequently there has been little opportunity for respectable whites to express outrage at their language.

True, some of the articles written these days about the "rhetoric of violence" are inspired by its use by young white radicals for whom it is a conscious choice, but the Lords speak the way they do not to shock anyone but because that is simply the way they and their people speak. To "deal" is to be active in a confrontation with the police and "to lay in the cut" is to shy from it, lively variants we should all be able to appreciate, but it may take real knowledge of conditions in the Barrio and the black ghettos to understand that sometimes only a four-letter word carries sufficient descriptive force.

Coming to the Promised Land

Americanization Fails

The arrival of Cuban refugees from their native land since 1959 has been described as one of the most successful resettlements in history. The American press has generally held up the gains of Cuban exiles as a prime example of the American dream come true. According to Business Week, *for example, "In the ten years since Cubans began fleeing to the United States from Castro, they have made faster progress in their adopted land than any other group or groups of immigrants in this century." The proof offered to support this view is the fantastic economic advances Cuban exiles have achieved within the capitalistic system as opposed to the communist system. But as recent events have made clear, there is more than one side to the Cuban exile story.*

As part of their heightened ethnic awareness in the 1970s, second-generation Cubans have begun to question seriously the reasons for their material advancement and the impact it has had on the Cuban community. The essay below notes the important and unique role played by the American government in easing the economic problems of relocation by providing large subsidies to the Cuban community.

Like other ethnic groups, Cubans have also begun to decry the loss of their culture as they accommodate to the new society. In the second part of this selection, "Americanization Fails," a young Cuban who arrived as a teenager in 1961 reflects the bitterness that some Cubans harbor toward America. He denounces the image of America as the land of opportunity and freedom as it has been painted by older Cubans and the American press. This young man accuses the United States government

"Coming to the Promised Land" and "Americanization Fails," *Cuba Resource Center Newsletter* (July, 1972). Reprinted by permission of Cuba Resource Center.

of stripping Cubans of their heritage. He finds among second-generation Cubans a realization of the evils of Americanization and a readiness to reassert their Latin American ties. They also stand ready to join with the Cuban revolution and liberation movements inside and outside the United States to stop the spread of capitalism.

COMING TO THE PROMISED LAND

The Cuban exile population in the United States is not like any other immigrant population, even those to which it bears superficial resemblance. It is not like the huge waves of immigration which came to this country around the turn of the century with nothing, people who were used and abused by a budding United States capitalism with pretensions of democracy operating through machine politics; it is not like the steady stream of sister Caribbean exiles who move to the United States for economic gain and must face the fact that color prejudice makes them part of the last hired/first fired syndrome; nor is it even like the occasional groups of political refugees who are encouraged by the United States to flee communism, whether in Hungary or North Vietnam. The Cuban exile community is instead a remarkably privileged group of "self-imposed political exiles" (the phrase is Richard Fagen's), an exile community not simply encouraged to flee Cuba, but transported and given scholarships to the United States.

Until the defeat of the CIA-organized Bay of Pigs invasion in April, 1961, United States foreign policy for Latin America was fixated on the forceful overthrow of Castro. Invasion from without and subversion from within until the regime was toppled, so ran the scenario.

The contingency plan, should invasion and subversion fail, was initiated with the December, 1960, opening of the Cuban Refugee Emergency Center in Miami. The aim was to destroy Cuba from within by encouraging its professionals and trained workers to leave. Emptied of its skilled personnel, upper and middle class, the internal structure of the economy was expected to collapse, thus undermining Cubans' confidence in Castro's leadership.

The Cuban missile crisis ended with the United States giving up further plans for the forceful overthrow of the Cuban government, in exchange for the removal of Soviet missiles. The future was set—the United States would try to rid itself of Communism in the Western Hemisphere by weakening the Cuban economy through the exiles. Thus the CIA-funded Radio Swan (a parallel of Radio Free Europe) encouraged Cubans to leave "Communist oppression" for the "freedom and higher standard of living of the United States." The United States government provided planes to carry the dissatisfied to Miami, and made cash payments on their arrival.

. . . .

Whatever the reasons, United States encouragement coupled with personal dissatisfaction has led some 650,000, or one out of every fifteen Cubans, to migrate to the United States during the past fourteen years.[1] This influx occurred in three phases, the first of which involved more than 150,000 people, most of whom left by commercial air flights. The second phase began with the Cuban missile crisis, when flights between the United States and Cuba were terminated. During the period from October 23, 1962, to November 30, 1965, the Cuban government established a special port from which relatives in the States could pick up by boat those who wished to leave. The third phase begins with the "Memo of Understanding" between the United States and Cuba, negotiated by Switzerland, which established the airlift to reunite separated families.

. . . .

There is no way to estimate the total number of dollars United States citizens have paid, through taxes, to support more than 60,000 Cuban exiles over the last fourteen years. . . .

The Cuban Refugee Program, from 1961 to 1971, has cost $730 million, more per capita than for any preceding refugee group. The administration's request before Congress is $161 million for fiscal 1973, $22 million more than the amount approved for 1972. The appropriation for 1971 was $112 million. These figures, supplied by the office of Rep. William L. Clay, represent a 300 percent increase in the funding of the refugee program since its inception in 1961. And this increase is accelerating even though fewer exiles are entering the United States now than at any time since the airlift began.

The $730 million figure represents only direct program subsidies from the Department of Health, Education, and Welfare. There is no way to estimate the cost of CIA operations—probably $200 million for the Bay of Pigs invasion and the ransom of those captured. (Figures for CIA-sponsored "mini-invasions" cannot be estimated; nor for such miscellaneous items as the electronic equipment which was to be planted in the offices of the Democratic National Committee headquarters.) There are also no known figures on the amount Cubans have deducted on their income taxes for losses in Cuba due to expropriation. Such a special deduction was approved by Congress. In all, the amount of tax dollars supporting Cuban exiles approximates the nearly $1 billion worth of corporate assets nationalized by the

Cuban revolution. And since a good portion of overseas investments is actually generated, through tax write-offs and other techniques, with our tax dollars, our erroneous foreign policy vis-à-vis Cuba has cost tax-paying citizens (remember, most large U.S. corporations pay few taxes) at least $1.5 billion since 1959.

Cubans have done well in this country also because federal tax dollars have subsidized an array of coordinated programs aimed specifically for them, and tailored to their economic and social needs. These programs include: assistance to voluntary relief agencies for providing daily necessities; provision of useful employment opportunities; assistance for resettling exiles; basic maintenance requirements (welfare); essential health services; local public school operating costs; training and educational opportunities, including scholarship aid to every Cuban applying to college; aid for care of unaccompanied children; surplus food distribution; and business credit and lending at reduced interest.[2]

In effect, whether it was an English-language program, a job-training skill, welfare assistance, or a loan to go to college, almost every need of the exile has been anticipated, so that his adjustment to the American way of life was, and still is, cushioned every step of the way.

The examples abound, but here are three. A special program at the University of Miami School of Medicine was established and funded by the United States government in order to provide Cuban doctors with the necessary knowledge to become licensed by the states. A little less than one-half of the reported 2,200 doctors who have left Cuba have completed this program. (Those who neither entered it nor completed it are, more than likely, hired by state and federal institutions, such as mental hospitals and prisons, where such a license is not required. Thus, their salaries are paid by the taxpayer.)

Another example of preferential treatment comes from a keen observer of the Dade County scene and should be set in context of the political clout Cubans have had behind the scenes in Florida: "By decision of the rural-based Florida legislature, until very recently (1969) the top welfare payment to a (Cuban) family was $85.00 per month. Thus, one could envision a local Negro mother with eight children getting less money than a recently arrived Cuban family ($100 a month plus $85 for other adult individuals). If enough even destitute Cuban relatives lived together for even a short period and secured several jobs, they could achieve a financial breakthrough level to slip out of the clutches of poverty. The Negro families could not. Add to this that since federal funds were available, the full range of surplus foods were given to Cubans but could not be given to Negroes because the state of

Florida did not seek the necessary federal funds. Refrigerated articles, like cheese and butter, were available to Cuban refugees only."[3] In 1969, local Dade County civil service jobs were opened to noncitizens. "Unfilled openings forced this policy change to hire Cubans."[4]

...If there is any doubt about the effects of this preferential treatment, consider what would happen if the same facilities for transportation, resettlement, job training, and automatic welfare payments were offered to politically and economically discontented people elsewhere in Latin America and the Caribbean. About 1.5 million Puerto Ricans have made their way on their own to the United States. In the New York City area alone there are some 100,000 Dominicans, and probably some 200,000 Haitians. An estimated 1.5 million Chicanos, Haitians, Dominicans, and other Latin Americans have entered the United States illegally. Since United States regulations define "refugees" in anticommunist terms, all others are subject to stiff quota restrictions. Unquestionably, were quota restrictions removed and support offered, the United States would be flooded by millions of immigrants, seeking to make their way in the "land of opportunity." In other words, the presence of Cuban exiles in the United States has very little to do with humanitarian compassion for suffering peoples and is based on a clear policy of assistance to those resisting communist-inspired change. And, more than likely, the press will continue to churn out stories on how the exiles have "pulled themselves up by their own bootstraps."

AMERICANIZATION FAILS

The integration of most Cubans into United States society began with economic and political seduction by the United States media long before the revolution. "They made us marry a lie, and we were forced to live with it," said Fidel. The biggest lie is the image of America, the land of opportunity, freedom, and justice.

Just as there is the myth of America the Beautiful, there is now the myth of the Cuban exile: a respectable, innocuous person who lost every penny to the Communists, came to the United States to save his children from being processed into canned meat in the Soviet Union, worked hard to get ahead, and is now proud of being a comfortable and secure Yankee citizen. A picture of the Cuban family smilingly posed by a color television often appears in official publications from the Cuban Refugee Center. They have been "resettled" in a cold climate, stripped of their identity, bought off with worthless gadgets and welfare, and molded to the needs of United States propaganda. But they do not regret it: the caption under the photo explains that the children feel no affection for, or attachment to, their land of birth.

But every success story has a shabby side. Often the family suffers unforeseen consequences: the corruption of the younger ones, unattended medical problems, psychic disorders. Many wish they had never left; the Cuban government forbids their return.

The pervasiveness and insidiousness of United States colonization can be seen best among some of the exiles that were proletarian before leaving the island and that continue to be proletarian. Firmly convinced that they should oppose "communism" everywhere, they permit the established order to oppress them, discriminate against them, humiliate them, and annihilate them as a community, while still commanding their obeisance. These Cubans are not properly *gusanos* (worms) but unfortunate victims of stupidity. From their ranks the Americans are able to recruit some of the soldiers that die first in fighting the Vietnamese, together with a disproportionate number of blacks and Puerto Ricans.

Young Cubans brought up in the collective hysteria of anti-communism fostered by their parents, and submerged in the massive conditioning of schools, newspapers, radio, etc., find it very difficult to arrive at an independent and intelligent conclusion about their situation. Estranged from their traditional values and Cuban history, truly counterrevolutionary young Cubans are a noisy but small minority. Judging from their grandiloquent statements, one could easily misread the militancy of political convictions of young Cubans generally. Most aspire toward the same plasticity—parties, drinking, drugs, clothes, shopping and souped-up cars—and political indifference, as do the sons and daughters of the native middle class (only more so). Some will pay lip service to the ideas of rabid anticommunists, but fail to articulate a coherent rationale for these ideas.

The blockade, the confiscation of Cuban films, suppression of information about the revolution, and the distortions of United States news reports are essential for the transculturation of Cuban youth and their political manipulation, but these efforts of the imperialists have failed miserably to convince a small but potentially important sector of Cuban youth. These young Cubans reject the middle-class, reactionary mentality of their parents, identifying instead with the Cuban revolution and the liberation movements within and without the United States. After developing a sharpened political consciousness with a Marxist content, as a result of their experiences in this country, these radical young Cubans have committed themselves to struggle with various movement organizations within the United States and Puerto Rico. They discredit the myth of the Cuban exile by signaling the terrific failure of the "American way of life." The words of Jose Martí are relevant to these young Cubans, for they "have lived inside the monster and know its entrails."

How many more young Cubans may eventually *exile* themselves from their involuntary exile and commit themselves to the struggle against imperialism will depend upon increased access to truthful information about the revolution and increased travel possibilities. Repulsion against American decadence and the exiles' servility may increase on the part of intelligent young Cubans, but this can lead to alienation unless there is a viable alternative for political participation. Many young Cubans shrink at the thought of confronting *gusanos* without adequate means of physical self-defense. Moreover, the revolutionary potential of young Cubans may have been blunted by some confusion due to the suspicion with which they are viewed by the Cuban government. But in spite of Cuban youth's odd position within the historical process, their "Americanization" has a crack down the middle, and it runs from Los Angeles to Washington to Miami.

"You're a Cuban?" people used to ask. "Yes, but not a *gusano,* not anymore," we would respond. That was a couple of years ago, when there weren't many of us, we were scattered all over the country, and the Cuban exile population was looked upon by people in the movement as a totally negative force.

Then, we began finding each other...in a movement activity...at the local university's "radical" class...or simply through a friend who knew more than one. What we sometimes jokingly but always truthfully call "the phenomenon of the Cuban radical" is no longer so rare.

"How'd you get radicalized?" we would ask each other first. It was usually through our antiwar feelings and disenchantment with the "American way of life." Then would come long discussions about Cuba, Latin America, Fidel, Ché, the Church. "Where did you live in Cuba?" "Is the family left there integrated into the revolution?" Then, inevitably: "Did you know so and so from such a school on the island?" and "Who do you know in Miami?"

We strove to develop a tight bond and got down to a deeper analysis. After much thought, we formed the Cuban Socialist Youth. Our first action as a group was to march in March, 1970, with our Puerto Rican comrades in New York to commemorate the Ponce Massacre. We have written articles, and our call to the Cuban youth has appeared in many underground newspapers. We talk anytime and anywhere we get a chance to let people know about us. We have leafletted in Puerto Rico, an experiment well received by progressive Cubans and seen as a big threat by *gusanos*. Nevertheless, we consider it of the utmost importance that everything possible be done to reach all the youth that are still confused and looking for alternatives. We feel very close to the history of struggle of our Cuban brothers and sisters and a very strong duty to continue their work wherever we find ourselves. In the words of Ché, we say, "The present is of struggle, the future will be ours."

SECTION 3

The Resurgence of Ethnicity

NICHOLAS PILEGGI

Risorgimento: The Red, White, and Greening of New York

Italians were the last of the major white immigrant groups to come to America before the advent of restrictionist legislation in the 1920s. The majority of these newcomers were unskilled peasants from southern Italy who were poor, uneducated, and firmly attached to their Old World traditions. They encountered discrimination from many different quarters. The brand of Catholicism Italians practiced differed substantially from what Irish coreligionists considered proper. Intense friction was the result. In the wider society Italians were castigated for an alleged proclivity for violent crime.

Despite such handicaps, these industrious immigrants soon spread to every part of the nation. They settled most heavily, however, in the urban centers of the East, where large numbers of their descendants are still found today. It is generally agreed that Italian Americans constitute America's second largest white ethnic minority. This impressive size and relative concentration has not often been translated into political or social advantages for the ethnic group. Indeed, it has only been since the late 1960s that Italian Americans have organized to correct this and begin demanding a greater share of influence and power from American society. Nowhere has this trend been more noticeable than in New York City, one of the largest centers of Italian people in the world.

Nicholas Pileggi has written perceptively of both New York and its Italians for many years. In this article he details the remarkable rise of the Italian American Civil Rights League, an organization formed by a reputed Mafia head-man, Joseph Colombo, in 1969. The League was modeled in many respects after the Jewish Anti-Defamation League and it sought many of the same goals. What is noteworthy is that the Italian ethnic group has never had a tradition of group-wide organization or action like the Jews. The response nonetheless to Colombo's League was immediate and widespread. Supportive rallies drew thousands of ordinary citizens of Italian descent who proudly, and loudly, endorsed the message of ethnic pride that the league sponsored. It was clear to even the most myopic observer that the organization was answering deep-seated needs. It gave a framework and a focus to many of the frustrations and anxieties that were affecting Italian American city dwellers.

The Italian American Civil Rights League suffered a fatal blow in 1971 when its leader was shot by an assassin during a huge rally in Columbus Square. The goals of the organization, however, have not died, and many observers of the ethnic scene see a continued willingness by Italian Americans to organize and strive for common goals. Despite its ignominious end, the league made an important contribution to an emerging Italian American consciousness.

No one can be certain just when the Italian American revolution began. It could have been September 21, 1969, when Mario Puzo's *Godfather* nudged *Portnoy* off the top of the *Times* bestseller list; or maybe June 29, 1970, when a real godfather, in the name of unity, gathered 50,000 people around him at Columbus Circle. Perhaps it was last July, in time for the 1970 ethnic vote, when Attorney General John Mitchell ordered FBI agents to stop using the words "Mafia" and "Cosa Nostra" in their press releases; or maybe it will not begin until June 28, [1971], and the second Columbus Circle Unity Day rally, at which police expect a crowd of at least 150,000.

Whatever uncertainty there may be over the exact day, there is no uncertainty over the fact that sometime within the last two years New York's Italians, after seventy-five years of benign residence in their own neighborhoods, have become restive. In the suburbs, while conservative, vowel-voting Italians [voting for candidates with Italian names] have begun to take over the political apparatus of Nassau, Suffolk, and Westchester counties, their children have been reading *The Greening of America,* just like the rest of their college friends, and have brought the middle-class Italian family its first taste of pot and filial estrangement. Those heartwarming stories in the *New York Times* about Tony the elevator operator who was given an "honorary doctor of transportation" degree upon retiring from Baruch College, are not sitting so well with the current generation as they did with the last.

In the city, meanwhile, where prominent judges, ex-congressmen, and daybed manufacturers have traditionally watched over working-class immigrants and their heirs like benevolent Sicilian landowners, a forty-seven-year-old Brooklyn-born real estate salesman, identified by the FBI as a Mafia boss, has suddenly taken over. In New York today, it is Joseph Colombo of the Italian American Civil Rights League—not Surrogate S. Samuel DiFalco, ex-Congressman Alfred E. Santangelo, or sofa-king Bernard Castro—who is appearing on the Dick Cavett Show. It is Colombo who is being taken seriously by the *New York Times,* being interviewed by Walter Cronkite, discussed at the Leonard Bernsteins'. And it is Colombo's son who now meets with officials at City Hall while the sons of the *prominenti* cool their heels.

Like most of the city's Jewish leaders who have been embarrassed by Meir Kahane's street-brawling Jews, Italian leaders, too, have begun to feel threatened by their own roots. All those rowdy truck drivers, embittered cabbies, and boisterous construction workers, abandoned by the middle class in Throgs Neck and Canarsie less than a generation ago, have suddenly and noisily arisen. Beckoned by Colombo and his Civil Rights League, working-class Italians have come out of their tenement apartments and backyards in unprecedented numbers to shout "Italian Power" in front of FBI headquarters and march past Bonwit's to Saint Patrick's wearing KISS ME I'M ITALIAN buttons. Recently, when Colombo's league publicly formed an alliance with Kahane's JDL, the *Times* editorial writers and most of the city's ethnic establishment were shocked. They shouldn't have been. Colombo and Kahane had been sharing picket lines, membership, and one attorney, Barry Slotnick, for months. Their followers had signed each other up during lunch breaks in the garment factories where they work. They had shared neighborhood candy stores and the elevated stops of Borough Park and Bensonhurst with each other for generations. They had played stoop-ball, three-man basketball, and Dyker Park hardball together as kids. Today, they drive for the same cab companies, pay off the same loans to First National City, and bet with the same neighborhood bookmakers, who are always Italians or Jews.

The alliance between Kahane's Jews and Colombo's Italians was the result of more than ethnic ego-building. Both men have, perhaps unwittingly, stepped into a leadership vacuum that has long existed among New York's low-income white working classes. They are providing a vehicle of outrage for all those borough-bound neighborhood people, most of whose kids are not getting draft deferments by going to college, whose already low incomes (63.2 percent of all white ethnic families in New York earn less than $9,400) are being shrunk even further by inflation and who have grown bitterly resentful of even the token assistance doled out to black and Puerto Rican communities to deal with many of the same problems.

In spite of their dubious backgrounds, Colombo and Kahane speak to the two-job sons of immigrants who must compete with blacks and Puerto Ricans for that bottom third of the city's job market, the 1.3 million New York jobs that pay less than $100 a week. It is their children who battle with black and Puerto Rican youngsters for school playgrounds and Coney Island beaches. While Kahane's young men are fighting blacks for lunchroom space at Brooklyn College, Colombo's Italian families are reporting the highest white drug addiction rate in the city and, next to the Puerto Ricans, the highest dropout rate in the city's school system. It is in Italian neighborhoods, despite the anti-welfare ballyhoo of their own representatives, that welfare cases have increased by 16 percent in the last two years, as compared with a 10 percent rise in predominantly black and Puerto Rican neighborhoods. And it is in Italian neighborhoods, too, that old-age benefits have jumped 87.3 percent in the last two years because the heads of families, no matter what old-world traditions dictate, can no longer afford to support their own parents.

While New York's Little Italies have helped make the urban scene more livable for the occasional visitor, it is their permanent occupants who have had to pay the price. And it is in precisely these neighborhoods, from Bensonhurst, Canarsie, Coney Island, Sheepshead Bay, Ridgewood, Elmont, Corona, Wakefield, Williamsbridge, Soundview, Fordham, Greenwich Village, East Harlem, and the increasingly troubled working-class suburban ghettos of Nassau and Westchester, that Joe Colombo's chartered buses are being filled. When the congregation of Fifth Avenue's Temple Emanu-el snubbed Kahane, and Fortune Pope barred Colombo from the Columbus Day parade, and the *Times* editorial writer found their alliance "unlikely," "unsavory," and "a matter of public revulsion," New York's establishment had failed to see the greater significance of their appeal.

Politicians claim they first felt the rumblings of Italian discontent back in the late 1960s when Vito Battista initiated his taxpayer's revolt among small homeowners. When John Marchi beat John Lindsay for the Republican Party mayoral nomination in the spring of 1969, it was apparent to some that great numbers of traditionally Democratic Italians were, most uncharacteristically, registering Republican. When Marchi and Mario Procaccino, even in defeat, showed they could poll 58 percent of the city's vote, almost all the city's politicians began watching the returns from Italian election districts. And, after Arthur Goldberg's resounding defeat last November, it was apparent that no candidate could again disregard the Italian vote with impunity. In that election, though neither party listed an Italian on the ticket, Rockefeller romanced Italians just as assiduously as Goldberg avoided them. Rockefeller ate pizza, attended street fairs, and organized the "Columbia Coalition," which listed as his supporters almost every prominent Italian American politician in the state. Goldberg, meanwhile, not only avoided Italian neighborhoods, but, supported by three Jewish running mates and innumerable Jewish organizations, publicly scolded one of his few Italian audiences for demanding that he stoop to ethnic politics.

The district-by-district analysis of the vote after Goldberg's defeat stunned political experts. They found, for instance, that Italians rarely moved. They found that long after the city's Irish and Jewish neighborhoods had been abandoned, Italians were still living in large numbers in the same borough-wide communities they had occupied in the 1920s. They read polls that showed that 40 percent of Italians continued to live in the same neighborhoods as their parents, compared with 14 percent of the Jews and 17 percent of the Irish. Italian Americans, now well into their third and fourth generations, were approaching 20 percent of the city's population while there had been a noticeable decline in the populations of other white ethnic groups. There were, for instance, as many Italians in the northeast Bronx as there were blacks in Harlem, but somehow they had gone unseen by the media and unacknowledged by liberal politicians. Italian American children were now almost 18 percent of the city's public school population, 25 percent of the current freshman class at City University, and more than half of the Fordham student body. They found that it was the Brooklyn piers, controlled by Italian locals, that now dominated the New York waterfront, not the traditionally Irish longshoremen's locals of the moribund West Side docks. The predominantly Irish New York archdiocese found that Italian Americans were now the majority of their parishioners and their children made up the bulk of parochial school students. Italian American lobbyists, after years of watching Irishmen and Jews roam through the corridors of the state house in Albany, began demanding state aid to parochial schools and coaxing construction contracts for their own builders. Italian Americans were not only the largest nationality bloc in the state, but as a result of the last election, now accounted for 40 percent of the Albany legislators.

The political effect of all this has been immediate. Within a month of Goldberg's defeat, and after four years of bitter wrangling, the city suddenly reversed its condemnation proceedings against sixty-nine Corona homes owned by Italian Americans and decided to move them, shingle, stucco, and stone, to what had previously been considered municipally sanctified Parks Department land. After two years and 180 attempts, the Congress of Italian American Organizations, one of the city's only social-action Italian coalitions, received city approval to sponsor day-care centers and after-school and senior-citizen programs in predominantly low-income Italian neighborhoods. For the first time in CIAO's five years, Mayor John Lindsay attended its annual dinner-dance in Brooklyn. When introduced by its president, Mary Sansone, who like many of the five hundred attending the dinner had supported Procaccino in the last campaign, Lindsay was surprised to hear himself being cheered.

The American Jewish Committee, in an effort to find out more about its own working class, recently sent two carloads of sociologists to Mrs. Sansone's Bensonhurst home, where they interviewed Italian American workingmen, legal aid lawyers, teachers, and an OEO health center doctor. The National Urban Coalition has detached urban affairs specialist Ralph Perrotta from its Washington office to work with Italian American organizations in New York and involve them in dealing with the problems of drug addiction, school dropouts, day-care centers, health care, and other social problems facing the white working class as well as the black. In Manhattan, meanwhile, actors Ben Gazzara and Robert Loggia have been looking for filmscripts about the Italian American immigrant experience that avoid the traditional Statue of Liberty sappiness. "Sometimes," Gazzara says, shaking his head glumly, "I look at the way so many of those men were torn up by leaving their homes and I wonder was it worth it, after all." Columbia University's Casa Italiana, a Renaissance-style building that houses an organization devoted exclusively to study of Italy's cultural life, held a discussion on Italian Americans last May 2, the first since the Casa was founded in 1927. And, along more practical lines, the Center for Migration Studies, housed on the Flagg estate on Staten Island, led by the Reverend Silvano Tomasi, a Scalabrini priest with a Ph.D., has begun to collect sociological, demographic, and legislative studies on the migrations of various ethnic groups. "In the last four years there have been 160 articles and 40 books on Italian-Americans, including my own," the Reverend Tomasi said, "and that is more than there had been in all the years since Robert Foerster's classic on Italian emigrants in 1919."

There has also been the emergence of a new generation of neighborhood politicians, radically different from the cigar-smoking *padroni* of the past—the neighborhood-born white ghetto politicians with an expertise in filtering social benefits into generally barren communities, while circumventing the obstacles thrown up by threatened local leaders. In Manhattan, typical of these new young men is independent Democrat Frank J. Russo, a key member of the downtown reform movement. Russo stunned reform Democrats when he carried his Mulberry Street district for Congresswoman Bella Abzug in the last election, and missed ending the thirty-one-year reign of district leader Louis DeSalvio by only sixty votes. In Carroll Gardens, Brooklyn, an independent Republican like Salvatore (Buddy) Scotto is following a similar path and threatening long-entrenched neighborhood fixtures.

Despite all the political scurrying and scholarship, however, it is still Joseph Colombo's Civil Rights League that has been most responsible for focusing attention on New York's Italians. Led by an extremely vulnerable Italian, the league has succeeded in attracting the media where other Italian organizations have failed. The league has filled Madison Square Garden, raised close to $2 million, opened chapters around the country, enrolled fifty thousand members, and pinned everyone from Nelson Rockefeller to William Kunstler as honorary members. The size of the league's rally in Columbus Circle last year was so impressive that the city has been forced to give the league permission to use the area again this year, despite the fact that environmentalists within the administration had earlier been turned down for the site because their plans were considered too disruptive. The league's success in silencing the FBI has spread to other kinds of Mafia-watching. It got "Mafia" and "Cosa Nostra" deleted from the *Godfather* script, but the real victory was forcing Paramount to agree to this demand on the front page of the *New York Times*. Since then, the league has also dealt with what it considers gratuitous slights and insults in television commercials. It has threatened to boycott Alka-Seltzer because of its "Datsa soma spicy meatball" commercial; a canned tomato sauce for which Enzo Stuarti intones "Datsa nice"; and Ford automobiles because they sponsor the *FBI* TV series. As a result of the league's actions most magazines and newspapers stopped using the terms "Mafia" and "Cosa Nostra" immediately, and even the *New York Times,* after several bitter internal policy battles, began covering organized crime with greater restraint than it had during the booming Valachi years. In fact, Nicholas Gage, hired to replace retiring Charles Grutzner as the newspaper's Mafia expert, has not found the same kind of editorial enthusiasm for Mafia stories as his predecessor did.

In private, officials of the league admit that they have been astonished by their own success. Most of them believe the cachet of Mafia power attached to the man who leads them has lent the organization credibility among the neighborhood rank and file. They have been more astounded to see that his mob credentials carry some weight with the establishment too. The publisher of the *Daily News,* for instance, apparently conditioned by his own paper's rhetoric, became extremely agitated recently when he received a form letter from the league asking the paper to cease publication on June 28 in honor of Italian American Unity Day. Rather than dispose of the request with a polite but perfunctory reply, the nervous publisher passed the letter on to his managing editor and the managing editor raced with it to the city desk and the city desk discussed it, photographed it, and ran it through a copying machine. Finally, William Federici, a *News* crime expert, was ordered to devote a day to calling his contacts in the league and pacifying them in advance.

On other occasions, however, the league has taken matters into its own hands. During preparations for last year's Columbus Circle rally, for instance, the city was confused as to whether the Department of Water Supply, Cultural Affairs, Parks or the mayor's office had the authority to order the monument's fountain turned off to make way for the stage. When the city did not move quickly enough to suit the league, unidentified plumbers, armed with blueprints of their own, turned off all the proper nozzles and valves themselves. "Sure, we were impressed," one city official said. "Most of our own guys wouldn't know how to turn that thing off."

This year, city officials are even more concerned. At the end of a series of meetings between the Department of Parks and officials of the league about the use of the southwest corner of Central Park, a Colombo representative said:

"Oh, by the way, could we chop down those three trees near the wall? They block the view of the stage."

"What!" the Parks representative screamed. "Those trees are eighty-year-old maples. They're landmarks."

"That's okay," the league representative winked. "We could send somebody over late at night. Nobody would know."

The league's approach can be alarmingly direct for those used to the circumlocutions of government and social agencies. Evangelical in spirit, the league's meetings are noisy and argumentative until Colombo personally takes command. Debates between the various officials and their supporters end only when Colombo rises from his seat, walks toward the microphone shaking his head, and begins to address the various sides like a stern father. He has never yet been contradicted or challenged from the floor.

>Joe had a little thing in Brooklyn the other day, [an observer recalled]. The tickets were $100 to get in, and he raised $25,000 for a boys' home right then and there. That's the way he does it. Somehow he's always got a bunch of guys in there with long pockets. I was there one night and this guy from Pakistan said he needed earthquake money. The guy walked out with $7,000. Joe raised a half-million last November at the Felt Forum. He's got another half-million from dues. In March they made him Man-of-the-Year. Whacko. Another hundred grand. Ads for a testimonial dinner for six guys—he picked them out of the audience the same night he announced it—bang, another $170,000.

>One night he raffled off a chinchilla coat. He had a stack of raffle tickets in his hand. In a matter of minutes, he had $14,400 on the coat. Everyone just threw the money on the floor at his feet. He was standing in the middle of a dance floor and his shoes were covered with money. The band leader won the coat.

>Joe has changed since this thing's gotten so big. He's gone preacher in a lot of ways. One night he got a thousand guys who were picketing the FBI to march all the way with him to Saint Pat's. I knew a lot of those guys, and they hadn't been in a church in years. Only he could have gotten them to go there. He's like an Elmer Gantry of the underworld. Joe, himself, is sincere. He's like the old-fashioned guys. He's a truly religious man.

Italian Americans have always been a puzzle to outsiders. Even State Senator John Marchi, who has often emphasized his northern Italian ancestry, is confused by them. It is clear to Marchi, as it is to many other Italian Americans, that Joe Colombo is essentially repeating in twentieth-century New York what the Honored Society has been pulling in Sicily since the 17th century. Colombo has managed to convince thousands of honest men and women that whoever defames the Honored Society also defames them. Marchi has very clearly pointed to the hole in Joe Colombo's boat, but he has offered nothing to the men and women on board by way of alternatives. Obviously Colombo and Kahane speak for a segment of the city's working population that has never felt comfortable with Marchi's Florentine style, or the kind of social activism represented by B'nai B'rith's princely Jews or John W. Gardner's most *un*Common Cause. It is Colombo's league, no matter how disreputable its leader, that has activated New York's traditionally disenfranchised working-class Italians.

Patrick Moynihan and Nathan Glazer, in their second edition of *Beyond the Melting Pot,* were only the latest in a series of social scientists who have wondered why Italians have failed to make a larger impact on the city. Since the 1960 census, Italians have been the largest ethnic group in the city next to the Jews, yet they have remained almost leaderless. There is no large or powerful upper-class Italian group or professional middle class that has taken on leadership in education, the media, politics, or even the church. There was, for instance, only one Italian name among the one hundred prominent businessmen organized last February by Loew's Corporation President Robert Tisch to help deal with municipal problems. (He was Joseph Grotto, a nearly anonymous real estate executive with Brown, Harris, Stevens.) Lindsay aides, who have been on an Italian American talent hunt since the Goldberg defeat, have reported that most of their first choices want no part of the round-the-clock City Hall routine Lindsay people seem to enjoy. "Look around your own office," one of the Italians they approached explained in rejecting an offer. "Most of you are divorced or splitting up, your kids never see you, and your parents read about you in the papers. That's no life for a family man."

Sociologists have repeatedly laid the blame for Italians' being of less social, economic, and political importance than their numbers would indicate to their overly developed sense of family. Theirs is a cultural style that has preserved the life of the old-world village but also prevented Italian Americans from thrusting themselves into municipal and national prominence. This social backwardness is so basic a characteristic that today, while almost one-quarter of the freshman class at City University is Italian, neither the chancellor, deputy-chancellor, four vice-chancellors, four university deans, nor any of the twenty college presidents is Italian. In fact, only 14 out of 165 of the university deans, and less than 6 percent of the city's college-level teachers, are Italian. Of the ninety high school principals in the city's system, only one is Italian, and he is on leave, and less than 10 percent of the city's 60,000 schoolteachers are of Italian ancestry.

"For most Italian Americans it's a big thing to get elected to some office, like the state legislature," said former Assembly Speaker Joseph Carlino. "A young, attractive Italian American thinks he's reached the millennium when he becomes an assemblyman. And what does he want next? What does he dream of? A judgeship!"

"Why don't they seek higher office?" he said. "Well, first of all it's a hard thing for an assemblyman to get to higher office. It's difficult to get money from Italians. I guess it comes from their working hard to get where they got. But they don't give to the average campaign, just as they don't give to charities. Italians save everything. They work at home. Become conservative. They are the ideal suburbanites."

In addition, 90 percent of New York's Italian Americans are descended from the impoverished Italian provinces of Calabria, Apulia, and Sicily, and many are burdened with a deadly regional Italian fatalism. They are the heirs of Italians who have been convinced, by hundreds of years of unrelieved woe, that nothing good is ever going to happen. Mothers prepare their daughters for the worst, fathers advise their sons against aiming too high, and proverbs always tell of the unhappiness that awaits the overly ambitious. For those who have not escaped the tenements the dour parents often proved right.

There is just no way to deal with Italian Americans in New York without also dealing with the phenomenon of organized crime, the Mafia, Camorra, Unione Siciliana, mob, or whatever one wants to call it. Although it has been inflated and promoted by the press and law enforcement agencies beyond reason as far as its national influence, profits, and wiles are concerned, it still has extraordinary power in the city's ghetto Italian communities and in some of the commercial areas in which Italians work. It cannot be discounted. In working-class Italian communities, it is probably the single most important form of local government. Dr. Irving Spergel, currently a professor at the University of Chicago, has spent years detailing and attempting to classify certain delinquent groups in New York. In a number of his books he has characterized Italian neighborhoods as "racket subcultures," identifying them as:

> Any community in which there exists lots of money and in which rackets are rife and an inherent part of the family structure. A neighborhood in which a dozen stores are converted into social clubs or meeting places for bookmakers, policymen, and loan sharks. A neighborhood in which racketeers and the rackets are considered a local way of life. A neighborhood in which candy stores and luncheonettes have little equipment, almost no supplies and, except for male adults hanging around, no business whatever....

> In an area where the racket subculture predominates, delinquent groups tend to be organized as an outgrowth of juvenile play groups. Members have known each other for many years. Their families have lived in the same neighborhood and even on the same block for one or more generations; the youngsters have gone to school together and attend the same church. Brothers and cousins may be members of the same group, and its ethnic composition tends to be homogeneous.

Italians came to their homogeneous tenement communities in the greatest numbers between 1890 and 1920, and they immediately set about recreating in New York's slums the same densely packed, overwhelmingly insular southern Italian towns and villages they had just escaped. They brought with them their own kinds of food, the apparatus to make their own wines, and a form of southern Italian Catholicism much too superstitious and saint-burdened to be tolerated by the Irish Catholics of that day. The southern Italian also brought a healthy skepticism for any form of government. On the early Calabrian and Sicilian immigrants, the Italian government had practiced a form of regional genocide not much different from the kind it practices today. But southern Italian émigrés today can at least be assured passports. At the turn of the century, millions of southerners immigrated to the United States bearing a slip of paper with the name of the *padrone* or work foreman to whom they had been assigned and through whom they would be indentured to railroad gangs and factories. It was on these slips of paper that immigration officials rubber-stamped "WOP" (With Out Passport) for Calabrians and Sicilians.

The distrust of southern Italians for the Italian government had affected every aspect of their lives, and when they arrived in a strange land they brought their suspicions with them. They remained in their own enclaves, hiding from the alien society that surrounded them, very much as their ancestors had hidden from Saracens, Bourbons, Visigoths, and Greeks. They moved into specific tenement buildings and onto certain blocks already filled with relatives and friends from not only their own provinces, but from their own villages and towns. In these extraordinarily insular communities Italians adhered to their own rules. They lived according to their own standards and old-world habits, resisting public housing, overhead expressways, indoor push-cart markets, compulsory education, the English language, and American food. Differences were adjudicated by their own judges, not by strange men who mistook Anglo-Saxon law for justice. It was these men, these elderly gentlemen of respect, who sipped black coffee in the social clubs of New York's Italian ghettos and watched over their streets like vengeful shepherds, from whom advice was, and very often still is, sought.

It was the local Mafia boss who was the most savvy man on the block in matters of marginal morality. It was through him that payoffs to policemen were arranged by the newly arrived resident who wished to make wine in his basement, play cards on the street in front of his tenement, or live with his family in the rear of his tiny shoe repair shop.

It was to these local Mafia bosses that the fathers of compromised girls went for marriage or revenge, where the insulted were mollified and business contracts were sworn to or dissolved. The local priest might advise, but the local Don could *order.*

Francis A.J. Ianni, of Columbia University's Teachers College, recently wrote of these men in *The Public Interest:*

> The base of Mafia power is the personal relationship, for the Mafioso reduces every social relationship to a personal level, a level in which he can feel and perform in a manner superior to that of other men. The Mafioso operates as a middle man in a vacuum of political values, structures and organizations. He is a broker—although not always an honest one—who operates as a network builder and monitor between and among elements in an unstable system.

It has not been for the residents of Italian communities alone that these men have administered local affairs. The City of New York itself has repeatedly reached out to them for assistance with particularly sticky problems involving Italian Americans. The police, during the Wagner administration, went to the old men and asked them to keep Mulberry Street youngsters from assaulting demonstrators who were picketing an official building that happened to be in Little Italy.

"After three nights of rioting and the pleas of priests, teachers, and parents, we went to a couple of the clubs and explained that the whole thing was bad for business," one high police official recalled. "The next night there wasn't an Italian kid to be seen."

In the Lindsay administration, former Relocation Commissioner Frank Arricale managed to defuse a potentially disastrous confrontation between black and Italian youngsters that started over the integration of a predominantly white high school in Brooklyn. Hundreds of police had been assigned to the area for days, thousands of youngsters roamed the streets brawling, looting, and burning whatever they considered enemy territory. In a final effort to end the madness, Arricale contacted the Gallo brothers, through their attorney, and made arrangements for them to get through police lines and, hopefully, to convince the young Italian American toughs to go home. Larry Gallo, who with his brothers was involved in a widely publicized gangland war at the time, arrived at the intersection that had served as headquarters for the Italian American gangs in a black Riviera. To youngsters and policemen alike, he was a genuine celebrity. Only the mayor's arrival the day before had aroused equal excitement. Gallo approached the young men he knew had influence with the white gangs and told them to go home. To stop.

"But the niggers are. . ." one young white began, and suddenly, Gallo smashed his fist into the youngster's face, sending him to the ground. The disturbances ended that night.

For their services to the communities in which they live, the gentlemen of respect have always exacted some kind of tribute—from a few dollars handed an elder for adjudicating a business matter to a whole community's conspiracy of silence to guard him and his friends from prying strangers and hostile cops. The Mafioso had always been, if not welcome, at least at home, in New York's Little Italies and he has been far more at home in the United States than he ever was in the impoverished villages he came from. He is, in a sense, ideally suited to New York's eat-thy-neighbor business morality. He has become the perfect conduit for the kinds of vice America's law-abiding citizens insist upon enjoying. His success in New York today, after all, depends not only on the reliability of his bread-and-butter services (sports betting and usury), but upon the loyalty of his satisfied non-Italian customers. He has filled the gap between the letter and the spirit of unrealistic, unenforceable, and unpopular laws, and to consider him an aberration, rather than a reflection of America today, is like blaming congenital obesity on an ice-cream manufacturer. Neighborhood Italian Americans have understood this viscerally for many years; therefore when Joseph Colombo went out to picket the FBI in 1970, the day his son was seized, they were not surprised at a Mafia boss's expressing moral outrage, but at the fact that he had come from behind the traditional cloak of secrecy and had stepped before the public and the press for the first time.

Andrew Greeley, the sociologist, had cited six major steps in the American acculturation process. They include the first cultural shock of a new group, when survival is really the only practical issue. This is followed by the beginnings of organization and an emerging self-consciousness. The newly arrived become semi-skilled workers, develop key community figures, and grow unmistakably American while preserving old-world customs and traits. The third process Greeley calls the assimilation of the elite—those who have reached the middle class and shun their ethnic past. Militancy follows when the group is fully middle class, has its own sources of power, and becomes excessively patriotic. This is the time, Greeley pointed out, when Irish Catholic Fordham men began investigating the loyalty of WASPs at Harvard. When a group develops a substantial economic upper middle class, however, that Yankee Doodle militancy dissolves and young professionals, economically integrated into the rest of American society, deplore the narrow provincialism of the past. It is at this point that the most devastating criticism is aimed at every aspect of an ethnic tradition and every institution that strives to keep the old-world culture alive. This period of self-hatred, Greeley says, is followed by an emerging adjustment.

The Italian Americans in New York today, using Greeley's scale, are spread in disproportionate numbers across the third, fourth, and fifth stages of acculturation. Their paranoid elite has been partially assimilated, their emerging middle class has decorated its automobiles with American and Italian flag decals, and the sons of the middle class grow increasingly resistant to that kind of ethnic aggression.

"It is not a static situation," the former Lindsay commissioner Frank Arricale explained. "Italian-Americans right now are almost our last hope for making New York a truly pluralistic community. Their numbers are large enough to make a discernible impact. Their defense agencies, like the league, have shown them that they can be Italian and still American, psychologically. The reform movement, which destroyed the neighborhood clubs, the only real avenue Italians had to enter politics, must now provide an alternative without trauma."

"Otherwise," said Arricale, "Italian-Americans could be seduced into what is already discernible as a neo-fascist, black-shirt, law-and-order puritanism."

Unquestionably, there is a white working-class revolt going on in New York today that is more economic than ethnic. The few politicians who have spotted it had not recognized it just a few months ago. During the battle over open enrollment, for instance, there were no politicians to point out to the white working class that Lindsay's open college enrollment policy would help them even more than it would help blacks and Puerto Ricans. Conservative spokesmen wandered through low-income neighborhoods unchallenged, explaining to white parents who could not afford to send their poorly schooled children to college anyway that the admission of blacks and Puerto Ricans would lower academic standards.

Today, the views of some liberal politicians are changing, and New York's 1.6 million Italian Americans are a key factor in that change. Similar ethnic revolts are taking place in other urban centers where the common needs of poor whites are breaking down barriers of ethnic xenophobia.

"Nobody has done anything for the white working class since Social Security," Msgr. Geno Baroni, the director of the Center for Urban Ethnic Affairs in Washington, D.C., said. "Today, there is a budding national movement of white workers wonderfully parallel to where the blacks were a few years ago. My hunch is this one is going to move even faster."

If Baroni is right, white ethnics will not only be the next glamour issue socially, but the basis for the kind of broad redistribution of economic power that every social revolutionary from Lenin to Bob Kennedy talked about. In New York, however, that working-class revolt will not have been sparked by the Central Labor Council, poli-sci radicals, or the *New York Review,* but by a renegade rabbi and a Mafia boss.

Violence: Is This Any Way
for a Nice Jewish Boy To Behave?

Among the first of the new immigrant groups to utilize the organizational techniques and demonstration tactics of the black revolution was the Jews. This trend was most clearly seen in the rise of the Jewish Defense League, an activist organization which proclaimed its intention to push forcefully with violence, if necessary, for Jewish rights. Organized by Rabbi Meir Kahane, the group has made headlines almost from its inception. The JDL first attracted national attention in 1969 when it issued a formal challenge to militant civil rights leader James Forman, after he announced his intention to exact "reparations payments" from churches and Jewish synagogues. The JDL rejected the legitimacy of Forman's demands and, in an unprecedented move, promised to break both his legs if he came to New York's wealthy Temple Emanu-El to order payment. Such behavior indicated a new direction in Jewish American life. The incident has also been viewed as another step in what some observers regard as a growing anti-Semitism among blacks. Thrown together in an urban environment, Jews and blacks have not had tranquil relations during the turbulent last decade.

In the section below Kahane explains the importance of the Forman incident to the development and growth of the JDL. He also explains the rifts that his organization has caused within the Jewish community itself. Kahane's forceful writing style and his advocacy of direct, confrontation politics seemed to augur a future trend in minority relations. The JDL has not, however, grown significantly since its inception and it remains a small, but very vocal, minority in the Jewish

From *The Story of the Jewish Defense League,* by Rabbi Meir Kahane. Copyright 1975 by the author. Reprinted with the permission of the Chilton Book Company, Radnor, PA.

world. Yet its capacity for making news continues intact: witness the efforts of Kahane to stop a recent Nazi march in the heavily Jewish Chicago suburb of Skokie, where seven thousand survivors of Nazi death camps live.

Kahane has written numerous books and articles about Jews in American society including Our Challenge: The Chosen Land *(1974). He continues to offer an alternative approach for Jews to the problems of group accommodation.*

The story is told of two Jews being taken out by anti-Semites to be shot. As they were both placed against the wall, blindfolds were placed over their eyes and one cried out: "The blindfold is too tight!"

At which point the other frantically whispered: "Quiet, don't make trouble...."

The advertisement appeared in the *New York Times* on June 24, 1969. Over a picture of a group of tough-looking pipe-wielding youngsters was the question: "Is this any way for a nice Jewish boy to behave?" The question did not wait for an answer. That followed immediately:

> Maybe. Maybe there are times when there is no other way to get across to the extremist that the Jew is not quite the patsy some think he is.
>
> Maybe there is only one way to get across a clear response to people who threaten seizure of synagogues and extortion of money. Maybe nice Jewish boys do not always get through to people who threaten to carry teachers out in pine boxes and burn down merchants' stores.
>
> Maybe some people and organizations are *too* nice. Maybe in times of crisis Jewish boys should not be that nice. Maybe— just maybe—nice people build their own road to Auschwitz.

The text went on to state the problems that had arisen and unorthodox militant solutions to them. It ended with the words: "We are speaking of Jewish survival."

The ad was placed by the Jewish Defense League, which had decided to "make trouble," and after its appearance the Jewish community was never quite the same. The reaction was, to put it mildly, explosive.

The very next day, B'nai B'rith's ADL [Anti-Defamation League] erupted in a fury that must have stunned its members, who had never seen such energy on behalf of Jews in years. ADL general counsel Arnold Forster declared: "The Jewish Defense League is a self-appointed group of vigilantes whose protection the Jewish community does not need or want." Within less than two years, Forster was to become famous as one of three major Jewish establishment functionaries who refused to appear in the same room with JDL during the televising of a David Susskind program. JDL wags, mindful of similar Arab refusals to sit with Israelis, immediately circulated a rumor to the effect that Forster was really an Iraqi. The ADL continued by accusing the JDL of "imitating the mindless tactics of racial hoodlums," thereby increasing "the danger of explosive riots." Not to be outdone by his employee, ADL national chairman Samuel Dalsimer said, "We find the group's paramilitary operations and sensationalist appeals to raw emotion an embarrassment and a potential danger."

The umbrella group that represented all Jewish "human relations groups," the National Jewish Community Relations Advisory Council (NJCRAC), condemned all groups that threatened "violent and coercive tactics" in defense of "Jewish security and Jewish interests," thus reviving memories of similar attacks by the group on the former Jewish underground Irgun and Sternists. NJCRAC went on to elect one Jordan Band as its chairman. Band was to gain his own measure of fame two years later by appearing at yet another NJCRAC conference to complain that Jews were beginning to look inward too much, were becoming too separatist and parochial (read: becoming too Jewish and worrying too much about Jewish problems). He then advised them to stop this trend and to start to concern themselves with "what is happening to our fresh air and fresh water, with poverty (non-Jewish, of course) and drug abuse."

The day after the advertisement appeared, the *Times,* in an act that gave us more publicity, members, and money than we could have gotten in three years of hard work, made the tiny JDL the subject of an editorial. The editorial stated:

> Some thirty self-appointed vigilantes, armed with chains, lead pipes, and baseball bats, mustered defiantly in front of a house of worship in Manhattan one evening last month to protect it against a Negro militant petitioner whom the rabbi and his congregations were prepared peacefully to receive.

> A few weeks later, another "goon squad," as they have been rightfully labeled by Rabbi Maurice N. Eisendrath, President of the Union of American Hebrew Congregations, tangled with a neo-Nazi gang on Fifth Avenue, marring a parade which was being held to mark an Israeli anniversary.

> "Is this any way for nice Jewish boys to behave?" asked an advertisement in the *Times* yesterday.

> The answer is an emphatic "No"—not Jewish boys, nor

Christian boys, nor white boys, nor black boys, nor any kind of boys.

The same day, the *Times* ran a major story on the League. A similar one appeared in the mass-circulation *Long Island Press, Time* magazine carried one under the heading "Jewish Vigilantes," the *National Observer* carried a huge article, and radio and TV crews descended upon us. Not bad for one ad.

What was all the excitement about? Narrowly speaking, it centered around an incident involving JDL, Manhattan's prestigious Temple Emanu-El, and a black militant. Broadly—and more to the point—it revolved around Jews and violence, or, precisely, the heading of the ad: "Is this [violence] any way for nice Jewish boys to behave?"

Once upon a time, the Jew was not a member of the ADL—neither in form nor in spirit. It was not in the role of Mahatma Gandhi that the Jews fought at Massada; the men of Bar Kochba and Judah Maccabee never went to a Quaker meeting. The Jews of old—when Jews were knowledgeable about their religion, when they turned the page of the Jewish Bible instead of turning the Christian cheek—understood the concept of the Book and the Sword. It was only in the horror of the ghetto with its fears, neuroses, and insecurities that the Jew began to react in fright rather than with self-respect. That is what the ghetto does to a Jew.

And this un-Jewishness became institutionalized when the ghetto walls came down and the Jew fled from his faith to the great light of emancipation and assimilation. Not only did he now *actively* shun Jewish concepts but his ignorance of anything Jewish compounded by his exposure to gentile culture created within him an assimilation of intellect that led him, in his ignorance and that of his leaders, to believe that so many of the liberal pacifist and universalist ideals that he swore were Jewish were in reality foreign, gentile, and at total variance with true Judaism. Indeed, assimilation begins not with the *shikse* but with the Idea, and more Jews than know it are already foreigners and assimilators within their own ignorant selves.

But more of this later. The immediate cause of the reaction and the advertisement was an incident that had taken place in front of prestigious Temple Emanu-El on Manhattan's posh Upper East Side, whose distance from struggling fellow Jews on the Lower East Side is measured not in miles but in light-years.

There, at 5:00 on the afternoon of Friday, May 9, 1969, stood the most unlikely group of Jews imaginable; indeed, had they remained in front of the temple for a few more days, property values on East 65th Street and along Central Park would have plummeted. Some had baseball bats, some had iron pipes, none smiled; all waited, waiting for Forman....

Forman was James Forman, the militant black who had shocked America by demanding half a billion dollars from churches in reparations for wrongs done unto blacks and adding threats of violence, unless.... While many muttered angrily, Forman declared that he would show up at prestigious Riverside Church to speak from the pulpit and make his demand. He appeared, was allowed to speak, and eventually a number of churches gave him sums of money. A similar demand was made in Philadelphia by the local neanderthal, one Muhammat Kenyatta, who barged into a church and swept various objects, including wine, from the altar.

We had our own academic feelings about the Formans of the world and their demands on the churches when the militant suddenly announced that he was also including synagogues and Jews in his extortion. And when leading Reform Rabbi Maurice Eisendrath, quoted so favorably by the *Times,* declared that he saw merit in Forman's demands (Eisendrath continued to favor Jewish reparations until the end), our position was that it might very well be that Eisendrath had had Baptist slaveowners for ancestors, but, as I told the press, "Most Jews came here in galleys long after the blacks were freed. Blacks deserve nothing from us and that is what they will get." I added, "If anyone is talking about reparations and if anyone deserves it, we Jews are first in line." The shadow of the Crusades, the Inquisitions, and both the Catholic and Martin Luther's massacres of Jews were difficult memories to erase.

We had no intention of asking for reparations and even less of giving them to an extortionist who was of that school of militants that preyed on the guilt feelings of the white gentile and on his cowardly reparations to pay him off so as not to "cause trouble." If churches wanted to pay, we pitied the poor congregants who were burdened with such "leaders," but that was their affair. When the threat turned to synagogues, it became ours.

And so, when on Thursday, May 8, we learned that James Forman had contacted the biggest and the richest of the Temples, Emanu-El, and informed them that he would appear at their Friday evening service to speak and make his demand, we decided that he would not, and I so informed the rabbi of the Temple, Dr. Nathan A. Perlman (Perlman was actually only one of several rabbis that the Temple was able to support in the manner that certain kinds of rabbis have become accustomed to). Dr. Perlman was most unhappy with the news and made a number of efforts to dissuade us from coming down. It was obvious that he was of the "Quiet, don't make trouble" school.

At the same time we attempted to contact Forman and when we could not, we asked the SNCC (Student Nonviolent [sic] Coordinating Committee) with which he generally associated, to please inform him that if he showed up with his extortion demands "we would break both his legs."

Let it be clearly understood why we did this. To begin with, the Forman incident had to be seen against a background of years of growing violence and Jew-hatred that had erupted among a significant section of the black community. This had manifested itself in a bitter teachers' strike that had unleashed open and blatant anti-Semitism. It had carried on in the form of harassment, arson, and murder against Jewish merchants in predominantly black neighborhoods, in crime that had made Jewish fringe areas nightmares of violence and fear, and in demands for black and Puerto Rican quotas in schools that would have destroyed the merit system and eroded Jewish rights and power to an alarming degree. Indeed, at that moment, City College of New York, once one of the finest schools in the country and which, under the merit system, had given *deserving* youth an opportunity to both be benefited and benefit the country, was in the throes of a month-long takeover by black students which had seen a total capitulation by the timid President Buell Gallagher and a riot in which a number of Jewish students had been beaten over the heads with lead pipes.

The reaction to all this was even more frightening than the problem. New York City Mayor John V. Lindsay, with his presidential aspirations, backed away from confrontation after confrontation in his long-range effort to acquire a reputation as one who had kept the city "cool." The price he paid was not out of his pocket, but out of the pocket of the little citizen and particularly the Jew. In general, the White Anglo-Saxon Protestant establishment that ruled the city was more than happy to let a small Jewish merchant's store burn rather than Wall Street, and it paid black blackmail in Jewish coin.

But the reaction of the Jewish establishment was even more horrendous. Coupled with their ghetto complexes and fearful neuroses was a liberal guilt feeling and inability to place Jewish interests over "universal" ones. We were beginning to pay in very practical terms for the gentilization of the Jewish establishment. Men like Eisendrath emboldened and encouraged the Jew-haters and symbolized the tragedy of the Jewish community.

We were not interested in whether Temple Emanu-El was willing to capitulate. We couldn't care less whether Temple Emanu-El wanted us there or not for in reality we were not there to defend Emanu-El. To be perfectly frank, I was not overly worried about what happened to the assimilated Jews there who had turned their backs on both Judaism and Jews decades earlier, and whose kitchen probably cost more than the Forman demands. We were not there to defend Temple Emanu-El as such but rather the *synagogue* as a concept. Forman did not know the difference between an Emanu-El and any other synagogue and he did not care. He chose it because it was famous, prestigious, and wealthy. If Emanu-El capitulated, as they would and easily could, since it was much simpler to pay blackmail than cause problems, then a precedent would have been set and other synagogues, neither willing nor able to pay, would be the next targets. In any event, the Formans of the world would have to learn that *no* synagogue and no Jew would ever again be the target of threats without reacting.

Thus it was that 5:00 P.M., Friday, May 9, 1969, found the motley, ugly, and beautiful group of Jews gathered at Emanu-El. It should be added that Emanu-El *always* held Friday "Sabbath eve" services at 5:30, whether the Sabbath began at sunset at 4:30 P.M. in winter or at 8:00 P.M. in late spring. The reason was that they broadcast their "services" over radio station WQXR, also owned by the *New York Times,* whose family, when it prayed, descended on Emanu-El. The radio station could not keep shifting its time schedule and so the Sabbath had to make way for radio and was frozen all year round at 5:30 P.M.

An army of police was on hand urging us to move across the street. We kept refusing, insisting that we had "come to pray." The police were almost outnumbered by a small army of newsmen, radio, and television people who had come to see the incredible sight: Jewish hoodlums. To each one I said the same thing. "Yes, if he shows up we'll break both his legs."

"He" never showed up, doubtless on the very correct theory that he could always find some other Jewish "patsies" and why risk one's legs? A similar train of thought must have chugged through Kenyatta's mind in Philadelphia, because he never dared do to a synagogue that which he had done to the church.

No, it was not from the non-Jew that the screams arose but from the Jew. Within a week, Eisendrath issued a blistering report to the Union of American Hebrew Congregations (UAHC) Board of Trustees. The UAHC is the governing body of Reform Jewry, and the latter was the most criminally guilty of failure to fight for Jewish rights while at the same time pouring funds and efforts into the causes of the whole world. In the report, which merited a full column and a half in the *New York Times,* Eisendrath called us "batsmen" who were "spoiling to commit assault and battery." He added:

"Jews carrying baseball bats and chains standing in phalanxes like goon squads in front of synagogues, led by rabbis, are no less offensive and, in essence, no different from whites carrying robes and hoods, led by self-styled ministers of the gospel, standing in front of burning crosses."

If an argument could have been made for the existence of a self-styled rabbi, or Jew, Eisendrath would have been the mold. The man whose ignorance of Judaism was transcended only by the more abysmal boorishness of his congregants—that is truly the *mazal* of most Reform rabbis—had in the past written a book against the idea of a Jewish state (in the 1930s, of course); spoken up for and raised money for every non-Jewish cause while condemning any Jew who did not bleed for the whole world; never once marched for Soviet Jews, Arab Jews, poor American Jews, or the suffering Jew of Brownsville (one wonders whether the man who could pinpoint Hanoi knew where the nightmare of Brooklyn Jewish neighborhoods was); and passed away in 1973 minutes before he was to give a speech condemning American Jews for shying away from attacking President Nixon simply because they were afraid it might hurt the Jewish state he never wanted.

When Eisendrath asserted that "neither Jews nor Christians nor America need such protectors," he certainly was not speaking for the Jew of the troubled neighborhoods where he did not live and which he had not seen in years. He certainly did not speak for the victims of crime in the South Bronx, for those who feared rapists and muggers in Williamsburg, or for those who feared to go outside after dark in Crown Heights. He certainly did not speak for the threatened Jewish teachers, students, and civil servants, for the little Jew, the lower- and middle-class Jew. He did not speak *to* such people and never had and never would speak *for* them. The Eisendraths and other Jewish establishment leaders lived in their own world, the gilded ghettos surrounded by unseen walls that nurtured the illusion that the gentile loved them. They preferred the company and adulation of the gentile; the richer, more prominent, and more prestigious, the better. If they could never join the WASPs, they could at least become WASH (White Anglo-Saxon Hebrews). These people were irrelevant to Judaism, to Jews, and to the crisis. So we ignored them and moved on "from outrage to outrage."

The Jewish Defense League began to throw itself seriously and concretely into the struggle to protect Jewish rights as the 1968 teachers' strike dragged New York City and the Jews through an agony of hate that in no way ended with the formal conclusion of the strike. The schools, teachers, and students remained hotbeds of hate, openly and officially. Thus *Forum,* the publication of the African-American Teachers Association (ATA), carried an editorial in its November, 1968, issue that declared:

> How long shall the black and Puerto Rican communities of New York City sit back and allow the Jewish-dominated United Federation of Teachers to destroy our every effort to rescue our children from those incompetent teachers whose only goal is stifling our children's intellectual growth? For years we have whispered that it's a shame that so many Jews have entrenched themselves in high positions in the educational hierarchy here. Not because they are Jews [sic] but because their attitude toward our children has been unremittingly hostile....
>
> Eighty-five percent of the teachers are Jews. Ninety percent of the principals are Jews. It is these very same persons who must bear direct responsibility for the systematic exclusion of blacks and Puerto Ricans as teachers and principals. We know that current fashion holds that one does not dare criticize Jews. One may criticize anyone else.... Anyone, that is, except a Jew....
>
> And the Jew, our great liberal friend of yesterday, whose cries of anguish still resound from the steppes of Russia to the tennis courts of Forest Hills, is now our exploiter! He keeps our women and men from becoming teachers and principals and he keeps our children ignorant.

This kind of talk from an official teachers' group in the city public schools brought not a word from Lindsay or the city. The presence in the school system of men like Leslie Campbell, who had written an article (also in *Forum*) calling whites "devils" and had threatened Jewish teachers during the strike, likewise brought forth only silence from the city and pleas of patience from the Jewish establishment and Jewish liberals in general. Thus, Dore Schary, chairman of the ADL, according to the *New York Times* on September 9, 1968, "cautioned the American Jewish community not to exaggerate fears of Negro anti-Semitism."

"Let us be crystal clear," said Schary, "the statements of a few must not be attributed to an entire people. Negro anti-Semitism presents none of the dangers of fascism." Mr. Schary then went on to condemn the city of Chicago for its "overkill" during the street violence at the Democratic National Convention. An ADL official named Schultz warned against Jewish "extremists" in the schools. Mr. Albert Vorspan, director of the Reform Jewish movement's Commission on Social

Action, decried "inflammatory" reactions by Jews that were bringing us "to the very brink of hysteria." A group calling itself the Council of Jews for Racial Justice condemned the "anti-Semitic scare" and quoted approvingly from an article by one Michael Scott who said that he was born in Germany (one can wager, not with the name "Scott") and was rescued by Youth Aliyah. He then explained away the anti-Semitism by saying that blacks are being pushed to the wall, equated it with the Jewish underground groups in Palestine, and then asked "why do we demand that black people be so much purer than we?" Jason Epstein, intellectual and Jewish self-hater in residence at the *New York Review of Books,* viciously attacked a book on the strike that had dared presume that there was anti-Semitism. Finally, the *New Republic,* liberal to the end, carried an article by Joseph Featherstone titled "Inflating the Threat of Black Anti-Semitism."

All this tolerance took place against a background of threats to carry Jews out of schools in pine boxes, vicious anti-Jewish leaflets stuffed in Jewish teachers' mailboxes, and Afro-American Society Black Week program at CCNY which saw an "Oppressed People's Theater" put on a performance that carried among others, the deathless line "Hitler didn't burn enough Jews," and much more.

HELENA ZNANIECKI LOPATA

Polish America's Relations with the Rest of American Society

Among the groups of the new immigration, Polish Americans have long had an active interest in their heritage and past. They have not until recently, however, been assertive in presenting the positive sides of their background and combatting unfavorable stereotypes. Helena Znaniecki Lopata, sociologist, researcher, and daughter of Florian Znaniecki, analyzes the causes of increased Polish American activism in the essay below.

Lopata notes that in the late 1960s and early 1970s, when Polish Americans were moving away from the behavorial aspects of their working-class, peasant backgrounds, there was an increase in negative stereotyping. Exemplified by the "Polish joke," these barbs tended to emphasize precisely those characteristics of group life about which Polish Americans were most sensitive. These ethnic jokes have had a major impact on the Polish community's commitment to change its image in American society. Simultaneously, Polish Americans have also attempted to enhance the entire nation's appreciation for things Polish, including that country's literary and artistic heritage. Lopata notes that there exists now an active protest movement attacking prejudicial labels, and for the first time Poles are making effective use of political pressure. Although Polish Americans remain "underrepresented in the upper echelons of the American economic and voluntary association hierarchies," Lopata is hopeful that the trends set into motion during the past decade, along with the changing demographic

Helena Znaniecki Lopata, *Polish Americans: Status Competition in an Ethnic Community,* © 1976, pp. 68–81. Reprinted by permission of Prentice-Hall, Inc., Englewood Cliffs, New Jersey.

characteristics of the group, will alter this fact. The term "Polonia" as used in this essay refers to the Polish American community, estimated at six million persons, and its subculture.

Helena Lopata lives in Chicago, where she is director of the Center for the Comparative Study of Social Roles, University of Chicago. She is the author of Occupation: Housewife *(1971),* Widowhood in an American City *(1972), and* Marriage and Families *(1973).*

"To gain influence and stature in the American society Polonia must involve itself in the mainstream of American life."[1] This conclusion, reached by a Polish American conference, reflects several aspects of Polonia's current definition of its situation, particularly its status as an ethnic community within a larger society. First, it implies that Polonia has not been in the "mainstream" of American life, but that it should now move in that direction. (This assumes that the mainstream consists of ethnic communities rather than a core of nonethnic American life.) Second, it implies that Polonia wants to gain influence, since the statement is preceded by the strong declaration: "Another deplorable circumstance is the limited influence of Polonia in American political life."[2] Finally, it points to dissatisfaction with Polonia's stature in American society.

In the Polish American Congress newsletter of July 20, 1970, its Commission on Civic and Political Activities reported "shocking discrimination" against Polish Americans in the state government of Illinois, and Congressman Pucinski in the federal government. Pucinski recommended that "all State Divisions (of the PAC) start a 'talent bank' which would give all of us a steady reservoir of capable Polish Americans who are willing to take on responsible positions, both in the government and in the private sector." Other stories concern themselves with "anti-defamation activities" and the concern that "there is so much to be done to uplift the Polish American image," including "stimulating the interest of our youth in their Polishness." The board of PAC was told of the "action and steps aimed at enhancing Polonia's standing and prestige in American life" by the organization's president.

While Polonia was developing its unique structure and culture and formulating its relations with Poland, it also had to interact with the American national society and the political state within which it is located. Relations of an ethnic community with the country of settlement can be on the community or individual level.

Several characteristics underlie these relations. In the first place, Polonia is not an independent community, able to survive without interaction with the larger society. It is a functional component of the society, regardless of how much it has identified itself as a separate subsociety. The members of the community are influenced in their private and community life by the political, economic, religious, educational, and recreational life that is emerging, existing, and changing in the larger society and its other social groups. In spite of the ideology developed in Polonia in the 1930s that pictures American society as a mosaic of different ethnic groups with no central core, there *is* a distinctive American way of life. It would be hard to imagine anyone in urban America claiming total independence from American institutions and associations. The culture pervades the home through radio and television and the actions and reactions of those members of the family who return home after participating in school or work roles on the outside. Although Polonia has developed a complex set of institutionalized alternatives to segments of American institutions, the lives of its central core of organizational personnel and leaders are heavily American in structure and action. The recent revitalization of interest in Polish national culture rather than folk or ethnic culture does not negate the fact that Polonia is an ethnic community whose lifestyle heavily resembles the rest of America. Movement from folk or national Polish culture to American culture has been gradual, but definite.

A second characteristic of Polonia's relations with America has been an underlying acceptance of the greater society and of the democratic political process. Whether applying pressure on society, or objecting to some of its actions, Polonia has functioned as a reform group rather than a revolutionary group, aiming to change, not to overthrow. Unlike Poles living in Germany or Russia (who, for many years organized extensive efforts to sabotage society), Polish Americans identify with the system and operate within its political institutions, even when they feel angry (as over the Yalta agreement), or hostile (as over prejudice directed against them). Part of the general friendliness toward America has been due to the fact that the larger society left immigrants alone to build their own community. Poles came here voluntarily and American society accepted them, made room for them in its cities and factories, and allowed them to build their own churches and schools.

In fact, the third characteristic of Polonia's interaction with America has been until recently a mutual neglect (not entirely benign) except at times of emergency. Polonia neglected America because of the awareness that it was difficult for the foreign born and even second generation Polish Americans to achieve status in American society. Only during wars and over peace settlements did Polonia attempt to change or direct the action of American society. In addition, there were some sporadic attempts to elevate Polish Americans to positions of higher prestige in the religious and political systems. This neglect of America has diminished in recent years because of the improved probability of positive responses and the changing composition of the Polish American population.

The in- and out-flow of prejudice has colored much of Polonia's life. Since they first settled in America, Polish Americans have been aware of the prejudice of non-Polish Americans toward them and toward other recent immigrant groups. Prejudice against immigrants has a long history in America; Benjamin Franklin stated that although America needed the Scotch, Irish, and Germans, he was worried about having so many of them and about their behavior. Forgetting that they themselves had been the objects of prejudice, or perhaps still reacting to it, the descendants of the groups now considered the "old immigration" in turn expressed strong negative attitudes toward the "new immigration" from southern and eastern Europe. In the first quarter of the 20th century the Immigration and Naturalization Service and many nongovernmental agencies sponsored or conducted studies which negatively portrayed immigrants of those years as illiterate, often mentally deficient, and criminally inclined or victimized by their own people. In addition they were said to be experiencing serious health problems, individual and family demoralization, and to be inwardly clannish and unwilling to Americanize. Sociologists and other supposedly value-free scholars often expressed negative judgments regarding the new immigrants, a large number of whom were Polish. W.I. Thomas, an eminent American professor at the University of Chicago, used a policeman's stereotype as one of the reasons for wanting to study Polish Americans:

> They were the most incomprehensible and perhaps the most disorganized of all the immigrant groups. This may be illustrated by what the American police call "Polish warfare." A policeman might enter a saloon where there was a noisy crowd of Poles and say, "You men be quiet," and they might subside immediately or one of them might draw a gun and kill him. This was due to the fact that the Pole in America has two attitudes toward authority. One of these reflects the old peasant subordination to authority. They were called "cattle" by the landlords and submitted like cattle. The other attitude reflects the conception that there are no limits to the boasted American "freedom."[3]

Bias is indicated in Thomas's report of his first contact with his future coauthor Znaniecki, who "was in charge of a Bureau for the Protection of Emigrants, which means advising all who planned to emigrate as to the desirable destinations and guarding them again[st] exploitation, especially in South America. Incidentally, it meant also, as I understand it, keeping the best elements in Poland and facilitating the departure of the remainder."

Even an American historian, Woodrow Wilson, advocated the reduction of Polish immigration to the United States:

> ... but now there came multitudes of men of lowest class from the south of Italy and men of the meaner sort out of Hungary and Poland, men out of the ranks where there was neither skill nor energy nor any initiative of quick intelligence; and they came in numbers which increased from year to year, as if the countries of the south of Europe were disburdening themselves of the more sordid and hapless elements of their population, the men whose standard of life and of work were such as American workmen had never dreamed of hitherto.[4]

On the other hand, some social scientists questioned the validity of such portrayals of new immigrants. Taft analyzed criminal statistics of the 1930s and reiterated a prior finding that the foreign born were not highly criminal, having rates lower than the native born. He also concluded that the high second generation rates were due to the age distribution of the population. The new immigrant groups' second generation males were highly concentrated in the "criminally significant" ages, as compared to the old immigration second generation youth. Hourwich attempted to dispel myths concerning the labor force and social behavior of the new immigration, including the Poles. However, their efforts were not very successful in decreasing prejudice against the Polish immigrants and their children.

Polish Americans could not be oblivious to the statements made about them or to the significance of the quota acts which were, after all, designed to keep people like them from entering America in any but minimal numbers. They reacted at first by ignoring the society of settlement and turning their attention to Poland and to Polonia's internal life. Withdrawal from identification with Poland was very difficult for Polonia while it faced negative prejudice from Americans, and it took many years. Polonia's realization of its low status in relation to other groups was reflected in the anger and frustration of its pronouncements of the 1930s and 1940s:

> The great declarations of freedom in the United States are only empty watchwords. Statements are made by the Nordics: "You Pole are as good an American as I." However, when the same Pole wants to take a place on an equal level as this Nordic, then

> he meets another side of his character: "What, you foreigners want to be equal with?" The Pole is supposed to be satisfied with slogans. That is why the [Polish National] Alliance must widen its services and waken the emigrant group to a recognition of itself and the role it has to play in the land of Washington. The Alliance must made the slogans become real.[5]

Changing the status of Polish Americans in American society was, however, very complicated. One internal problem was that Polish Americans did not have a positive image of themselves; in short, they suffered from a major inferiority complex. Rather than dealing with prejudice through positive action, Polonians simply became angry, withdrew from competition in American society, or dropped all ties and identities with Polonia and created a non-Polish family history.

According to a Polish writer of the new emigration, Alexander Janta, Polish Americans' feelings of inferiority were due to their ignorance of Polish culture and the anti-intellectualism which prevented them from breaking through this barrier of ignorance.

> At the root of this deficiency lies a profound misunderstanding of the meaning of culture among the majority of Polish leaders, and, consequently, among the masses as well. . . . In spite of the efforts of a few national culture intelligentsia, . . . an overwhelming majority of Poles in America can express their "Polonism" in relation to the American background by little more than costume, dance, or food.[6]

Thus, Polish Americans lived as a separate entity within society, preserving the folk culture and the language, but ignoring the literary and artistic culture of Poland. The latter could have been of interest to Americans and might have helped change the image of Polish Americans and also of Poland as a limited and peasant-dominated land. "It is disappointing to realize that between the two wars too little was done to reverse this trend. No solid educational program has been conceived and developed [in Polonia] and no investment into its establishment was attempted from the Polish side."

The inability of Polish Americans to fight prejudice resulted in one Polish author writing a book about them entitled *The Silent Emigration.* The few attempts to change the passivity did not have a profound influence on Polonia. Bishop Rhode pleaded, "If we forget our Polish heritage we become nothing but ships in the wind without anchors."[7] The Polish National Alliance kept telling Polish Americans, "We can not change ourselves into hybrids, because then our worth would be completely lost. We must convince ourselves of the worth of our spiritual possessions and of our Polish history. . . ."[8] However, only recently have observers of the Polonia scene reported an interest by youth in learning more about the Polish national culture.

One accomplishment of the Polonian leaders assisting the preservation of the community was the development of an ideology defining America as a pluralistic society as early as the 1930s, long before such a view became popular with the waning of the melting pot theory.

The ideology looked at the United States as a group of subcultures—minority groups with no highly visible, permanent, and distinct majority. Accordingly, not only did American society lack a central core of nonethnics, but the other ethnic and racial groups had been aware of this, were well organized, and had effectively concentrated their attention toward improvement of their relative statuses. Polonia, in the meantime, was involved only in Poland and in its own internal affairs. Within this frame of reference Polonia's low status in the society was admitted but was attributed to its long-lasting insistence on being the "fourth province of Poland" and its failure to establish a satisfactory community status in this society, rather than to any "inherent" inferiority. The other ethnic groups were internally better unified and organized in their efforts at status achievement, and the lack of "Polish power" (as it is currently being called) is thus reversible with proper effort and cooperation.[9]

It is here in the ideology, however, that some hesitation is voiced, as to Polonia's ability to unify. Many Polish Americans who still identify with their Polish background believe in a Polish national character than makes sustained cooperation difficult, if not impossible. The main features of this national character are individualism, independence, and competitiveness. The ideology thus provides a loophole for the lack of status achievement in the outside society. Not only were other groups more established on the status ladder than were the late arriving Polish Americans, but they benefited from the absence of the "Polish character" which was likely to handicap Polonia in its bid for superior or at least equal status in the future.[10] On the other side of the coin, the positive consequence of the national character was an internal appreciation of the dynamism of individualism and competitiveness. Feeling these sentiments and beliefs about themselves, recognizing their status in American society as low, and assuming a powerlessness to change it because of their very "character," Polish Americans who continued to identify with the community (from World War II until recently) were mainly concerned with individual and family participation in community life and in its lively and engrossing status competition.

Although Polish Americans have not concentrated all their efforts on changing their status in American society, they continue to remind people of their cultural contributions to American society. They do this in three ways. First, they select individual Polish Americans for dramatic publicity as positive representatives of the community; second, they make declarations of loyalty; and third they try to "enrich" American culture with elements of Polish culture.

The first of these activities was based on the assumption that certain types of people and certain activities are more highly valued in the society than are others. Early in Polonia's history, the two persons most often selected as reminders of Polish contributions to America were the Polish generals Pulaski and Kosciuszko who became heroes in the American Revolution. References to these men in mass communication media and the erection of statues to them attempted to anchor American memory of Polish contributions to the past, capitalizing on the society's idealization of its own history and length of residence or involvement by members on this side of the ocean. It also served as a reminder of the historical presence of men of upper classes in a land from which most of the Poles who emigrated were of the lower classes. More recently, outstanding sports figures, film stars, successful businessmen, artists, and scientists have been chosen as representatives.[11] The publicity emphasizes that these individuals have achieved not only American but cosmopolitan reputations. Their idealization is expected to infiltrate the image of the total community.

Declarations of loyalty have also been used in attempts to change the image of Polish Americans. As one of the speakers at a 1938 joint convention of the Polish Medical and Dental Association of the United States of America and the Polish Lawyers Association of the U.S.A. stated:

> Our first and most important duty is to be good Americans, take an active part in all phases of life here, and take advantage in full of all opportunities and privileges as are rightfully ours, not as a numerous minority but as mutual originators and participants in the common good of the American Republic.[12]

At this same convention Starzynski stated that Polish Americans have another set of obligations:

> Our second and no less important duty is to enrich our common American life and newly forming culture. This American culture is the total of contributions of all those national groups which live here. We can not be beggars, with hat in hand. We cannot take, giving nothing in return.[13]

Several groups such as the American Council of Polish Cultural

Clubs or the Kosciuszko Foundation undertook the selection, development, and dissemination of cultural items to the broader society. However, not until very recently has there been a concerted and dramatic effort to change the status of Polonia in American society by changing the image of Polish Americans. As far as can be determined from Polish leaders and the ethnic press, this effort is a direct consequence of the "Polack" or "Polish" jokes (although other factors played an important role). The humor of these strongly negative stories centers on the lower-class background and peasant culture of the immigrant. Use of this humor increased dramatically in the late 1960s and early 1970s when most Polish Americans had moved away from behavioral aspects of peasantry (which are exaggerated by the jokes) into the upper segments of the lower class and into the middle class. This increase has been attributed to the mobility itself which has made the ethnic group more visible in the society. It has also been attributed to the anti-Polish sentiment of the Jewish community, many of whose members are writers and performers.[14] "More and more Americans of Polish descent are complaining of the malicious anti-Polish articles written by members of certain Jewish groups, and of the constantly growing discrimination against Poles and Americans of Polish descent by these groups. The more judicious individuals of the Jewish community are ready to help in the goal of changing this situation, but they need facts on this subject." The Kosciuszko Foundation in New York asked their readers to send data documenting discrimination or prejudice with names, dates, places, and descriptions of the event. Although the foundation could not directly follow up each incident, it promised to find ways of helping other groups to do so.

Whatever the real and attributed reasons for their emergence, Polish jokes have had a profound influence on Polonia—more so, in fact, than all of Polonia's previous efforts at expanding the Polish American and American knowledge of its Polish heritage. The campaign against these jokes has been taken very seriously in Polonia for several reasons. In the first place, they were a jolt to a community that had been comfortably involved in its own status competition, only vaguely aware of and responsive to prejudice from the outside. Second, success in acquiring American status symbols served to increase interest in status competition outside the community. Third, the jokes affect not only the active members of the community but *anyone* who identifies himself or is identified by others as Polish American. They have reportedly been told to people with Polish names as if they would be specially meaningful, even when the recipient considered him- or herself successfully acculturated and, in Gordon's terms, structurally assimilated. The jokes thus come as reminders of the imperfection of such assimilation. They also serve as a rallying point for those who want to retain Polish or Polish American identity. The leaders are now able to say, "I told you so.... You must support us and the community to change this prejudice." The leaders are aware that the jokes may have a beneficial effect in forcing the youth and adults to identify and cooperate with Polonia. They have thus provided a source of revitalization of community efforts, a specific goal and sources for sentiments of peoplehood.

An official reaction to the current status of Polonia in American society is fully expressed in the report of the Committee for the Defense of the Polish Name (Anti-Defamation Committee) and states:

> Slandered, ridiculed and misrepresented in the media as "dumb Polacks," Polish Americans have, for the most part, remained silent. This silence, with all its implications of ineffectuality, fear, and intimidation, is the greatest problem facing the Polish American community today.
>
> Too many of us are content to cart around for a lifetime the psychological and emotional damage that has been done to us by a continuing barrage of negative images, slurs, and so-called "Polish jokes...."
>
> What the Polish American community needs more than anything else is an effective process of consciousness raising....[15]

Polonian leaders have tried to change the image of their ethnic community in five ways. First they consulted members of the intelligentsia (previously somewhat isolated from the community) to create ideologies and select cultural items which could be used outside the community to project a new image. The first meeting of political leaders and intelligentsia resulted in a set of recommendations as to such ideologies and items, and the methods to use in disseminating knowledge of Polish and Polonian culture internally and externally. Some of the recommendations were a push for high school and college courses in the language, history, and cultures of Poland and Polonia, teacher training programs at Orchard Lake Schools and Alliance College, publication of books and journals on the above subjects, a survey of attitudes of youth with a Polish background, excursions to Poland by the youth, the creation of speakers' bureaus, the hiring of a professional public relations expert, the collection and dissemination of information on all publications dealing with Poland or Polonia, and support of the Polish Museum in Chicago. The proposed studies of Polish American communities and organizations by the Polish Institute of Arts and Sciences in America is a direct movement in the direction of the recommendations, but many of the other ideas of the conference have not been acted upon because of a shortage of funds.

While these proposals and plans were being crystallized in the minds of Polonian leaders, other members of the community were undertaking public relations actions. For example, the Polish president of Mrs. Paul's Kitchens (a financially successful producer of frozen foods) decided to change the image of his ethnic group through direct advertising. The content of the advertisements was developed by the president of the Orchard Lake Schools and Seminary. Together, these men devoted a year to an intensive publicity campaign, reported on the front page of the *Wall Street Journal,* October 12, 1973, as follows:

POLISH AMERICANS HIT ETHNIC SLURS,
PRAISE THEIR CULTURE IN ADS

Was Copernicus Trying to Tell Us Something?
Yes, and It's Far From a Joking Matter

By Greg Conderacci
Staff Reporter of the *Wall Street Journal*

ORCHARD LAKE, Mich.—Have you heard the story about the Polish millionaire who spent $500,000 to help stamp out Polish Jokes?

It's no joke.

It's "Project: Pole," an effort to place a half-million dollars worth of pro-Polish advertising in newspapers across the country.

"Polish jokes should set up in a man a determination to prove they're not true," says Edward J. Piszek, president of Mrs. Paul's Kitchens, Inc., of Philadelphia and the man bankrolling the campaign. "In a positive way, it's an answer to the jokes—instructively. You eliminate the opportunity to originate the joke by proving it's not true."

So today a pilot campaign, in the form of a half-page advertisement, will appear in Detroit newspapers with the headline: "The Polish astronomer Copernicus said in 1530 that the earth revolved around the sun. What was he trying to tell us?" The answer, Mr. Piszek says, is that Polish Americans are every bit as good as any other Americans.

A third form of action designed to change the image of Polish Americans is the joint celebration of important Polish events. In 1973, Poland and Polonia celebrated the Copernican Year, declared as such throughout the world by business, religious, intellectual, and political leaders of Poland and its "colonies" in other countries. The celebrations took place in many cities (including Chicago and Philadelphia in America) and involved the unveiling of statues of the Polish astronomer. Many leaders of larger societies as well as ethnic leaders gathered for the ceremonies. The very erection of such statues, an expensive venture, involved concerted effort and a great deal of publicity and cooperation with various individuals and organizations. In addition, Poles are participating in events significant to Americans. In trips to Jamestown and other American cities in connection with the bicentennial celebration, Polish American leaders stress that "the Poles have been in the United States since 1608."[16]

Besides stressing Polish contributions to American society and shared culture, Polonia's efforts at changing its image in society includes many gestures of interethnic cooperation. Polish Americans have repeatedly been accused of prejudice against other minority groups, particularly those with which they are apt to have come in direct contact at community boundaries. The history of relations between Polonia and the Jewish community is one of mutual dislike and attempts at cooperation are relatively infrequent. In recent years Polonia's members have been increasingly angry over what they define as a deliberate attempt by Jews in mass communication media to prejudice the rest of society against them, and the relations between these two communities tend not to be very cordial, especially in recent years.

Initial settlement of Poles in America placed them in virtual isolation from blacks but recent years have evidenced a movement of blacks as well as Puerto Ricans into traditionally Polish neighborhoods, accompanied by an increase in anti-black and anti-Puerto Rican prejudice on the part of Polish Americans. The expansion threatens the status-invested property so painfully gathered by the immigrant, his proof of success of upward mobility. The value of property diminishes as the black community expands, because of panic selling and moving, and negative feelings in older Polonian communities that have been dissolving is very strong. The status loss created by the geographical expansion of groups Polish Americans consider below them in the American status hierarchy, and the black civil rights movement of the 1960s and the societal response to it, angered Polish Americans. They had worked hard to bring themselves up to their present position and now society was threatening these gains by helping blacks up to a similar position while Polish Americans were losing money and property because of the expansion of the black community. Aware,

however, of the accusation of anti-black prejudice in, for example, Greeley's work, community leaders have attempted both to decrease that feeling in Polonia and to develop and document instances of black-Polish cooperation. If fighting blacks and ignoring Italians and other groups in a similar position did not benefit Polish Americans in the past, then cooperation in solving community problems deserved a try. An example of cooperation to solve common problems without a history of cultural contact is the Black-Polish Conference of Greater Detroit—a combining of forces of two low-status groups to increase the status of both.

Polish organizations have met on numerous occasions with representatives of other ethnic groups for special events or in order to meet specific goals. For example, Poles, Czechs, and Hungarians distributed ten thousand fliers with an open letter to the Secretary General of the Soviet Communist Party, Leon Brezniew, demanding freedom for the "captive nations." The joint effort included the three countries which had tried to revolt against Soviet influence or power in Europe.[17] Other intergroup activities which have been institutionalized include participation in the Intercollegiate Council by Polish students, decoration of a Polish Christmas tree in museums, participation in ethnic festivals (Detroit), international trade fairs (Chicago), and singing and dancing competitions.

The current popularity of the ethnic movement in America and the society's interest in it is documented by the Ford and Rockefeller foundations' grants and governmental support of such centers as Andrew Greeley's Center for the Study of American Pluralism and the Center for Immigration Studies at the University of Minnesota. Poles themselves received a Rockefeller grant to study Polonia through the Polish Institute of Arts and Sciences in New York. This interest has guaranteed greater cooperation between Polonia and other ethnic groups or the society at large. The society, in fact, is now coming to Polonia and its organizations and representatives, asking to xerox its files of newspapers for permanent preservation and to obtain information as to its ethnic identity and the content of the ethnic culture.

The final form of action aimed at changing the image of Polish Americans has been active protesting—by mass communication or through public representatives—of any known prejudicial statement. The anti-defamation committee's guide specifies what data are needed to start a protest, the best methods of doing so, and the best methods for communicating with the committee so that it can reinforce the protest. For example, strong protests have been sent to NBC for sponsoring "Laugh-In" because its comedians repeatedly use "Polack jokes." In fact, the case against the company has been brought before the Federal Communications Commission.

Thus, Polonia is now very actively involved in efforts to prevent negative images of Polish Americans from spreading in American society and to create its own positive image of Poles and Polish Americans, and Polonian and Polish culture.

HARRY KITANO

Japanese Americans
on the Road to Dissent

During the early years of the ethnic resurgence, Japanese Americans were often overlooked. It is not difficult to understand why this was so. Considered by most Americans to be quiet, fully assimilated citizens, Japanese Americans were unlikely candidates to be affected by ethnic appeals. Yet, this assessment was proved wrong.

Anthropologist Harry H.L. Kitano has analyzed in the essay that follows the generational and cultural factors which have shaped the Japanese American response to current developments. He finds, for example, that there have been a wide variety of responses to prejudice, discrimination, and segregation among Japanese. Generally, however, he believes the first generation, the Issei, have sought "to make it" in America and, as a consequence, have been a very passive group. This has also been true of the children of Issei. Only the Kibei, among the second generation born in America, have preferred to retain their ethnicity. The Kibei were Japanese children who received their early education in Japan during the 1930s, the era of Japanese nationalism and militarism. Despite the presence of the Kibei, widespread discrimination, and the wartime evacuation, Kitano argues that the acculturative process was so strong in the Japanese American community that only "2 percent of the 110,000 Japanese evacuees" chose repatriation to Japan after World War II.

The 1960s and 1970s, Kitano contends, have seen a significant change in the traditional passivity of the Japanese community. It was during this period that the accommodationist position of the Issei and Nisei

From Joseph Boskin and Robert Rosenstone, editors, *Seasons of Rebellion* (New York: Holt, Rinehart and Winston, 1972). Used by permission of Joseph Boskin.

"became more dramatic." Anxiously seeking to become more American and to forget things Japanese, "they have run directly into the racism of the American social structure." Whereas previous generations would have ignored or rationalized such racism, the third generation has instead chosen to challenge it by joining such activist organizations as the Asian American Political Alliance.

Harry H.L. Kitano is the author of Japanese Americans *(1969),* American Racism *(1970), with Roger Daniels, and* Race Relations *(1974). Kitano himself was among the Japanese Americans relocated during World War II. He received his high school education at the Topaz (central Utah) Camp.*

For the past several decades, the image of the Japanese American has been one of quietness, docility, orderliness, and conformity, despite a long history of frustration in the United States, including a mass evacuation to relocation camps during World War II. This behavior has led to generalizations that certain groups or cultures are immune to overt dissent, regardless of the provocation. Clearly, this is an oversimplification. In fact, the pattern of Japanese American behavior has been due to cultural factors, which are now in the process of change. As the Japanese American becomes more acculturated, the possibility of his joining protest movements will increase.

An analysis in terms of generational dynamics will shed light on the question of why Japanese Americans have failed to become significantly involved in protest politics in the past, and will suggest why their behavior may change in the future. This approach will focus upon the experiences of specific generations.

The Japanese can be conveniently divided into Issei immigrants who came to the United States between 1895 and 1924; their Nisei, American-born children who grew up during the depression years of the 1930s and survived the wartime evacuation of 1942–45; and the Sansei, the American-born children of the Nisei. Estimated current ages of the generations are as follows: Issei, over 70; Nisei, 30 and over; Sansei, under 30.

It is simple to support the generalization that Asian immigrants— first the Chinese (1850–1870) then the Japanese (1895–1924)—were among the primary targets of racial hostility, especially along the West Coast. Prejudice, discrimination, and segregation faced the Japanese; they were considered unassimilable, and were compared to dogs and other animal life.

A particularly vicious quotation conveys the depth of feeling that some Americans held toward the Japanese: "They exist like the yellow, smoldering discarded butts in an over-full ashtray, vilifying the air with their loathsome smells, filling all those who have the misfortune to look upon them with a wholesome disgust and desire to wash."[1]

But in a short while, these low-life immigrants became competitors for land, business, and a desire for equality so that the Honorable James D. Phelan, United States Senator from California, wrote in 1921:

> We are willing to receive diplomats, scholars, and travelers from Japan on terms of equality, but we do not want her laborers. We admire their industry and cleverness, but for that very reason, being a masterful people, they are more dangerous. They are not content to work for wages as do the Chinese, who are excluded, but are always seeking control of the farm and of the crop. . . .[2]

The senator represented the beliefs of many Californians concerning white-nonwhite relationships. Citizenship, ownership of land, "normal" family lives, and other benefits were thought to be primarily "white" prerogatives, and the thought of Japanese immigrants enjoying these "rights" was actively resisted.

Laws were passed attempting to limit Japanese entry (generally successful); to deny them citizenship (successful against the Issei); and to erect boundaries that would limit participation and upward mobility in the larger society. The culmination of anti-Japanese hostility was the wartime evacuation (1942–45), when the West Coast population of the Japanese, both citizens and aliens, was placed in concentration camps.

It is within this context that we present the possible goals faced by the Issei and later the Nisei. The general model is presented in table 1.

TABLE 1. GOALS OF THE ISSEI IN AMERICA

	Active	
Model A (Makino)		Model B (Okumura)
Ethnic retention ———————————		———— Acculturation
Model C		Model D
	Passive	

The Issei had several choices—to actively or passively seek to become Americans or to remain Japanese in terms of loyalties, values, and lifestyles. The decision for each of these goals was associated with certain strategies, techniques, and behavior, including overt dissent. Each choice had specified outcomes. We would like to emphasize that although these choices were similar for the Issei, Nisei, and Sansei, the meanings and the consequences differ so that what was meant by ethnic identification or acculturation by the Issei was different for other generations. Therefore, the current use of pejoratives to describe other generations is often unfair; "Uncle Tom," "reactionary," or "radical" might describe a position using today's definitions, but does not necessarily correspond to the realities of a different era. As we will illustrate, each generation defines goals and positions which sound similar (for example, acculturation) but which involve a different constellation of factors so that they are multidimensional rather than unidimensional in character.

To illustrate the styles of adaptation related to the goals of the Issei, we will present individuals who represent some "ideal types."

Fred Makino served as a model for those Issei who played an active role in retaining an ethnic identity.[3] We have taken some liberties with Makino's life in order to formulate a model for this category.

Makino came to Hawaii from Japan in 1899 and soon began to perceive some of the problems that faced his ethnic group. He saw Japanese being exploited by white Hawaiian plantation owners, whereupon he helped Japanese workers to organize their own unions. He started lawsuits against discriminatory practices and was willing to go to jail for his convictions. He felt that the best protection for a relatively small, powerless minority group was to organize and to *actively* fight to protect its interests, rather than to quietly fade into the background.

Makino's primary emphasis was to heighten ethnic awareness, to promote ethnic identity, and to foster ethnic group cohesion. Consequently, one of the main tenets in his program was to open and maintain Japanese language schools. Here the Issei and their children (the Nisei) could learn their native language, understand their own culture, and resist attempts of the Americans to "rob" them of their native heritage. He felt it was important that Japanese build up pride in their ethnicity, that Japanese values (of the Meiji era) be held superior to those of the American culture, and that Japanese institutions and culture be preferred and maintained. He advocated political organization, "bloc" power, and felt that group pressure was the most effective means of dealing with the white man. He was a strong believer in developing and maintaining a cohesive ethnic community based primarily on Japanese culture. Popularity and acceptance by the white man were not important to Makino's strategy.

Another Issei, living in Hawaii at the same time as Makino, was Takie Okumura. He perceived the problems of the ethnic community differently and advocated an active, acculturative position. By this, he meant acquiring American culture.

For example, Okumura felt that one of the major barriers to acceptance by the white group was the maintenance of Japanese culture. He felt that living conditions, manners, habits, and customs that were primarily ethnic should be discarded. Therefore, smelly Japanese foods, noisy Japanese festivals, loud conversation in Japanese, and prominent Japanese architecture were defined as hindrances to acceptance. Any behavior (especially in public) that "offended" the American should be controlled, or eliminated.

Okumura's position was in most instances the opposite of Makino's; Japanese language schools, ideals, values, entertainment, and recreation were to be discarded as constant sources of embarrassment.

Perhaps the most pertinent guideline for Okumura was the concept of the Japanese as "guest." As guests in America, he felt that Japanese should conduct themselves accordingly. They should do nothing that would damage their image with their hosts—they should go to American schools and be taught and trained as Americans. They should avoid such unpopular acts as labor strikes and slowdowns and should continue to work loyally for their employers no matter what the provocation.

Okumura might be expected to say, "If we expect to be Americans, then we must be Americans in every way. We must associate with them, learn their language, and go to their schools, for the only way for a small minority to become successful is to merge with the host culture."

Choices C and D represent the passive end of the goals of acculturation and ethnic retention. Persons in the C category would be those living quietly within the ethnic community, learning little English and belonging to all-ethnic organizations. They would patronize ethnic resources and carry on a style of life little removed from their homes in Japan.

Issei in the D cell would be characterized by a minimal attempt to come to terms with American life in terms of acculturation. While their more active peers (cell B) might be attending courses in English or Americanization, their reading in English might be limited to a vocabulary of street signs, shopping messages, and billboards. Most would begin to dress in a more Americanized fashion, but several years behind in "style," and American foods might begin to appear at their table. Although never dreaming of becoming an integral part of the American community, most had cut their ties with Japan to such an extent that they knew their future would be in this country.

The passive approach to problems of ethnic retention and acculturation was characteristic of most Issei. Probably the greater proportion of rural residents chose cell C, while a higher proportion of urban Issei were identified with cell D.

From our model, we hypothesize that dissent would arise primarily from those choosing cell A—Japanese searching for an active ethnic identity. For those most concerned with retaining their ethnic separateness, there was always the alternative of returning to Japan. Most others preferring ethnic retention went about it quietly, so that Makino was an unusual individual.

There were other factors that limited the amount of Issei dissent, aside from their numerical smallness. Those choosing the active ethnic category possessed a minimal amount of English and most had only a superficial knowledge of the American social scene. Further, adherence to the values of Meiji Japan was not particularly conducive to active dissent. Therefore, the stereotype of the Issei as nondissenters had a degree of validity—those who were likely to dissent were limited to their ethnic enclaves and could barely be heard by the outside world.

The background faced by the Nisei was similar to that of the Issei with one important difference—the Nisei were American born and were therefore United States citizens. They were educated in American schools, and were consequently exposed to strong acculturative influences. Also, many of them were pushed farther along the acculturative path by Issei parents (cells B and D) who transferred their desire of "making it" in America to their children. It is important to

TABLE 2. GOALS OF THE NISEI IN AMERICA

	Active	
Model A ("Kibei")		Model B (JACL)
Ethnic retention ———————————————————— Acculturation		
Model C		Model D
	Passive	

conceptualize the role of the Issei generation as it affected the model of acculturation, ethnic retention, and dissent for their children.

Table 2 has the same parameters as the Issei. Different groups are presented as falling into different cells.

of interest and the emphasis on "telling it like it is" is seen as one primary goal. Therefore the need for a more accurate history of ethnic groups, the need for a strong ethnic identity and alliance among all Asians, are important concerns. We therefore have labeled this cell ethnic identity rather than ethnic retention. It is different from the Model A of the Issei and Nisei.

TABLE 3. GOALS OF THE SANSEI IN AMERICA

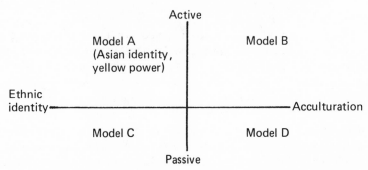

The search for such an identity has led to the formation of different groups. By the end of the 1960s, groups with such titles as the Asian American Political Alliance, the Council of Oriental Organizations, the Yellow Brotherhood, the Third World Liberation Front, and the Red Guards were emerging from the Asian communities. The Asian American Political Alliance stated: "...The crucial question facing us today is not that of integration. Now there is the more compelling question...What is this society which we have sought, too often with ludicrous fever, to become integrated into [sic]?"[6]

Central to most of these newer groups are concerns of racism and discrimination, and the shift away from an accommodationist-acceptance mode toward an emphasis on ethnic identity and autonomy. A newspaper titled *Gidra,* produced by Sansei of the college-age generation, challenged the local Japanese, Chinese, and other Asian establishments by advocating stands on such "controversial" issues as student demonstrations, yellow identity, and yellow power.

There were attempts to establish coalitions among all Asian groups, whereas in the past nationality differences were barriers to an overall Asian identity. It is difficult to ascertain the numbers, the representativeness, and power of these newer groups. Nevertheless, the ethnic identity cell A, as with the Issei and Nisei generations, is one where overt dissent is likely.

There is one major difference. Previous residents of cell A were unacculturated and lacked a strong acquaintanceship with American culture. Therefore much of their effectiveness in presenting their problems to the larger American social system was lost, and instead, much of their effort was limited to intragroup conflict. Although there remains a similar problem, there are also many Sansei in cell A who are college students, well acquainted with the American culture and articulate. Thus, for the first time, many of the "hidden" problems of the Asian community are being exposed to the larger community.

The meaning of becoming an American especially in the urban setting has changed. Whereas for the Nisei it meant conformity, denying or minimizing one's ethnic background, and overachievement, for the current generation it may now include overt dissent and coming to terms with and/or recognizing one's ethnicity. Therefore, many Sansei in Model B are also capable of overt dissent—they have taken up many of the causes that have distressed large numbers of the younger generation. The war in Vietnam, pollution, the campus riots, and the generation gap are the ambience of the young, especially among those who have become most "Americanized." Some have become part of more radical groups so that even though dissent may be similar to [that of] those Sansei following Model A, they may be motivated by different issues. Whereas the Sansei in Model A are talking about ethnic identity and ethnic studies, those following Model B may be thinking about larger societal changes and issues rather than solely the ethnic one.

For example, the Free Speech Movement (FSM) riots in Berkeley in 1964 saw two Sansei faces. They did not belong to individuals identified with the ethnic movement (the ethnic movement did not really start for the Japanese until several years later); rather, they were drawn from highly acculturated Nisei Model B parents.

We hypothesize that very few Sansei belong in Model C, the passive quest for an ethnic identity. Perhaps the most visible group of present Japanese who fall into this category are the new immigrants from Japan and Japanese business representatives.[7] Many retain their ethnic customs, shop at ethnic stores, eat ethnic foods, and go about their lives in a quiet Japanese way. They do not actively recruit others into their styles of life, but since many of the forms of the new "Japanese culture" are similar to the American, there are no sharp points of conflict between the two. Many of them will return to Japan after their tour of duty is over.

The majority of the Sansei fall into cell D, the passive acculturative position. They are still in the process of acculturation and by most measures are quite successful. They do well in school, are obtaining good jobs, and are moving to the suburbs. All of their entertainment, speech, and styles of life are "American." They identify as Americans and have almost no knowledge of Japan. Nevertheless, many are "embarrassed" by the role of the activists, and would no doubt prefer to merge quietly into American culture in a manner similar to their parental generation.

Whereas dissent for the previous two generations came from only one cell, A, probabilities of overt dissent for the Sansei come from two cells, A and B. Therefore, it is highly probable that more visible dissent will be forthcoming from the Japanese American—from those who are actively concerned with their ethnic status and those with a focus on the societal problems faced by all members of the younger generation.

Two examples follow that illustrate changes we have discussed. They involve two Japanese personalities in America—S.I. Hayakawa and Thomas Noguchi.

There is little question that the appointment of Dr. S.I. Hayakawa to the presidency of San Francisco State College would have been greeted with unanimous acclaim by the ethnic community during the prewar days, for he would have epitomized the model of integration—a Ph.D. with a Caucasian wife and now the president of a large educational institution. [At publication of this book he was the junior senator from California.]

Even today, for the majority of Japanese he is probably a hero—but it is not quite unanimous. In Disneyland in April, 1969, there was a large ethnic assemblage to pay him honor. Over five hundred people were on the inside, and they greeted him with a standing ovation. But while older Nisei were applauding, a smaller but visibly younger Asian group was on the outside, with signs such as "Hayakawa is a banana—yellow skin but white inside" or "Hayakawa is not our spokesman." Such overt expressions would have been rare several years previous, and impossible decades before.

President Hayakawa has been able to temporarily unite two groups of dissident Japanese. One group are the Sansei concerned with ethnic identity (Model A); the other, a more heterogeneous group of highly acculturated Nisei and Sansei (Model B) who remain critical of his handling of the San Francisco State situation.

The case of Dr. Noguchi, County Coroner of Los Angeles, also occurred in 1969. Dr. Noguchi was dismissed from his position by the Los Angeles County Board of Supervisors on numerous charges, ranging from drug taking to mental illness to incompetence. In a previous era, he would have quietly resigned and accepted an alternate position that was offered. The ethnic community would have been embarrassed over the whole affair and would have preferred for the physician to remain quiet and to accept the "demotion."

But instead, Noguchi chose to challenge his dismissal. Even more important, the ethnic community supported the coroner. They quickly raised over $40,000 for a defense fund. A large number of small contributors probably reflected the many Japanese who felt that they had been ignored or passed over in their own job situations. Dr. Noguchi was eventually reinstated as County Coroner. Japanese were practicing atypical "Japanese behavior"; rather than acceptance and accomodation, they were practicing challenge and confrontation. Noguchi's support came from *all* generations and from *all* models.

Why, after decades of acceptance, accommodation, assimilation, and inward aggression, was there the beginning of overt dissent in the Japanese community in the latter 1960s, especially when things were going so well?

It would be impossible to pinpoint one single factor. However, from our proposed goal model, we can suggest several possibilities.

First, some general social-psychological explanations are pertinent in discussing the beginning of dissent. One relatively consistent social science finding is that periods of dissent, strain, and rebellious behavior often occur when social conditions are improving, whereas extreme deprivation is usually associated with apathy. Perhaps concerns for sheer survival under depressed conditions take precedence and are accompanied by low expectations and a feeling of hopelessness. Conversely, as opportunities increase, expectations rise, often at a quicker level than actual improvements in social conditions, which in turn sets up strain and a background for dissatisfaction. For example, the Women's Liberation Movement is strongest in the United States, where the role of the female is perhaps more "liberated" than in most other systems; the Watts "rebellion" occurred in Los Angeles where treatment of the blacks has been presumably "milder" than in other sections of the country.

The current "success" of Japanese falls into this pattern. Previously, expectations of equal opportunity and of equal treatment was pegged at a low level so that a modal reaction to discrimination and prejudice was that of resignation, apathy, acceptance, or avoidance. Now, expectations have changed and the disjunction among expectations, opportunities, and the means used to attain objectives provides strain and the beginning of overt dissent.

Another hypothesis is based on social learning theory. Learning takes place through exposure to other models, and the influence of other groups has not been lost on the Japanese. Questions of identity and power, of techniques used to create change, and development of newer organizations are learned behaviors. The most important influence has been that of the blacks; however, other models have also been incorporated. Open dissent and confrontation by student groups, both in the United States and Japan, have been another source for modeling. The generation gap has not escaped the ethnic community.

Therefore, a model picture of the Japanese dissenter may be the following:

a. He is young (primarily Sansei) and a college student.

b. He belongs to newer organizations (that is, Third World groups) that may be patterned upon other ethnic models.

c. He asks questions concerning identity and power.

d. He advocates open discussion and dissent and is searching for relevance and an overthrow of racism.

e. He follows Models A and B.

Perhaps the strongest influence in shaping the current mood is related to a shift in goals. As long as Japanese maintained an integration-assimilation perspective, the probabilities of open dissent were minimal. To want to become "American" according to the parameters of the melting pot was associated with concepts such as "proving one's worth" and "visitors or guests" and behaviors of conformity and docility. Questioning of these goals has led to less conforming behaviors even though alternate goals are seldom clearly articulated. "What is so desirable about becoming a middle-class, white American?" is the question that provides impetus for a change in adaptive techniques.

Our model, presented independently by generations, is in practice an interactional one so that definitions, goals, strategies, and techniques for one generation have influenced each of the others. And the causal relationship among cells is not a linear one—followers of Model A for the Issei do not necessarily lead to Model A for the Nisei and Model A for the Sansei. It is precisely this assumption that has led to the name calling and pejorative "Uncle Tom" labels that have become a part of current day rhetoric.

For example, if Japanese were still segregated into insulated ethnic ghettos, changes would be neither as sharp nor as dramatic. If we hark back to the arguments of Christian missionary Okumura (Model B) and Mr. Makino (Model A), the irony of their positions becomes clear. The missionary, an advocate of the acculturationist-accommodationist-assimilationist mode, probably contributed more to current dissent and the call for an ethnic identification than Makino, the overt dissenter in that era. If Japanese had followed Makino's model, they would have retained much of the formalism and structures of Meiji Japan. They probably would have remained more isolated from the larger community, less prone to acculturation, and more "Meiji Japanese." It is our observation that those Japanese and their children who have followed the early model of Makino by retaining much of the older ethnic culture (Model A, Issei and Nisei) are probably the most conservative about current dissent in the Japanese community. There is no causal linkage in Model A by generations.

But the irony of the past accommodationist-assimilationist mode appears even more dramatic. Counseled to forget things Japanese and to become American, they and their children have come full circle— assimilationists have acculturated and they have absorbed American values. In their quest, they have been exposed to various groups and to newer American models, including disruption and dissent. And by their closer interaction with larger culture, they have run directly into the racism of the American social structure.[8] Whereas previous generations often avoided, rationalized, or repressed their encounters with racism, those who have been the most active toward assimilation have realistically perceived the limitations of the melting pot. We hypothesize that the most active dissenters are those whose parents (the Nisei) were the most assimilationist in their orientation. The primary call for a reawakening of ethnic identity, of behaving in "unpopular" (nonstereotyped Japanese) ways—in short, many of the stands taken by Makino—comes primarily from the descendants of his antagonist, Okumura.

WILLIAM V. SHANNON

The Lasting Hurrah

Throughout their history in the United States, the Irish have held a unique position among minority groups. They were the first large non-Protestant group to arrive in this country. Although they spoke English, they were subject to intense, often irrational discrimination from native Americans. Nativists accused the Irish of, among other things, plotting to overthrow the nation in the Pope's behalf. Discriminated against in the types of employment and the kinds of housing they could find, the Irish turned to politics to protect themselves and to provide social mobility. Their unusual success in politics at the city and state level added to their uniqueness as an ethnic group. Ironically, it was when the country elected an Irishman, John F. Kennedy, as the thirty-fifth president of the United States that the Irish appeared to lose their ethnic distinctiveness and join other immigrant groups in the melting pot.

William Shannon suggests in the following essay that the view that the Irish have indeed melted and lost their uniqueness as a political, social, and cultural force is an erroneous one. While noting that few Irish Americans are caught up in the Protestant-Catholic crisis in Northern Ireland, Shannon argues that "the American Irish community's sense of identity" is still shaped "by the tragedies in Ireland's past." Their distinctiveness as an ethnic group has also been molded by their experiences in America. In particular, Shannon describes the curse of alcoholism, the lack of a business tradition, and the loss of able men and women to the Church. Despite these difficulties and the intense nativism they encountered, Shannon points out that the Irish have achieved widespread economic success in America, today ranking second only to the Jewish families among all ethnic groups in family income. Moreover, they still exhibit a flair for politics, a commitment to their faith, and a contentiousness that sets them off from the rest of the populace. In this period of heightened ethnic awareness, Shannon contends, the Irish "are still a definable group" because "these intangibles of national character and moral outlook persist."

William Shannon is presently the American ambassador to Ireland. He has served as a member of the editorial board of the New York Times *and has written several books including* The Truman Merry-Go-Round *(1950),* The American Irish *(1964),* The Heir Apparent *(1967), and* The King Could Not Be Trusted *(1974).*

The farewells were premature. For a generation, it had been the fashion to assert that the Irish are fading out as a discernible group in American life, their representative character types disappearing into the bland conformity of suburbia, their characteristic political creation—the Tammany-style big-city machine—in irreversible decline, and their dominance of that powerful cultural force, the Catholic Church, soon to be a thing of the past.

Then along came Daniel Patrick Moynihan, all six feet, five inches of him, plus jaunty tweed hat. In seven months as United States ambassador to the United Nations, Moynihan stirred more excitement outside, and raised more blood pressure inside, that glass palace than the previous five American ambassadors combined. What Moynihan had done with regard to the Negro family and welfare reform, he did for the U.N.: he did not solve the problem but he transformed it from something boring and intractable into news and fluent drama. The Irish gift for controversy was clearly still alive.

In politics, meanwhile, recent elections have demonstrated that although the old machines have indeed disintegrated (the Chicago of Mayor Richard J. Daley being always the baroque exception), American Irish politicians are showing a notable capacity to adapt their style to changed circumstances. They govern the two most populous states, California and New York. Hugh Carey has brought back to the New York political scene the blarneying, street-wise, fast-moving executive style of the Irish politico not seen since the days of Al Smith and Jimmy Walker. With his strong-featured face and solid body, Carey looks like everybody's conception of an Irish cop. If Pat O'Brien were still making movies, it would seem type-casting to star him in "The Hugh Carey Story." Taking over a state entangled in an unending skein of financial horror stories, Carey in fifteen months in office has impressed observers with his ability to learn and master complex briefs and with his finesse in maneuvering among such diverse personalities as Abraham Beame and Gerald Ford, William Proxmire and Albert Shanker. Whatever the bottom line may ultimately be on New York's finances, Carey has put on a dazzling demonstration of the politician's art. A biased observer might say a very Irish performance.

On the other side of the continent, Edmund G. (Jerry) Brown, Jr., is giving a political performance of quite another kind. With a high style blending fiscal austerity and individual idealism, Brown is offering the counterculture's response to the post-Vietnam disillusionment with big government, big business, and big unions. Where liberals used to say, "Make no small plans," Brown says, "Think small." Eclecticism prevails as he draws upon the thinking of the environmental movement, the discipline of yoga, and an ex-Jesuit novice's conviction that, after all, our kingdom is not of this world.

Carey and Brown hardly exhaust the range of Irish political styles. Do you want a right-wing revolt against establishment liberalism? Kieran O'Doherty and J. Daniel Mahoney organized New York's Conservative Party in 1962. Having failed to block John V. Lindsay from City Hall by running that superb controversialist William Buckley for mayor, they subsequently plucked off one of New York's Senate seats by running his brother James.

Do you want a left-wing alternative? Michael Harrington, out of the St. Louis Irish by way of Holy Cross College and Dorothy Day's Catholic Worker Movement, is national chairman of the Democratic Socialist Organizing Committee. Tom Hayden, another scion of a middlewestern Irish Catholic family, is running in California for the Senate seat now held by John V. Tunney.

Sick of the two old parties and looking for a new one? Eugene McCarthy, who in 1968 adumbrated some of the themes that Jerry Brown is now developing, is again running for president, this time as an independent. He hopes with the aid of petition-circulating volunteers to get on the ballot in every state.

Do you want a young reformer trying to govern an old central city? Consider Paul Jordan, mayor of Frank Hague's battered stamping ground, Jersey City, or Kevin White, trying to hold together busing-torn Boston.

Do you want canny veterans running Congress? Representative Thomas P. (Tip) O'Neill of Massachusetts is majority leader of the House, and Senator Mike Mansfield of Montana is majority leader of the Senate.

Or do you simply want the most controversial man in American public life, the man whose personal history and presidential qualifications are certain to be the subject of argument at almost any dinner party? Take it away, Senator Kennedy.

If the Irish seem ubiquitous in national politics, they are also still highly visible in numerous fields where they long ago made their names, such as labor unions (A.F.L.-C.I.O. president George Meany), law (Edward Bennett Williams), law enforcement (F.B.I. director Clarence Kelley), literature (James T. Farrell), journalism (Red Smith, Jimmy Breslin, Mary McGrory), business (Peter Grace of W.R. Grace & Co., Wallace Carroll of Katy Industries, Edward Gallagher of Western Union, Thomas F. O'Neil of RKO-General) and the church (Cardinal Cooke of New York).

The Irish continue to be underrepresented in pure science as distinguished from medicine and engineering. Fortunately for them, they have long since been muscled out of any power they once had in crime and racketeering. As they have moved up the social ladder, they have largely changed in sports from producing heavyweight boxers and all-American fullbacks to champion tennis players (Maureen Connolly, Jimmy Connors). This shift from brawn to agility is actually a return for the Irish to one of their sports traditions. When football in this country was still a monopoly of gentlemen at Ivy League colleges, the Irish were prominent in track-and-field events. The first American to win an Olympic event was an Irish immigrant, James Connolly, in 1896. His event: the hop, step, and jump.

The Irish even have what every ethnic group needs to keep its self-consciousness keen—that is, a fighting issue in its ancestral homeland. In theory at least, the fact that Ulster, comprising one-sixth of Ireland and one-third of its people, is still ruled from London more than fifty years after the rest of the nation gained its independence ought to nourish feelings of grievance among the American Irish.

In reality, however, this is not the case. The American Irish are less emotionally engaged by the fate of Ulster than are most American Greeks by the Turkish occupation of Cyprus and much less than are most American Jews by the danger to Israel. The explosive headlines about the continuing political crisis in Ulster and about the killings by the Irish Republican Army and the rival Protestant gangs dominate the news from Ireland. Funds from America help finance this strife but, as we shall see, only a very small and diminishing number of American Irish contribute money or feel directly involved in the Ulster crisis.

The great majority are not so assimilated that they no longer think of themselves as in some sense Irish. But it is the tragedies in Ireland's past, not those of the present, that shape the American Irish community's sense of identity.

As a group, the Irish are one of the most successful in American society. Estimates vary, but approximately 14 million to 16 million persons, 6 to 7 percent of the total population, are entirely or predominantly of Irish ancestry and usually of Catholic faith. U.S. Census Bureau studies report that almost 30 percent of all Irish hold high-level white-collar jobs, compared to only 19 percent of the adult population as a whole. According to a study by the National Opinion Research Center, Irish Catholic families in 1974 were second only to Jewish families in average income and in educational attainments. They outrank not only Italian, German, and Slavic Catholics but also, more surprisingly, all Protestant groups. The study noted that Protestants of British ancestry are ahead of all Catholics in "occupational prestige" because they are heavily represented in high positions in the financial community and on the boards and staffs of the great private universities and foundations. If a substantial majority of the American Irish are middle-class in status and income, a sprinkling of families—the Buckleys, Cudahys, Kennedys, Murrays—are rich.

The relative success of the Irish is readily explicable. They were among the earliest immigrants and most of them arrived already familiar with the English language. But why, it might be asked, have they not been even more successful? Why, for example, do they lag $1,000 a year in average family income behind the Jews, who, in point of time, were a little behind them in the queue arriving in this country? The probable explanation is composed of three parts: the tragic, the institutional, and the historical.

Alcoholism is the Irish tragedy. Why this is so is difficult to determine, for there seems to be a complex interplay of cultural, psychological, and genetic factors involved. But the facts of disproportionate alcoholic addiction among the Irish are plain enough. Their significance is magnified because the Italians and the Jews, two groups with whom the Irish are in competition on the urban scene, have notably low rates of alcoholism. Thus, one study of first admissions in hospitals in New York State for alcohol psychoses showed these results per 100,000 population:

Irish	25.6
Scandinavian	7.8
Italian	4.8
English	4.3
German	3.8
Jews	0.5

Drinking and its evils are part of the Irish folklore. As a result, some Irish men and women are zealous teetotalers. (A personal reminiscence: When I was growing up in Worcester, Massachusetts, the head of the local branch of the Women's Christian Temperance Union was a Swedish woman named Amanda Peterson, whom we did not know but whose letters denouncing alcohol regularly appeared in the columns of the local newspaper. My father was only a light social drinker, but my mother had seen enough of drunkards in the Irish community to feel obliged to lecture us children from time to time at the dinner table about the evils of drink. Whenever she started in on this theme, my father would josh her by saying, "Now, now, Amanda. . . ." It was a triumph for the medical profession when my mother's physician persuaded her in her very old age to have a "medicinal" glass of sherry before dinner.)

If one applies a purely secular standard of measurement, the Catholic Church drained off an extraordinary number of talented men as bishops and priests and women as nuns who otherwise might have been prominent in business and the professions. One has only to think of the vast structure of churches, schools, colleges, seminaries, hospitals, orphanages, and convents created and administered by the Catholic clergy over the last century and a half. Financing, constructing, and running these institutions as well as administering major religious orders with thousands of members call for executive talents of a high quality. A cynic might speculate that if the Irish had been, let us say, Unitarians, there would be no telling what worldly heights they might have scaled.

Historically, the Irish arrived in this country without a mercantile tradition and without much experience in owning property or administering large affairs. As a result, very few Irish of the famine generation of 1840–60 were able to enter business or penetrate the middle class. But if their ascent was slow, their integration into the American business scene proceeded smoothly and almost invisibly.

Professor Thomas N. Brown of the University of Massachusetts, who did a study some years ago of discrimination against the Irish for the American Jewish Committee, concluded:

> The point is an ironic one: the Irish benefited from the very peasant qualities that at first unfitted them for participation in middle-class American life. Without skills in business, the Irishman. . . could learn how to run a business only from his American boss. The Irish were apprentices to the Yankees, who indoctrinated them in the behavior and the ethical norms of Yankee society. When the process was completed, the Irish businessman was indistinguishable from the Yankee. There has

never been a stereotype of the Irish businessman.

Unlike Irish politicians, who seemed to challenge American political values, Irish businessmen glided to wealth and power without attracting attention unless they had marked personal eccentricities, like Diamond Jim Brady, or political ambitions, like the Kennedys and the Buckleys. The Irish initially concentrated on industries such as railroading and copper mining where the first generation of immigrants had provided much of the pick-and-shovel labor. More recently, their gift of gab has brought many of them success in advertising, public relations, television, salesmanship, and related fields where skills in writing and talking are important. But the public was unaware a decade ago that about one-quarter of the nation's railroad presidents were of Irish ancestry and knew little of a businessman like Cornelius F. Kelley, who for nearly forty years, until his death in 1957, was president and then chairman of the Anaconda Copper Mining Company.

Similarly, John Mulcahy, who came here as a youth fifty years ago and amassed a fortune in the steel business, is known, if he is known at all, only because his contribution of $550,000 in 1972 made him, next to Clement Stone, the biggest giver to the Nixon reelection campaign.

Wealthy Irish Americans usually become Knights of Malta, contribute to Catholic charities, receive a few honorary degrees from Catholic colleges, and stay out of sight. But as Professor Brown noted, it is basically their lack of a distinctive business style that accounts for their lack of fame. That is one reason why Stephen Birmingham's book about the rich American Irish, *Real Lace,* is so inferior to his study of wealthy Jews, *Our Crowd.* The latter was as much a work of business history about a distinctive group of entrepreneurs as it was an account of the marriages, scandals, and charities of a social set. The Irish, having no business tradition, starting late and rising slowly, have entered the upper class, but theirs is a series of individual success stories having no common theme.

Yet what is true of Irish businessmen is untrue of the Irish in many other fields. One has only to listen to Pat Moynihan at the U.N., observe George Meany or Hugh Carey at a press conference, or read the writing of Jimmy Breslin or Mary McGrory to recognize that they are in some sense Irish in the same way that McGeorge Bundy and Elliot Richardson are Boston brahmins or David Dubinsky and Norman Podhoretz are Jews. But how does one divine the sensibility, the attitude toward life, the traits that make them Irish? What is it that they share and how to account for it?

It is not a language or a culture. The British did a thorough job of eradicating the Irish language, and recent Irish governments have had only modest success in reviving it. Except for a fistful of recipes, the Irish have no cuisine and no large body of national customs. What they share is a pair of intangibles: an outlook on life formed by centuries of defeat, subjugation, and alien occupation of their native country and a Catholic religion darkened by that same past.

"The Irish," wrote Macaulay, "...were distinguished by qualities which tend to make men interesting rather than prosperous. They were an ardent and impetuous race, easily moved to tears or laughter, to fury or to love."

Whether this was originally the authentic Irish character is open to doubt. But it is the character the Irish developed as a result of repeated military defeats and relentless exploitation by the English during the 17th and 18th centuries and condescension by the ruling Anglo-Irish ascendancy families in the 19th. This unhappy history produced a people with marked tendencies to be contentious, ambitious, proud, and easily offended, yet with contrary and self-defeating tendencies to be pessimistic and fatalistic, to make extravagant gestures, and to drink to excess.

As soon as the Irish reached the United States, their gifts of eloquence and organization were liberated. They erupted into politics. It was as if they were working off centuries of frustration and could at last have a government, law courts, and a police force of their own to run. Having been powerless for so long in their own country, they exhibited a marked instinct for power. Adlai Stevenson once said, "Better we should lose the election than misgovern the people." It is hard to think of an Irish politician expressing such a sentiment. Irish politicians tend to have a well-developed sense of the practical side of politics, what it takes to move a voter to go to the polls, how coalitions are contrived, how issues have to be sharpened. Since they recognize that power is going to be exercised by someone and that some mistakes will be made whoever is in office, they are not reluctant to accept responsibility, and they are strangers to utopian ideals or perfectionist illusions. Like Hugh Carey talking his way through New York's financial maze, they figure they can cope. One of Pat Moynihan's collections of essays on government is called just that, "Coping," in the belief that most public problems can only be managed, not solved.

Since there are rebels against every consensus, the Irish produce their radicals and revolutionaries. In the McCarthyism frenzy of twenty-five years ago, few realized that Communist Party leaders W.Z. Foster and Elizabeth Gurley Flynn were Irish.

Irish political attitudes take account of the human realities in any situation, the feelings of loyalty, dependency and nostalgia, the human quirks and foibles. They are suspicious of reform and long on understanding. At best, this can mean compassion, "government with a heart"; at worst, sentimentality and tolerance of corruption.

Being a religious people, the Irish see the hand of God in human affairs. They allow for the mysteriousness and inscrutability of life. Although good at worrying, they ultimately trust in Providence. The really important things in life, like good health or a happy marriage or the gift of love, cannot be planned for or bargained for. So why not leave them to God's decision? In different circumstances, this folk wisdom can be taken for fecklessness, fatalism, or simple courage.

A child reared as a Catholic is inculcated with a deep sense of moral responsibility for his own acts, an awareness of his mortality, a sense that sin is a relevant concept.

He retains this moral outlook even if, as an adult, he drops out of the Church. As biographer Arthur Mizener wrote of F. Scott Fitzgerald:

> He had been brought up a Catholic, with all that means in the way of habitual convictions.... His unfaltering sense of life—especially his own life—as a dramatic conflict between good and evil was cultivated, if not determined, by his early training.... It takes a sense of sin which lies far deeper than any nominal commitment to a doctrine to be as powerfully affected by immoral conduct as Fitzgerald was.

This moral training helps explain distinctive Irish attitudes on public affairs. The majority of the Irish are bread-and-butter liberals supporting Democratic Party candidates, and in presidential contests this level of support can rise to 75 percent, as it did in 1960 and 1964.

But whether they remain Democrats or join the growing minority who vote Republican, the Irish basically do not accept the liberal idea that the social environment is the largest determinant of individual behavior. In their view, a home in the slums is no excuse for sticking up a gasoline station. A youth who loses his job does not thereby acquire a license to be a mugger. A girl who gets pregnant does not owe herself an abortion because she does not want to have the baby.

There is clearly a conflict between the pragmatism of the Irish political tradition and the moralism of their ethical code. This tension, irreconcilable perhaps on an intellectual level, is dissolved or at least considerably diminished in practice. For the Irish, politics is a functioning system of power and not an occasion for acting out abstractions, moral or otherwise. When they are in power, their politicians tend to appoint liberals to administer conservative policies and vice versa. If a program proves obsolete or unworkable, they are likely to allow it to die on the vine rather than virtuously chop down the vine for all to see. Where there are mitigating factors, they will take them into account, recalling the old maxim, "Hate the sin and love the sinner." Notwithstanding the Irish political instinct for accommodation of opposing views and the Irish sense of human frailty where wrong-doers are concerned, the force of the underlying moral judgment still persists and helps account for distinctive behavior by some notable Irish Americans.

It is this sense of moral responsibility for one's own acts that impelled Eugene McCarthy to set out for New Hampshire to oppose Lyndon Johnson's war policy; that informed the passionate writing of Mary McGrory and Mary McCarthy against the war and later against Richard Nixon's Watergate crimes; that caused Robert Kennedy to heap scorn on Jimmy Hoffa and pursue his conviction in the courts with relentless zeal; that resonated through Pat Moynihan's eloquence about third-world hypocrisy; that can be heard in George Meany's harsh judgments on detente, and that makes James T. Farrell's *Studs Lonigan* and other novels into moral dramas of character rather than naturalistic slices-of-life. It is no accident that the last volume of the *Studs* trilogy is titled *Judgment Day*.

If the Irish in this period of heightened ethnic consciousness are still a definable group, it is because these intangibles of national character and moral outlook persist. Paradoxically, it is not because the American Irish are emotionally engaged by the struggle in Northern Ireland.

Prior to the settlement of 1922 that established the Irish Free State (now the Republic of Ireland), the American Irish had been intensely active in their support of the national struggle for independence. The old tradition of money-raising, gun-running, and political agitation never entirely died out. Since the ancient antagonisms in Ulster exploded again into violence seven years ago, this tradition has revived. Some of the money for I.R.A. weapons—how much is in dispute—flows from the American Irish. The Irish Northern Aid Committee, popularly called Noraid, is the major organization in the United States raising money for the dependents of I.R.A. men in Ulster. It is the suspected conduit, according to British government estimates, for $2 million to $3 million in aid.

Speaking to American correspondents in London in December, Prime Minister Harold Wilson said, "The fact is that most of the modern weapons now reaching the terrorists in Northern Ireland are of American origin—possibly as much as 85 percent of them. They are bought in the United States, and they are bought with American-donated money. Those who subscribe to the Irish Northern Aid Committee...are not helping their much-loved shamrock to flower. They are splashing blood on it."

Noraid is run by three old-timers, all of them veterans of fighting the British fifty-five years ago, who exiled themselves to this country because they did not like the terms of the peace settlement. None of them is from Ulster.

At 73, Michael (Mick) Flannery is the youngest of them. Although not a drinking man, he agreed to be interviewed at the Liffey, a bar near his home in Jackson Heights, Queens. A more improbable revolutionary in outward appearance could hardly be encountered. Until his retirement seven years ago, he worked for forty-one years as a training supervisor in the home office of the Metropolitan Life Insurance Company. Spare and erect, he wears a dark blue suit, white shirt, neatly figured tie, white breast-pocket handkerchief. He resembles Mr. Chips far more than Che Guevara. But his voice, though softly inflected, is firm and his keen brown eyes hint at his stubborn purpose.

Flannery characterizes Wilson's charge as "a malicious falsehood."

"We're registered with the Justice Department and we have to account to them for every penny we raise. It amounts to something more than $1 million. Now, I ask you, if every cent went for guns and not one penny for relief, how much of a civil war could you finance for a million dollars?" Flannery asks.

The American Irish politician most identified with the Ulster problem is New York City Council President Paul O'Dwyer, who observed recently:

> Harold Wilson made a tactical mistake attacking the Northern Aid Committee and talking about "the shamrock being splashed with blood." It tended to revive memories and the Irish have long memories when it comes to the British shedding other people's blood.
>
> There are many things that infuriate me—the hypocrisy and the unfairness of these attacks, for one thing. Wilson and the others think, "If we zoom in on the idea that this is all being financed by Irish malcontents in Boston and New York, we can focus attention on that rather than on our own incapacity to deal with the problem of Northern Ireland."
>
> Many people here and in Ireland are mad at me for not condemning violence. But violence is an effect, not a cause. Let's talk about the real causes. Let's talk about the real causes, the injustices, and indecencies of the last fifty-five years. Let's talk about discrimination in jobs and in housing. Let's talk about the abuses of the Protestant-controlled police force, the internment of Catholics without trial, the torture of I.R.A.

suspects. They prate about money from America when there was torture under the shadow of Westminster.

But O'Dwyer sadly avows that not 1 percent of the American Irish contribute money or in any way concern themselves with the civil strife in Ulster. Concern exists almost exclusively among first generation immigrants who arrived here in the two decades after World War II. The immigration reform law of 1965 drastically curtailed the admission of Irish to this country. Immigration, which used to average 15,000 persons annually, has now fallen to about 2,000. The educational and professional requirements of the new law have also altered drastically the demographic character of the immigration. Instead of the farm youths and working-class girls who used to come, the new Irish arrivals now are doctors, secretaries, students, and other middle-class persons who merge rapidly into the cosmopolitan American scene.

The middle-aged and elderly immigrants who gather to drink and talk of the old country at bars like the Liffey are immune to the denunciations of British prime ministers. On the contrary, such statements only excite them to increase their modest contributions to Noraid. But the ranks of these immigrants are thinning and not being refilled. There does not exist in the American Irish community the same need that there once was to identify with Ireland's aspirations. Most of those aspirations were fulfilled with the establishment of the Republic of Ireland. But, more fundamentally, only new immigrants who are financially impoverished and culturally disoriented need to come together in nationalist organizations.

As Oscar Handlin and other historians of immigration have observed, organizations such as the Ancient Order of Hibernians or the Sons of Italy do not exist in Europe. Nationalist sentiment is the cement that holds such organizations together, but their real purpose is to ease the transition of immigrants into American life. They make up for a sense of individual weakness by asserting group strength. Misunderstood by native critics even today, such organizations do not create "hyphenated Americans"; they serve to smooth away the hyphen. They promote adjustment to American ways and emulation of American ideals, rather than retard them.

The millions of American Irish have moved well away from that initial period of immigrant anxiety and adjustment. As Americans, they have the security to perceive the complexity of the Ulster problem and to view it from an emotional distance. For them to enter fully into the passions that convulse Northern Ireland would require a journey into the past they are reluctant to make. They are too involved with the American present and future.

SECTION 4

Criticism of the New Ethnicity

ROBERT ALTER

A Fever of Ethnicity

No one would question that the renewed emphasis on one's ethnic background has been a source of increased self-awareness and fulfillment for millions of Americans. It is equally true that this social phenomenon has produced deep-seated anxieties and social concerns at all levels of American society. Not everyone has viewed the reawakening of these primordial feelings with an equal sense of pleasure.

In the essay below Robert Alter, educator and social critic, has questioned the direction in which the new ethnicity seems to be leading the nation. Alter believes that America is in the throes of a collective identity crisis. Numerous citizens are being compelled by a "driven need to discover oneself." If American society should come to view everything "through the prism" of ethnicity, as Alter believes such authors as Michael Novak and Peter Schrag are suggesting, it could become a constricting, not expanding, force for identity. On the larger scene, Alter claims that such a development can lead to a balkanization of the nation's political interests and cultural life. He is also critical of the new ethnicity for its universal condemnation of the WASPs. Not all evils in society, he claims, have flowed from the actions and decisions of this segment of our population. In the last analysis, Alter warns us to be "wary of moves which promote atavistic feeling at the expense of reason."

Robert Alter is a member of the Hebrew and comparative literature department at the University of California, Berkeley. He has written

Reprinted from *Commentary* (June, 1972) by permission; copyright © 1972 by the American Jewish Committee.

Rogue's Progress *(1964) and* After the Tradition *(1969), and is a regular contributor to the magazine* Commentary.

More and more, America comes to seem the land of perpetual identity crisis. First there were the founding WASPs, outcasts, misfits, dissidents, and adventurers who in the momentous crossing of waters had torn themselves loose from the Old World ties of tradition and community. In the vast solitude of the American wilderness—as Oscar Handlin and others have contended—the new settlers had to live with a new kind of existential loneliness that called into question familiar assumptions of value and identity. The characteristic response to this insistent dread inspired by an unpeopled, disorienting new landscape was less a distinctive American identity than a distinctive American fantasy: a self-consciously masculine ideal of craggy independence, toughness, cool resourcefulness, and resolute self-discipline. By the 1950s, that ideal had become for many as factitious as its tinniest embodiments in Hollywood cowboy heroes and fictional private-eyes; and Americans, now no longer preponderantly WASPs, began to look elsewhere for images of identity.

The great vogue of *Yiddishkeit,* beginning in the late fifties and peaking in the mid-sixties, was the first signal break from WASP cultural hegemony, at least on a literary level. Whatever the falsifications and the sentimentality fostered by the vogue, Jewish Americans felt encouraged to look freshly at who they were in the light of their own distinctive experience, while other Americans (some of them undoubtedly WASPs) tried to see in the distorting mirror of Jewishness possibilities of selfhood neglected by the dominant WASP culture. The Black Power movement of the mid-sixties, and the more radical movements of protest of the late sixties, though often a response to particular grievances, could legitimately be seen as the violent throes of a collective identity crisis affecting certain vocal ethnic groups and social classes. Still more clearly, the emergence of a counter-culture in this same period reflected, as many commentators have noted, a vehement—and for the most part, filial—rejection of the values and models of identity of affluent America, whether old WASP or second-generation Jewish. The two major alternatives of identity, then, developed in the dissident movements of the late sixties were a submergence of individuality in some paramilitary collective identity among the dark-skinned minorities or revolutionary youth, and a flamboyant antinomianism among the proponents of counterculture. In both directions, one senses a frantic urgency to *become* in the face of all the forces that seem subtly or crudely to coerce the self, and much the same urgency is detectable in the current women's movement. Saul Bellow's Mr. Sammler nicely catches this special American quality of a driven need to discover oneself in one of his reflections on the more extreme manifestations of the counterculture:

> Antiquity accepted models, the Middle Ages...but modern man, perhaps because of collectivization, has a fever of originality. The idea of the uniqueness of the soul. An excellent idea. A true idea. But in these forms? In these poor forms? Dear God! With hair, with clothes, with drugs and cosmetics, with genitalia, with round trips through evil, monstrosity, and orgy, with even God approached through obscenities? How terrified the soul must be in this vehemence, how little that is really dear to it it can see in these Sadic exercises.

Sammler, one might note, does not coolly put down the new cultural dissidents but rather views them with a compassionate sadness ("How terrified the soul must be..."). The idea of the uniqueness of the soul—it is an idea to which I would like to return—seems to him true and excellent, but he is at a loss to imagine how uniqueness can be realized through an absolutism or originality, with no regard for models of emulation. Elsewhere in the novel, he pointedly observes that the programmatic abandonment of models leads only to the unwitting imitation of lesser models, the dream of autonomy translating itself into a grotesque rehearsal of derivative gestures and roles.

Now, the waves of upheaval on the cultural and political left of the late sixties generally were in one way or another reactions against the increasingly "rationalized" nature of American society, the growth of bureaucracy, large-scale if ineffectual social planning, computerization, corporate commercialism, mindless standardization through the media—all those tendencies that Norman Mailer, over a decade ago, with his characteristic combination of insight and irresponsibility, began to lump together under the rubric "totalitarianism." (Mr. Sammler, too, suspects that the "fever of originality" may be the result of modern collectivization.) The dissidents' vigorous reflex of rejection, as Bellow's analysis makes clear, revealed the depth of the problem of identity but offered no viable solution. It might have been predictable, then, that the politics of protest of the late sixties would be followed by a politics of identity in the seventies, one in which a different cultural and demographic base would be proposed for creating alternatives to both the old WASP myth of strenuous individualism and the depersonalized face of the new corporate America.

Two signs of the changing times are two new books that argue for the political implementation of cultural pluralism in America, Peter Schrag's *The Decline of the Wasp** and Michael Novak's *The Rise of the Unmeltable Ethnics.*** Schrag's book combines slick thinking with an abrasive manner, and since there is little in its argument that is not said more reflectively and more probingly by Novak, it need not be dwelt on here. One of its chief defects, however, does illustrate the principal virtue of the Novak book. Schrag, writing from a standpoint beyond ethnicity, as a Jew thoroughly assimilated into the new culture of swinging protest, exhibits not only icy contempt for the WASP patricians but also, despite his professed pluralism, a barely veiled disdain for the TV-trapped masses of the lower-middle and working classes. One comes away from his book with the impression that the most shamefully exploited Americans after blacks and Spanish-speaking people are university students. Novak, on the other hand, is a Slovak Catholic intellectual who, just recently involved in articulating a theology of radical politics, has now rediscovered his Slovak ethnicity in the full weight of its political implications; and he begins by reminding us that there are nearly 50 million Catholics in this country, perhaps 70 million descendants of immigrants from Ireland, Italy, Greece, Spain, Armenia, and the Slavic nations. His forceful argument against the Left in particular and the intellectuals in general is that the recent politics of protest has largely ignored the legitimate aspirations, sense of value and self-respect, and the pressing economic needs of these large groups, who have been written off as benighted hard-hats and proto-fascists, have been seen not as various human beings with a special role to play in this country but merely as "pigs," wielders of nightsticks and wavers of flags.

Novak's argument to the electorate at large is that the many millions of derided white ethnics are the swing vote of the future. They have at least as good reason as any other group of Americans to feel deep political resentment. Preponderantly working-class and preponderant in the working class, they constitute a looming proportion of the 70 million Americans whose annual family income is between $5,000 and $10,000; their real income as workingmen declined 3 percent between 1965 and 1970; typically, the chief wage-earner in the family of this group hits a permanent income plateau by his early thirties, and from year to year life becomes more of a treadmill of grubbing and frustration. On their television screens they are regaled with the expensive gimcrackery and luxury of activity of an upwardly mobile America, and confronted with the contemptuous rejection of their own values in the political protests of the children of the affluent. They

---

*Simon and Schuster, 1971, 255 pp.
**Macmillan, 1972, 321 pp.

themselves, by contrast, enjoy only the most limited economic or social mobility, while still clinging to a stalwart Americanism which now seems decidedly too American to the very educated classes that once encouraged them to adopt it. Simple prudence, Novak plausibly argues, should suggest that the needs of the white ethnic minorities be given considerable priority in future public policy.

Novak's new ethnic politics, however, goes far beyond the old ethnic politics of group self-interest ("Is it good for the Jews?") that has been such a fixture on the American electoral scene. I have called it a politics of identity because ultimately it proposes the tight texture of ethnicity as the one, the true and salubrious means to a viable sense of selfhood. The following rationale for ethnic belonging in America is characteristic of the argument as a whole:

> The emergence of "rational" universal values is dysfunctional since it detaches persons from the integration of personality that can be achieved only in historical symbolic communities. The "divisiveness" and free-floating "rage" so prominent in America in the 1960s is one result of the shattering impact of "forced nationalization" upon personality integration. People uncertain of their own identity are not wholly free. They are threatened not only by specific economic and social programs, but also at the very heart of their identity. The world is mediated to human persons through language and culture, that is, through ethnic belonging.

> The function of ethnic belonging is to integrate a person's sense of reality, the stories that tell him how to live, the symbols that move him. These are the matrix in which his conscience receives instruction. By contrast, the American system of individualization and rationalization leaves all but a certain human type profoundly deprived—deprived of initiative and symbolic thickness, unable to function in the nonconnected way demanded by the ethnic symbols of WASPs; individualism, competition, and merely rational interest.

This seems carefully considered, and whatever uneasiness the statement may elicit, it is an argument that needs hearing now. Intellectuals, accustomed to conceive the realization of self as a matter of individual choice, endowed as they generally are with the economic, geographical, social, and imaginative maneuverability to select from a whole spectrum of values and lifestyles, tend to forget that most people simply don't have that wide freedom of choice or energy of self-forging initiative. The alternative to Little Italy or Little Warsaw with their networks of close kinship and distinctive custom is usually not the riches of individualism but a fresh-frozen life in some pre-packaged suburb, Howard Johnson's on Sundays, Disneyland vacations, the cut-rate American dream of happiness out of an aerosol can. Against the corporate-wasteland vision of a standardized American, and against the dissident's extravagant dream of an absolutely original self, Novak suggests that our various ethnic subcultures can offer the self precisely the "models" that it needs—the images, gestures, rituals, memories, modalities of feeling through which a vigorous, confident selfhood can be realized.

Novak's aphoristic summary of his rationale for ethnicity is memorable: "People uncertain of their own identity are not wholly free." It is a point that will be vividly familiar to many Jews, a point, indeed, that has been made repeatedly over the last two centuries by nationally conscious Jews about the uneasy self-consciousness of assimilated Jews. For much of this period, Western Jewry has been conducting a precarious experiment in combining the preservation of cultural distinctiveness and group solidarity with full participation in the civic and cultural life of larger national communities. In the continuing tensions of this enterprise, Jews have often felt the preciousness of the very values Novak extols—family ties, com-munitarian closeness, tradition, collective pride. But the modern Jewish experience offers a double perspective on this set of values, for if Jews in some respects have remained exemplary traditionalists, they have also been the modernists par excellence, and it is precisely modernity that gets short shrift in Novak's plea for ethnic belonging. What his argument consistently neglects is that ethnicity can also be a constricting context for identity. The obverse of his aphorism would be equally true: "People preoccupied with their own identity are not wholly free."

Perhaps this truth is more readily perceptible among Jews because historically it has been not ethnicity but rather a sense of peoplehood— that is, an ongoing *national* identity, not just the recollection of common origins in a single "old country"—informed by religious covenant that has bound Jews together. Today, both the covenant and the peoplehood remain as possible options for Jews, together with two highly ramified Jewish intellectual traditions, the classical and the modernist, from which individuals can draw models of identification, resources of experience. Against this background of resonant possi-bilities, mere ethnicity—B'nai B'rith bowling leagues, Temple Sister-hood fashion shows, lox-and-bagel breakfasts—may seem empty and limiting, a cultivation of clannishness rather than the matrix for the development of a secure and open self.

The fact is that while a genuinely national identity has the flexibility to develop and change with history, ethnicity is by its very nature a conservative concept (keeping up dilute enclaves of the old-country ways in the new), and *The Rise of the Unmeltable Ethnics* is indeed a profoundly conservative book. I use the term not as an automatic pejorative, since some of what commands respect in Novak is bound up with his conservatism, but in order to locate precisely the implicit dangers of his outlook. I also do not intend the term in its ordinary journalistic sense, since Novak is clearly aiming his argument somewhere toward the left wing of the Democratic Party, and his ideas on the redistribution of national resources, as much as they can be inferred from his statements here, would put him not far from the social-democratic position of, say, Michael Harrington. The explicit world-view underlying this apologia for ethnicity is nevertheless fundamentally and pervasively conservative.

Novak believes, as we have already seen, that the best integration of personality "can be achieved only in historical symbolic communities." Again and again he exhibits a utopian nostalgia for the traditional communities of the past, never suggesting how those communities could stifle individuals within them, could exert cruelly coercive force on their own disadvantaged or dissident members. (Revealingly, he offers an idyllic image of the Jewish community through the ages as "a people who without governmental or coercively structured economic institutions nourish[ed] in their midst strong persons, strong cultural selves." In point of fact, Jewish communities were usually rigidly hierarchical, both economically and politically, and had their own internal institutions which could be harshly coercive—in recent centuries in Europe, the oligarchic *kehillah* organizations.) Again and again Novak stresses feeling over mind, past over present, collectivity over individuality. "When a person thinks, more than one generation's passions and images think in him. Below the threshold of the rational or the fully conscious, our instincts and sensibilities lead backward to the predilections of our forebears." There may be a nucleus of truth in the assertion, but one becomes uneasy with a language that presents the individual as a passive conduit for the collective past (the past thinks in him) and places such peculiar stress on what is nonrational (passions, instincts, sensibilities, predilections). The sense of uneasiness is confirmed when Novak goes on in the next breath to articulate a mystique of ethnic mentality: "Upper-class Quakers *think* and *feel* in a way I cannot think and feel; Jewish intellectuals tend to live and breathe out of writers, concerns, and experiences I can emulate as second nature, but not as first; certain Irish Catholics exhibit emotional patterns I can follow, but not find native to me."

The statement, of course, has a minimal and quite literal validity, but its grand sweep of implication is mere resonant nonsense. The easiest thing to convince yourself of, if you set your mind to it, is that ineradicable, deeply indwelling differences exist between others and you; it is the last thing intellectuals, who after all have succeeded in creating a genuine lingua franca at least among themselves, ought to be doing. I can enter into the thought and feeling of Edmund Wilson far more completely than I can enter the thought and feeling of the Satmar Rebbe; though I have in common with the obscurantist religious leader some Jewish experiences and two Jewish languages, I share with the literary critic an embracing realm of discourse with some of its implicit values, an engagement in American culture and modern experience, and to that basic commonality of enterprise the differential element of Wilson's WASP background is incidental. Or, to take an example closer to home, I can identify with Michael Novak's writing and thinking far more readily than with Peter Schrag's, though the latter is a Jew, the former a Slovak Catholic, because Novak, whatever his conclusions, respects the same linguistic and intellectual standards that I do, works within the broad modes of logic and conceptualization to which I am accustomed, while Schrag affects a souped-up prose and a turned-on sensibility that I can understand but which seem alien to me.

I risk the gratuitous absurdity of these comparisons to illustrate what is untenable in Novak's position—the implicit tendency to view everything through the prism of ethnic origins, with the social and political contexts of any particular act or statement, the individual psychology of the person or people involved, falling away before the "ultimate" fact of their ethnic identity. Eugene McCarthy's peculiar petulance and negligent manner in the campaigning of 1968 are explained not in terms of his idiosyncratic character but as expressions of his refusal as an Irish Catholic to play the WASP game of evangelical politics. Normal Mailer's attempt to create a "revolution of consciousness" in his writing (perhaps like that of William Burroughs, whom Mailer has much admired?) is seen not as a function of an individual writer's quirky ambition and imagination but as the reflex of a Jewish sensibility rejecting the images of identity of WASP America. Even a provocative gesture made by a female student demonstrator to a policeman is viewed not as an attempt to offend an armed representative of the establishment but as an insult directed squarely at the policeman's ethnic sensibilities. To be fair, Novak's book is by and large more carefully reasoned than these few examples might indicate, but they suggest the inherent danger in making ethnicity the absolute point of departure for all thinking about America. On the level of practical politics, such unrelenting insistence on the primacy of ethnic identity could lead, given the perverse logic of competitive interaction among people, not to a new American diversity but to a balkanization of political interests and cultural life. At any rate, in regard to the way we think about ourselves, the insistence on ethnicity tends to encourage certain unconstructive simplifications and misdirections of attention.

Thus, a major fault shared by Schrag's *Decline* and Novak's *Rise* is to overstate the case against the already abundantly berated WASP. To be sure, the WASP elite has much to answer for in American history, from the virulent Nordic racism it once promulgated to its hypocritical ideology of egalitarian individualism as a mask for privilege, and the denial of the dignity of new immigrants implicit in its myth of the melting pot. Nevertheless, both Novak and Schrag, from their different viewpoints, offer what is ultimately a racist reading of American history because, finally, all the ills and wrongs of the nation are traced to some sickness of perversion of the WASP spirit. Such highly industrialized urban societies as those of France, Germany, and Japan have done quite nicely in producing social pathologies similar to ours unaided by WASPs of their own. Yet reading Schrag and Novak, one infers that all we suffer derives from the arid puritanism, the estrangement from life, the competitiveness, the sexual insecurity, the hatred of the body, the emotional frigidity, the atomistic individualism, the mechanistic view of self and society, that are seen by these writers as the very body and blood of WASP ethnicity.

All this, of course, merely turns discredited ideas around 180 degrees: the nation is still divided into good guys (immigrants from southern and eastern Europe and dark-skinned people) and bad guys (the paleface descendants of Englishmen and northern Europeans). This sort of inadvertently Manichean division seems particularly bizarre in the case of a fundamentally reasonable writer like Novak. He implies that, given the imperative fact of ethnicity, there is no common American standard of discourse and value, but his own book illustrates the vigor of just such a standard. He repeatedly insists that the self is mediated by language, and the primary language for almost all ethnics in this country after the first generation is American English—if they choose to write, generally educated American English at that. Thus, the very categories Novak invokes to defend ethnicity—inner freedom, integration of personality, historical symbolic community, conscience, "imaginative and symbolic thickness"—are conceptualizations rooted in a common Anglo-American idiom of thought, if you will, in the dominant WASP tradition of discourse.

I would like to return to the conservative implications of founding a view of personality and history on ethnicity. Novak claims at one point hat he is not anti-modern, but the "skepticism" he repeatedly evinces toward modernity is so far-reaching that the line between skepticism and actual rejection blurs and fades. If modernization tends to break down traditional social structures, conceives of individuals as free agents, reduces family, clan, and ethnic group to mere options instead of necessary contexts, it must be viewed as a threatening, negative process: "Modern civilization—urban, fluid, democratic, determined to change history—is a Nordic invention. The men of the south and the east have long been skeptical about its outcome." The statement makes clear not only the grudging attitude toward modernity (including democratic process) but, more embarrassingly, the gross distortion of a racial reading of history.

Repeatedly, Novak imagines modernization as a pulverizing mechanical force that assaults traditional life from without: "The weight of every conceivable social practice and psychological instruction is to break up extended families and to atomize nuclear families. The fission of America seems to focus upon all organic, communal links." Though "atomize" and "nuclear" are of course intended in a sociological sense, their use here in quick sequence with "fission," set over against the idea of organic community, suggests a doomsday image of social change as a kind of slow-motion hydrogen explosion blowing apart the "natural" wholeness of pre-modern life. The metaphor of modernity as a destructive mechanism or a technological "processing" that threatens organic growth recurs elsewhere, and it may make one a little nervous, for it has been invoked before by others in the service not of a tolerant conservatism but of fanatic reaction.

Since intellectuals as a class have been the great catalysts of modernity, the social planners, the spinners of schemes for radical innovation, Novak devotes more than a third of his book to a critique of the intellectuals. It is precisely here that one sees most vividly both the positive value and the ultimate danger of conceiving culture and politics in terms of ethnicity. Novak, let me hasten to say, is not anti-intellectual but fits clearly into the tradition, going back to Burke and Tocqueville, of conservative attack against the excesses of the intellectuals. That tradition has recently been described by Peter Steinfels, an associate editor of *Commonweal,* as "counterintellectualism."* Counterintellectualism at its best, Steinfels writes, "is an antidote for the nonsense which the intellectuals are always capable of producing," and there obviously has been no slack in the production of such nonsense over the

*"The Counterintellectuals," *New American Review* 14.

past few years in this country. Novak seems especially sound in his sustained assault on the elitism of the intellectuals, their general failure to imagine as real people large segments of our population unlike themselves, their fondness for abstract schemes of social amelioration that are out of touch with the needs and desires of many of the people whose lives are being planned.

The notorious arrogance of the intellectuals, however, is for Novak merely a secondary manifestation of their primary error, which is nothing less than their adherence to "an image of history favoring the future," an image reflected in the very use of the metaphor of an avant-garde for the intelligentsia. From the ultimate viewpoint of a conservatism that seems theological as well as political, Novak sees this commitment to the future as a kind of anthropocentric heresy: "To be on the side of the future (a benevolent future, safeguarding the continuous progress of man) is the equivalent [for modern intellectuals] of standing in the presence of God." It has of course been a long time since such naive faith in continuous progress was a serious intellectual position, but one wonders why the intellectual aspirations to make the future more humanly livable than the past should be inherently suspect. Novak cannot be proposing that we simply reconcile ourselves to the bottomless misery and outrageous inequities of the present and the past; he surely does not want us to go back to the repressive feudalism of some *ancien regime,* or even to an America before the social legislation of the New Deal and its aftermath. Social planning and progressivist ideologies have been guilty of dismal blundering and unfounded self-assurance, but must that discredit the very attempt to use reason to construct a future which will not compound all the hideous mistakes of the past?

The intellectual's indispensable role, whatever his sins, has been to envisage alternatives, to imagine new possibilities. According to Novak, however, "his function is not to lead, in the way an avant-garde leads, or in the way planners, managers, and experts lead," but rather "the intellectual's vocation is to be a voice of the people—to put into words what they already know." Though Novak realizes that not everything in the people is admirable—what the intellectual will put into words will "terrify" as well as "illuminate"—he nevertheless comes disturbingly close here to a mystique of *Volkstum,* which hardly seems what we want to return to after all that has been perpetrated in its name in recent history. The individualistic assertion of self, beginning as far back as the Renaissance (and *not* merely among Anglo-Saxons!) has admittedly been one of the most tortuous enterprises of modern culture, but it also has been heroic, incurring great inner risks in order to realize a new order of inner freedom. In this enterprise, the assertive voice of the intellectual has often been abrasive or disdainful but it has been necessary, and I think one must strenuously resist any suggestion that the time has come for the intellectual to submerge himself in the people, or that the most valid realization of self can come only through the people.

It is simply wrong to say, as Novak does, that individual autonomy and personal authenticity are WASP concepts, limited to the assumptions of WASP ethnicity. They are, rather, key concepts of modern culture in general—paradoxically, without them Novak would hardly have written his book. Whatever the enormous difficulties in the realization of these ideals, the very currency they enjoy points to a new horizon of possibility for every human being. That horizon, as Novak justly observes, will scarcely beckon at all to large numbers of people; nevertheless one must be grateful for its mere existence, for the fact that a person can at least in part free himself from subjugation (in some degree it is always that) to the community and the past in order to realize his selfhood according to his own needs. Granted, the self always requires a social context and always used previously experienced models in creating its own goals: the dream of absolute originality, as Mr. Sammler reminds us, is a dream to drive men mad. But Mr. Sammler also knows that individual uniqueness is a true, an excellent idea; and modern individualism, whether as a social ideology or a pervasive style of intellectual discourse, has sustained the live and various possibilities of fulfilled uniqueness, however imperfectly and intermittently. Each of us must live between the relentless dialectic tensions of communal norms and the self's imperatives; to disallow either side of the dialectic is to expose the self to crippling impairment, from without or from within.

Ethnicity, to be sure, in no way implies the extirpation of individuality, but one is entitled to be suspicious of any political philosophy that might compromise or circumscribe the individual's scope for discovering his own uniqueness. At this point in American history, it seems less than helpful, and it could be pernicious, to promote atavistic feeling at the expense of reason; to proffer a thoroughly ahistorical ideal of innocent organic community as an attainable goal; to suggest that the highest vocation of the intellectual is to become the voice of the people; and, above all, to insist that the ultimate cause of our present national disarray is an ideal of individualism allegedly deriving from white Anglo-Saxon Protestantism.

RICHARD SENNETT

Pure as the Driven Slush

The power of the new ethnic labels to stimulate public debate has been enormous. Jimmy Carter's celebrated remarks during the 1976 presidential race, for example, about retaining the "ethnic purity" of neighborhoods produced a firestorm of reaction. To many it seemed that Carter was advocating the solidifying of communities based solely upon ethnicity. Critics foresaw the emergence of group chauvinism and extreme separatism. When these statements were related to the continuing debate over busing and black rights, they took on a more ominous tone.

New York University sociologist Richard Sennett is particularly critical of the thrust of the new ethnicity. He has observed, for instance, a tendency to indulge in an overly romantic celebration of the ethnic past. Such a phenomenon implies, he believes, a rejection of the present as a worthwhile existence and often leads to social and political programs based upon nostalgia. Sennett fears, moreover, that those who are involved in the efforts to revive ethnicity are in fact creating false and narrowly idealized pictures of what this heritage was like. The truth of the matter, he claims, is that the old life was often restrictive and unfulfilling in numerous ways. Similarly, a modern society that is truly pluralistic, with every group trumpeting its own glories and demands, would contain much that is undesirable and dangerous. Sennett is the author of, among other publications, Families against the City *(1970) and* The Uses of Disorder *(1970).*

A myth is an idea people need to believe in, whether or not it is true. All societies, from the primitive to the overcivilized, are held together by such ideas. One of the most powerful of these ideas is the myth of decline, the conviction that the present is inferior to the past. Today, American society is finding a new set of symbols to express a peculiar version of the myth of decline—symbols derived from the experience of ethnic groups.

The communal life of ethnic groups in America is interpreted by people across the political spectrum as something special and precious; ethnic groups are portrayed as warm, open, and caring among themselves. They are seen as threatened, like an endangered species, by all the homogenizing pressures of American society—upward mobility, mass culture, rootlessness. The virtues of ethnic community in the past have become a yardstick to measure present-day communal emptiness, and, not coincidentally, an ideological weapon to fight reforms like racial integration.

Given the actual facts of ethnic community life in America, there is something obscene about politicians like Gerald Ford or Jimmy Carter celebrating "our precious ethnic heritage." The history of most ethnic groups in America, white as well as black, is appalling.

Most European peasants who migrated here had no consciousness when they came of being "ethnics." They identified themselves as members of a village or shtetl; in America, unable to buy land and converted into an urban proletariat, they suddenly found their language, family patterns, even food habits, treated by the larger culture as signs of cultural inferiority.

Furthermore, the first generations of ethnics never experienced anything like the community "purity" these politicians speak of. The Lower East Side in 1910 was probably the most polyglot urban settlement in the world. Being an ethnic, any kind of ethnic, radically restricted where one could live as well as what one could work at; the ethnics found themselves jumbled together, among a mass of people who often could not stand each other's religions, understand each other's speech, or make sense of each other's customs.

That these tense, confused communities managed to work at all is the genuine tribute to be paid to the people who inhabited them. Celebrating ethnicity *per se* means celebrating the badges of cultural inferiority American society forced the agrarian immigrants to wear.

As the various ethnic urban groups gained a toehold in the American economy, they withdrew from each other. The pressures to make secure each ethnic group as a world unto itself were greatly increased by the coming of southern blacks to northern cities, for the latest migrants seemed to threaten to pull the Europeans back down into the chaotic world from which they had escaped. Granted that today the white ethnics' efforts to preserve ethnic homogeneity are more complicated and sympathetic than simple racial prejudice, nonetheless it is difficult to understand what a society has to celebrate when it forces people to act as if they were racists.

Finally, the issue of ethnic identity is a painful one between the generations in many ethnic families. People who have grown up in ethnic communities have often felt suffocated by them; when they leave, the old feel the ethnic culture is being abandoned because there is something unhealthy about it. This is more than a half-truth; in the extended families of many European ethnics, parental control of adult children is justified in the name of keeping up "tradition." The celebration of ethnicity ignores most of these realities.

Idealizing ethnicity fits into a pattern that antedates the large-scale arrivals of European peasants by more than a century. From the late 18th century on, concern about the eclipse or weakening of community is a constant theme in American writing. Madison, Tocqueville, and Olmsted all worried about the decline of community. Many progressives at the turn of the century feared ethnics because they feared that these outsiders threatened community life. By a perverse irony, modern-day ethnic consciousness is giving the myth of communal decline a new life.

The purpose of a myth of decline is not to revive the past but to create an attitude of resignation about the present. If what really matters has vanished, if community has broken down, then those left in the wake have some justification for feeling apathetic.

Americans are a peculiar people; economically aggressive, socially passive, not terribly interested in each other, convinced that the conditions under which people can live with some mutual concern are outside the bounds of practicality and that within these limits everyone has to take care of himself.

In celebrating as a precious heritage the horrors of the ethnic past, we give ourselves license to feel that the present is dead. It is not that we want to recover our real ethnic roots, but that we need to mourn the loss of them.

This is why the language of many of the ethnic revivalists is like the language of museum curators, talk of conservation, preservation, restoration. But a living tradition is not like a painting; it needs to be changed and retouched by each new generation. The ethnic revivalists speak as they do because they are obsessed with the idea that ethnicity is dying out. Whether ethnicity is in fact a living or a dead tradition in

America is altogether another question; people need to believe it is something precious that is absent from their lives.

Jimmy Carter's so-called blunder in talking about the old-time virtues of ethnic purity may turn out to be a stroke of genius. Blacks, and Jews with good memories, may find the phrase chilling, but for those who have dimmed memory of their own ethnic pasts, or who have never had such a background, these words may strike a sympathetic chord, its root deep in the American experience.

The leader gives people an image of how much more decent things once were, and they want desperately to believe him. The ability to arouse their longing makes him a credible figure, more credible than the politicians who want to talk about what should be done now.

My own conviction is that if someone like Carter comes to power on these terms, it will be the beginning of a real and irreversible decline. Nostalgia is not a very good preparation for survival.

NATHAN GLAZER

Ethnicity and the Schools

Nathan Glazer and Daniel Moynihan were among the first writers to note the continuation of ethnicity in America despite the pressures of assimilation. In this article Glazer readdresses the issue of ethnicity by asking what the resurgence of ethnic awareness means for American society. He wonders if the current wave of filiopietism is not just another name for racism. At first glance, he observes, one would argue that it is, but upon further examination it becomes apparent that substantial cultural differences between white ethnics and blacks have been important in shaping this response. He notes that "the culture of the Poles or of the Jews, for example, has not been seen by, say, the Italians to be as great a threat to their own culture as the culture of the blacks or Puerto Ricans whose traditions in many respects ran in almost the opposite direction. Against this threat the white ethnics have attempted to fight."

Glazer is especially concerned about the meaning the new ethnicity has for American education. Do ethnic studies courses actually help students in school? Glazer says he is not sure they do. In the last analysis, he argues, a student has to learn to read, write, and calculate, and the ability of a student to perform these functions is being impaired by a crowded curriculum. Glazer also believes a curriculum oriented by ethnic considerations may well create a "greater distortion than the one it sets out to correct."

Glazer suggests that immigrants who lost their language and culture were not necessarily deprived. Americanization, he believes, has been a

From *Commentary* (September, 1974) by permission; copyright © 1974 by the American Jewish Committee.

great achievement. He adds that one must remember that the United States is not and has not been a "nation of nations" but one nation created from many stocks.

It is not easy to find the words that would accurately describe the current wave of ethnic feeling which seems now to be sweeping over America. Even the word "wave" may strike some as exaggerated. We live in a world in which the interplay among mass media, scholars, foundations, and the general public is so subtle and rapid that we are often left confused as to what is "really" happening. Thus, we know that the Ford and Rockefeller Foundations are funding a number of projects in the field of ethnicity. Some are research-oriented, some are oriented toward community action, some are oriented toward directing preexisting bodies of ethnic sentiment into a liberal political direction. In making these grants, are the great foundations responding to a sense of neglect in ethnic communities (or those claiming to speak for them) who have seen so much foundation money going in the past ten years to black and other colored minority groups? Are those grants activated by the fear of an anti-black backlash among working-class whites, and the hope of heading it off? Or are the new projects the creation of scholars and organizers who, at a moment when urban studies are down on the foundation market, and black studies are increasingly limited to blacks, see in ethnic studies a possible new frontier of expansion?

Obviously these and other cynical explanations will continue to suggest themselves so long as we have no very solid empirical understanding of just *what* the ethnic resurgence amounts to. We look at a book like *The Rise of the Unmeltable Ethnics* by Michael Novak—a liberal Catholic intellectual of Slovak origin to whom ethnicity has assumed an enormous new importance—and we wonder how representative it is of the feelings of other Catholic intellectuals, and whether it reflects in any way what ordinary Americans of Slovak origin are feeling.

One of the reasons it is so difficult to answer such questions is that the meanings of ethnicity have become so various. We are not dealing here, for example, with a mass immigration of very distinct ethnic types who have no doubt as to their identity. Blacks, Jews, Puerto Ricans, and Mexican Americans have a sharply defined sense of identity, but for most other Americans ethnic identity is mixed and unclear. There are those Americans who have no ethnic identity at all, there are those whose ethnic identity is largely symbolic or latent (Germans? Scots-Irish?), there are those whose identities are strong but not sustained by organizational ties (Italians?), and those whose identities are weak but are so sustained (assimilated Jews?). No wonder we are at a loss in describing the present situation and projecting even slightly into the future.

Nevertheless, I think we can take as given the fact that ethnic feelings which not so long ago were dormant or latent or altogether nonexistent have in recent years become more evident, more urgent. Even if this has been stimulated or overstimulated by the mass media, the foundations, and the remaining caretakers of ethnic interests delighted to cash in on a slight movement in the chart of ethnic feeling by immediately labeling it a substantial rise, it remains a fact. Taking this fact as given, then, I want to raise two sets of questions about it. First, is it honest? That is to say, is it a cover for racism, a justification for anti-black prejudice, or even (more benignly) a defensive reaction to black pride? There are other ways of being dishonest. Is the new ethnic assertiveness deeply felt? Is it simply fashionable or faddish or a grab for funds and other benefits? Second, what does the new ethnicity mean for the relations among the different groups in America, and for the future of the country? Does it mean more prejudice and more conflict? Does it threaten a balkanized nation, neighborhoods, schools? And if so, how are we to avoid the worst of these consequences?

Seven or eight years ago, when Martin Luther King marched in Chicago and Father Groppi marched in Milwaukee, both in largely working-class, low-income, white ethnic areas, they were met with screams and posters declaring: "We want to save our homes," or "Get out of our neighborhoods." It was incidents like these that raised the question of honesty in connection with the new ethnic feelings. For what was there in the Polish or Lithuanian or Italian group and its culture that could justify such behavior? Most liberals answered, nothing. Just as the South had said it was protecting its culture in resisting desegregation, so was something similar now being said in the North, and for exactly the same reason: racism. In any case, how much Polish or Lithuanian or Italian culture actually existed in these areas? Who read Mickiewicz or Dante there? And if there was no real commitment to Mickiewicz or Dante, how could one pretend that those opposing black entry into their neighborhoods were fighting to maintain a culture?

Yet the word "culture" cannot be restricted only to the arts. It also means the way of life, the customs, the language—or if the language goes, the accent—the food, the stores, the weddings, the knowledge of how to approach a person on the street or how to address someone, and the comfortable expectation that one will oneself be approached and addressed in the same way. A known and experienced way of life is always of value to those who have been raised in it, and a reflexive effort to defend it demands at the least sympathy and understanding, if not necessarily acquiescence. It is true that any value may be inferior to any other and the Lithuanian neighborhood may have to go if another group is to have justice. But we cannot determine that in advance, and it is worth taking the initial claim seriously and sympathetically.

Those who believe that the new ethnicity was merely a cover for racism, however, advanced another argument. If, they said, the opposition in these neighborhoods to various forms of black entry were based on a desire to defend the ethnic culture, we would expect to find as much opposition to the entry of other ethnic groups. Yet those very areas in Chicago and Milwaukee that fought against King and Groppi were mixed. Lithuanians or Poles may have predominated in one or another neighborhood, but there were also Italians and Germans. Similarly, if we look at Canarsie in New York, where some years after the King and Groppi marches, a boycott was staged against the busing-in of more black students, we find that the opposing whites were not all members of a single ethnic group protecting its own way of life, but of two ethnic groups with very different ways of life—Jews and Italians. Surely, then, what we are dealing with here is white racism, pure and simple.

Once again—and without denying that racism played some part in these conflicts, though it is impossible to say how much or even how to determine how much—I think this is an inadequate explanation. For the truth is that certain forms of traditional behavior may be found among many ethnic groups, but not among all. Thus the kind of culture that was characterized by a strong position for the father, the obedience of the children, and the following by them of paternal occupations, the consequent rebellion of some against both the requirements of obedience and the insistence on respect for the parents' way of life and the father's occupation—this kind of culture was much better domiciled among the east European white ethnic groups than it was among American blacks or among Puerto Ricans and Mexican Americans. Consequently, the culture of the Poles or of the Jews, for example, has not been seen by, say, the Italians to be as great a threat to their own culture as the culture of the blacks or Puerto Ricans whose traditions in many respects ran in almost the opposite direction. Against this threat the white ethnics have attempted to fight.

One problem with their effort, and indeed with any effort to defend the values of an ethnic culture in America, is that we do not in this country have an ideology and a rhetoric to justify such action. We do, on the contrary, have an ideology—the ideology of the melting pot—

which justifies surrendering one's distinctive cultural traits, and assimilating to a common culture. This position has held sway in America for a very long time, but there are many indications that it is now crumbling. Consider, for example, that it was once axiomatic that all immigrants should be forced to learn the English language. Today a knowledge of English is still required for citizenship, but in New York State, at any rate, it is now possible to vote without demonstrating capacity in English. Bilingual education receives federal support. Whatever the future of Spanish will be, it already has a status very different from that of any earlier immigrant language.

Another aspect of this process of "Americanization" was the insistence that foreign loyalties be subordinated to American loyalties, or rooted out. This demand rings very hollow at a time when no one seems to know what *American* loyalties are any more. After what has happened to American patriotism in the last ten years, when our best-educated youth paraded with Cuban or North Vietnamese flags, on what grounds can anyone be upset if Jews demand support for Israel, Irish for Ireland, Greeks for Greece? (And, indeed, when anyone does get seriously upset, it is usually because he opposes the political implications of such demands and not because they are demands in favor of foreign countries.)

But if the model of the melting pot and the rhetoric of Americanization are gone, we are still not very clear as to what will take their place, and this is perhaps why we are all in such confusion over ethnicity. Just as a simple "Americanization" has been rejected (even by the Congress of the United States, as we see from all the recent legislation supporting bilingual education, ethnic studies, and the like), so, too, we are presumably rejecting a simple "separatism." Between the two are the misty reaches of "cultural pluralism." Cultural pluralism was never a widely accepted ideology in America. Its biggest moment came in World War II, when, because so many nations had been overrun by Hitler, it seemed that America could be strengthened most not by insisting that everyone forget his national origins, but rather that everyone (except, of course, the Germans) remember them. But cultural pluralism more or less disappeared after World War II, and it was only in the past few years that it began to be revived. If the people fighting King in Chicago and Groppi in Milwaukee had been able to lean on the ideology and rhetoric of cultural pluralism, they would have been able to explain themselves better and to defend themselves more effectively against the charge of racism. Instead, many of them threw up their hands in despairing frustration at their inability to give sophisticated voice to their feelings and said, "Very well, then, we are racists."

Yet even if the "pluralist" position of the white ethnic groups is not simply racism, or a cover for racism, the question of its honesty in another sense—the sense of depth or authenticity—still arises. Many spokesmen for the blacks and the Spanish-speaking groups doubt the sincerity of the white demand for special recognition of ethnic background, seeing it not as a cover for racism so much as a kind of "me-tooism" and a grab for federal and foundation funds. Where education is concerned, for example, many in the black and Spanish-speaking communities feel that they are more truly deprived than the white ethnic groups and that they therefore have a more solidly established right to an education which acknowledges their special cultural distinctiveness and which raises their group consciousness. The blacks point out that they were brought here as slaves, and the Spanish-speaking (Mexican or Puerto Rican) point out that they were conquered, whereas the white ethnic groups came as free immigrants. The blacks also say that their own culture was subjected to almost total destruction, whereas the white immigrants were allowed, if they wished, to maintain theirs—in churches, in afternoon schools, in parochial schools—and far from being forcibly deprived, voluntarily chose to assimilate.

I think there is a good deal of weight in the view that blacks and Hispanics (and American Indians) have a larger moral claim on American society than the white ethnic groups. At the same time, we should not exaggerate its weight. Many blacks, after all, were also free immigrants, from the West Indies and elsewhere. Most Mexican Americans were free immigrants or the descendants of free immigrants, and all Puerto Ricans voluntarily chose to enter an English-speaking environment. And if the argument is that the black and Spanish-speaking immigrants were forced to migrate for economic reasons, so were the immigrant ancestors of the present-day European ethnic groups.

The fact is that we cannot separate ethnic and racial groups into two classes: those who have suffered, economically and culturally, in America, and therefore deserve redress, and those who have not. Perhaps at the extremes we might make such a distinction, but each group's history is so special that no such broad separation makes sense. Consider the Asian Americans—Chinese and Japanese. They are neither European nor white; they did not come as slaves; they were not conquered; they did suffer race prejudice and, in the case of the Japanese Americans during World War II, confiscation of their property and even incarceration; they do well economically and their children do well in school. To which class of immigrant groups do they belong?

In considering this question, we are brought to a more powerful argument that gives special weight to black and Spanish-speaking claims where education is concerned as against white ethnic claims. This is the pragmatic argument that as a matter of fact black and Spanish-speaking children do poorly in school, and for that reason alone some special attention in the form of ethnic-studies programs is required. If the first claim is based on a past deprivation, the second is based on a present deprivation.

But since this is a pragmatic argument, there are pragmatic questions. Do ethnic studies actually help students do better in school? There are many reasons why they might, but none is decisive. According to one argument, the present curriculum is alien to the black or Mexican American or Puerto Rican child, and because he cannot "relate" to it, he does poorly. But would an ethnically oriented curriculum be more effective in bringing the black or Spanish-speaking child to competence in what we may call the general curriculum (sometimes and improperly called the "white" or "middle-class" curriculum—improperly, because the ability to read and calculate is a general human need, not based on class or color)? In my own case, growing up in a tenement in East Harlem, I read with wonder stories about children who lived in houses where they went *upstairs* to bed—to me that was romantic and the alienness made it all the more intriguing. But many children may be put off rather than attracted by the alien.

There is a second and quite different pragmatic argument for ethnic studies—not that they directly serve to make the curriculum more attractive and meaningful, but that they give a greater sense of self-respect to the child of a minority group and in so doing strengthen his ability to learn. And another variant of this argument says that if we have ethnic studies we will of course have more blacks and Spanish-surnamed teachers in the schools, thereby increasing the number of "role models," which will again indirectly encourage the child to achieve more.

All this may well be so. It is true that Chinese, Japanese, Armenians, Greeks, and Jews—and several other groups too—did well in school even though nothing about their own history and experience was in the curriculum, and even though their own people were entirely absent from the ranks of teachers and administrators. But there are many ways of learning: perhaps the children of some groups or some children in all groups do need direct contact through the curriculum and in the school itself with their actual ways of life, with their own ethnic histories, and with adults from the same ethnic background. Here again we see that ethnic groups cannot be regarded as being like so many peas in a pod.

Not only do they differ concretely from one another, but their differences may result in a variety of educational needs, such that some groups require ethnic studies and others do not. And if those who have no real need of such studies, or whose economic and political progress does not seem to have been badly hampered, ask for them anyway, is this not a case of "me-tooism," or faddishness?

Yet in contrasting Chinese, Japanese, Armenians, and Jews—who have done well in school even in the total absence of any public recognition of their culture and group life—with blacks and Mexican Americans and Puerto Ricans—who have done poorly and might be helped by a recognition of their culture and group life—we tend to forget that there are many groups in the middle—Poles and other east Europeans, Irish, Germans—whose achievement has neither been remarkable for speedy progress in the face of adverse circumstances, nor notable for backwardness. Would children of these groups be helped academically if recognition were given to their group character and their cultural background? Again it is hard to say. In any case, their demand for ethnic studies is generally based not on past political oppression or on present academic or economic deprivation, but rather on the idea that all cultures must be recognized as having equal significance and dignity and that all therefore deserve a role in education and in the curriculum.

Is, then, the demand for ethnic cultural components in the curriculum honest, serious, real? By certain standards the answer may be no, but the fact is that we are now living with a new standard of public discourse that forbids this kind of dismissal. A few years ago, when blacks demanded Swahili, it was simply not considered acceptable to reply that Swahili was not widely spoken, would not be helpful to future black economic and political progress, and was in any event not the ancestral language of American blacks. Nowadays, it appears, a cultural demand can no longer be weighed on the scales of seriousness and depth. Evidently all such demands are to be taken seriously. Indeed, the point about ethnicity and ethnic consciousness is that no group submits to the judgment of others. By their very nature ethnic claims do not allow of a universal scale against which they can be measured.

I am reminded of the first time Mao buttons appeared in Berkeley. They were then jokes—to those who wore them, and to those who saw them worn. A year later they were not jokes at all. They were worn with deadly seriousness, and those who wore them were ready to engage in desperate actions to demonstrate just how serious they were. Marx once said that the first time something happens in history it is tragedy, and when it is repeated it becomes farce. Today, in reversal of Marx, what starts as farce soon becomes serious—sometimes grimly and tragically so.

In short, with regard to the question of whether the new ethnicity is serious, my conclusion is that we (that is, informed public opinion) have given up the claim to know how to answer it. No matter how extreme or outlandish it may seem to begin with, if the demand is raised, persisted in, finds adherents, it *is* serious, or as serious as anything becomes in this world. There is no universal arbiter who decides which ethnic demands are serious and just and which are not, who honors those of the blacks, Mexican Americans, Puerto Ricans, American Indians, on the one hand, and rejects those of the Poles, the Irish, and the Italians on the other. Maybe there should be such an arbiter, but we would be deceiving ourselves to believe that there is.

Granted, then, that at least in principle and at least to begin with, all ethnic claims must be admitted, is this good for America? The question is so large that it may help to start with a more modest problem: is it good for education, for the curriculum? One difficulty already becoming visible is the crowding of the curriculum by the demand that all ethnic groups be recognized in, for example, the teaching of American history. Now, it is one thing to include American blacks, who were here at the beginning, who were the victims of the major institution of slavery, who were a crucial factor in the most tragic and bloody of all American wars, who were the very basis of the distinctiveness of America's most distinctive region, the South, and who were—and are— deeply involved in the urban crisis which has agitated the nation for decades and will probably continue to do so for a few more. Moreover, as 11 percent of the population—and 20 percent at the time of the American Revolution—they exert a powerful claim for inclusion in our social science curriculum.

But how powerful is the claim of other groups? Certainly the Irish and Germans played a role in the urban history of the 19th century and the history of the opening of the Midwest. It is, however, hard to say whether it was significant for American development that such and such an immigrant group wielded pickaxes and laid the railroads and opened the prairie farmlands, as against what Americans of British origin did. Despite the fact that I have spent my life in studying and pondering the role of immigrant and racial groups in America, I remain doubtful that this aspect of the national life should be accorded the same importance as the traditional content of American history—the settling of the thirteen colonies, the Revolution, the making of the Constitution, the expansion territorially of the nation, the struggle over slavery, the Civil War, the industrial revolution, the entry onto the international scene as a world power, and so on. If the American history that was taught in the 1930s and 1940s were replaced by one that sectioned it up among the ethnic and racial groups, and made their fate primary—which is what is beginning to happen in our elementary and secondary schools today—I myself would not consider this an improvement.

I believe the "Americanization" of the immigrant was a great achievement, an almost unique and unparalleled achievement despite its harshness and arrogance. I am not sure that the immigrants who came to this country willingly, to work and to become citizens of a new land, were deprived when they gave up an old language for English, old cultures for a new emerging culture, old allegiances for a new allegiance. I am not suggesting that ethnic studies would undo this achievement; perhaps they would only introduce a proper balance. But the danger exists that they will end by creating a far greater distortion than the one they set out to correct. For if in teaching the history of the American Revolution, for example, we make it appear that George Washington and John Adams and Thomas Jefferson were not much more important than Haym Solomon, Crispus Attucks, Pulaski, Baron von Steuben, and whoever else might be necessary to give every group in the nation a sense of sharing in our great founding event, we not only risk distortion, we risk weakening commitment to common political values, and we risk losing the sense of the United States as a country dedicated from its birth to distinctive and great ideals.

From the point of view of the schools this last may be the greatest challenge. The schools should be committed to honest teaching, but they also socialize children. With mathematics we have no problem, but with history and English we may have a great problem. In the universities it is clear that the analytical mode should prevail (though we are well aware that in recent years there has been a danger of advocacy dominating analysis in the colleges and universities, and not only in ethnic studies). In the elementary and high schools, however, we have always "advocated" democracy and liberty, and we have always inculcated a belief in the general goodness and rightness of our country and of its role in world affairs. This advocacy is justified to my mind by the socializing function of the schools. But the pressure on textbook writers in many states today is in the opposite direction. They are being asked to substitute a new kind of advocacy which emphasizes the racist and ethnocentric aspects of American life—the narrowness and the prejudices of the founding fathers, the oppression and suffering of all minority groups, with each competing for the distinction of having been treated the worst by the "Americans."

I believe a more honest picture can be given of our past and present, one into which the facts of ethnic diversity as a constituent part of American life, culture, and politics are introduced. But when each group can make a claim on the school to tell its story and highlight its role, distortion will inevitably enter it. The curriculum, like the voting districts, will be gerrymandered, and though no one yet proposes breaking it up to the point where each and every group gets its "proper share" (whatever that may be), we are already in danger of ending up with such a notion—and sooner than we might think.

There once were—there still are—mechanisms for reconciling the demands and needs in education of the larger community, with the demands and needs of each subcommunity. There was the afternoon school supplementing the common school, and there was the parochial school, which accepted, along with its commitment to transmit a distinctive heritage, the obligation to transmit the general tradition. There is a great deal to be said for these compromises, and we might well think of ways to strengthen them instead of importing the work of the afternoon or parochial school into the common school.

Undoubtedly our children will have a different picture of the American past in 1975 than American children had in 1965. But I hope we will find as many people to be as concerned with the distortions of 1975 as there were to be concerned with the distortions of 1965. Whatever the attractiveness of the phrase, the United States is not, in reality, "a nation of nations," nor do the overwhelming majority of Americans want it to be. One nation was created here, of many stocks. Some have altogether lost their original identities, some retain only nostalgic ties to what they once were, some are close to being peoples in the full sense. This is a complex reality, and it should not be suppressed. But neither should we be presented with a false and distorted picture in which every group is the equivalent of every other and in which our common heritage as a nation is either defamed or made to disappear.

NINA TOTENBERG

Discriminating To End Discrimination

The effort by the federal government to end discrimination in higher education during the 1960s led to adoption by universities and colleges of special admissions programs to aid minorities. Such programs, along with busing, have been among the more controversial and emotional aspects on the recent American scene. In the following essay Nina Totenberg details the case of Marco DeFunis, Jr., a white Phi Beta Kappa college graduate, who was denied admission to the University of Washington's Law School despite having a grade point average and Law School Aptitude scores that were higher than those of thirty-six minority students who were admitted. In reaction to his law school rejection, DeFunis sued the University of Washington, charging reverse discrimination.

The case has bitterly split the liberal alliance of labor, Jewish, and civil rights groups: labor and Jewish organizations have been joined by big business in opposing the efforts of civil rights groups to retain the quota programs at the nation's law schools. It has also created much consternation among white ethnic groups who are especially sensitive about preferential treatment for blacks. They contend, correctly, that they never received such assistance when they were on the bottom. Even the federal government has been divided from agency to agency.

A ruling by a lower court forced the university to admit DeFunis. While complying with this decision, the University of Washington appealed to the state supreme court, which upheld the university's initial action. DeFunis then appealed to the Supreme Court. Totenberg

212

notes that the university has consistently argued that past deprivation by American society has necessitated special treatment for minorities today. In addition, there is a critical shortage of minority attorneys throughout the nation. On the other hand, opponents contend that one cannot use race, color, or creed to discriminate and that this is precisely what Washington is doing to DeFunis.

Shortly after this article was written, the U.S. Supreme Court ruled 5 to 4, on April 23, 1974, that the case was no longer valid since DeFunis was about to graduate in June. DeFunis ultimately graduated in the top 10 percent of his class. The DeFunis case had great consequences in defining for the nation the major constitutional issues surrounding special admissions programs to colleges and universities. The arguments made in this litigation were later repeated in the case of Allan Bakke, an aspiring medical student who was twice denied admission to the University of California at Davis medical school. Bakke contended that he possessed credentials superior to sixteen minority students who were admitted under a special admissions program. In an unusual dual majority opinion, the court announced on June 28, 1978, that Davis's special admissions program was invalid and ordered that Bakke be admitted. It also ruled, however, that programs which protect individual rights under the Fourteenth Amendment can use race as a factor in the admissions process. Hence, colleges and universities will almost surely continue to consider race in their admissions policies, but they will be required to structure loose, informal guidelines rather than those which possess "target quotas."

Nina Totenberg is Washington editor of the New York Times Magazine. *She previously covered the Supreme Court for the* National Observer.

The two men walking across the University of Washington campus in Seattle looked like any two professors just chatting away. But they weren't. They were lawyers. Suddenly, the older, gray-haired man turned to his companion and said, "You know, Jim, if the regents don't let that kid into law school, I'm going to sue the university. It'll be a big case, and I'll take it all the way to the Supreme Court if I have to. And I'll win." The younger man smiled to himself, amused at his friend's saber-rattling.

Three years later, in February, the same two men, Joe Diamond and Jim Wilson, sat on the teams at opposing tables for counsel. The place was the United States Supreme Court, and the case that had been just a seedling in 1971 had blossomed into one of the potential landmark cases of the decade. At issue is the whole concept of affirmative-action programs—programs that give preference to minority groups in such areas as school admissions and employment in order to compensate for past discrimination.

The case involves Marco DeFunis, Jr., a white Phi Beta Kappa college graduate who was denied admission to the University of Washington law school in 1971. DeFunis's college grades and Law School Aptitude Test scores were higher than those of thirty-six minority students—blacks, Chicanos, Indians—who were accepted by the law school. DeFunis claims he was the victim of reverse racial discrimination. He asserts that racial discrimination of any kind is a violation of his constitutional right to equal protection of the law. The university claims that "benign" discrimination—discrimination to aid historically disadvantaged minorities—is within the law. It asserts that without an affirmative-action program to aid minorities, the law school would be "lily white," and that it is the duty of the law school both to provide a diversified student body and to help correct the appalling shortage of minority lawyers in the nation.

However the Supreme Court decides the issue—and even if the Court does not decide it definitively—the case of *DeFunis v. Odegaard* (the defendant recently retired as president of the university) has brought the Court and the nation to a painful point in history. No longer are the choices easy ones. No longer is it a simple choice of a crumbling old schoolhouse for blacks and a sparkling new school for whites; no longer is it a simple matter of a person's dark skin excluding him from a vote, or a drink at the soda fountain, or a job. The heart of American ideology is equality of opportunity and success based on individual merit. From its inception, this nation fought to undo the notion of aristocracy, at least in principle. At the same time the nation was discriminating officially and viciously against blacks and other brown-skinned groups, denying them a decent education, a decent wage, decent housing and, most of all, equal opportunity.

In 1954, the Supreme Court in its historic *Brown v. Board of Education* case pushed the country firmly down the path of racial equality. Since then, the Court, at every chance, has torn down remaining barriers to equal opportunity. But now the Court, like much of the nation, finds itself caught between two of its most cherished ideals. It must decide which is more important: to continue to do everything possible to correct the effects of centuries of racial discrimination, or to remain faithful to the American ideal of a strict merit system.

The question is so painful that it has split the traditional liberal alliance of labor, Jewish, and civil rights groups. Suddenly most of the Jewish and labor organizations are joined with big business in opposing civil rights groups, while the government itself is split from agency to agency. Indeed, the question is so painful that it has, on occasion, brought to the surface usually repressed feelings of racism and anti-Semitism.

DeFunis himself is a Jew, though he does not argue that the university discriminated against him because of that. The reason for all the emotionalism over the case is the accumulated resentment of every white man who believes that a black or a woman was given preference over him in getting a job or a promotion. Business has always disliked affirmative action because it means constant pressure to do this or that, from the government or some other outside group. But now business has been joined for the first time by hard-core labor, predominately white and male, which fears that affirmative action would take its jobs away. Jews have deserted the old civil rights coalition because they see the DeFunis case as a matter of quotas, and quotas are anathema to Jews because they were used for so many centuries to keep Jews out of universities.

Marco DeFunis's journey to the Supreme Court began in 1971 when he was rejected by the University of Washington law school for the second time. A resident of Seattle, he had received his college degree from the university and done a year of graduate work there, while working part-time for the Seattle Park Department. He had been accepted at four other law schools and had just about decided to go to the University of Oregon in Eugene, where tuition would be the same as at U.W. But there was a problem: DeFunis had lined up an office job in a Seattle law firm and neither he nor his wife, a dental assistant, could make nearly as much money in Eugene. They figured that his going to law school in Oregon would cost them about $1,500 a year in lost salaries; DeFunis's father, a furniture salesman, could give them only limited financial help.

Enter Craig Sternberg, a one-time college fraternity brother of DeFunis's who was already a practicing attorney in Seattle. Sternberg offered to help, and spoke to the senior law partner in his firm about DeFunis. The partner, Josef Diamond, was intrigued—partly because the situation offended his sense of rightness, and partly because he had a couple of well-to-do clients who had children not as qualified as DeFunis who were having trouble getting into law school. Diamond took over the DeFunis case. After numerous unsuccessful meetings with the law school dean, the admissions committee chairman, and the board of regents, he brought a lawsuit. Following a trial in a local court, the judge issued an order compelling the university to admit DeFunis to the 1971 freshman class. The university complied and then appealed to the Washington State Supreme Court, which reversed the ruling of the trial judge.

By this time, DeFunis was well into law school; he thought the university would probably let him stay, and wasn't enthusiastic about appealing. After all, being called the "house bigot" wasn't much fun; there were at least a couple of incidents, his lawyer says, when DeFunis walked into the library and encountered a group of black students who pointed him out as a bigot and promptly got up and left. But despite his uncomfortable position, DeFunis agreed to press his case when Diamond noted that the university was then legally free to throw him out. An appeal was brought to the United States Supreme Court, and Justice William O. Douglas issued an order that has kept him in school until the present.

Now twenty-five years old, he is expected to graduate in May. His legal education, however, will be far more expensive than he ever anticipated. Attorney Diamond is not charging his young client a fee. Just costs. But those add up to from $10,000 to $12,000 by Diamond's estimate. Why was Marco DeFunis, this Phi Beta Kappa, *magna cum laude* college graduate, forced to go to court to get into law school? The facts are fascinating and give a rare insight into the admissions process.

In 1971 more than 1,600 students applied for the 150 student slots in the U.W. freshman law school class. The Law School Admissions Committee, consisting of five faculty members and two students, used a preliminary system of ranking students according to their numerical records. A student's undergraduate junior-senior grade point average was combined with his Law School Aptitude Test (L.S.A.T.) score under a formula that was supposed to yield his Predicted First-Year Average (P.F.Y.A.). Applicants with P.F.Y.A.s above 77 were almost automatically accepted. Those with P.F.Y.A.s below 74.5 were generally rejected. The group scoring between 74.5 and 77 was put aside for later review. Two basic exceptions were made regarding P.F.Y.A.s under 74.5: All returning veterans who had previously been enrolled in the law school could re-enroll; and all minority students' files were held for further evaluation.

Marco DeFunis's junior-senior grade point average was 3.71 out of a possible 4. He took the L.S.A.T.s three times, getting 512, 566 and 668; the scores were averaged. His P.F.Y.A. was 76.23—in the middle-ground between 74.5 and 77.

Thus, when the preliminary accepting and rejecting was completed, DeFunis was still in the running, along with the others in the middle

group, a few applicants with P.F.Y.A.s above 77 about whom the admissions committee had doubts, and all the minority applicants. More subjective criteria then began to operate: the quality of the applicant's work in difficult, analytical seminars; his recommendations; the standards of the school he attended; his past employment; his extracurricular activities, and his racial or ethnic background.

The minority students, however, were essentially isolated into a separate class and evaluated in regard to each other, rather than as part of the group as a whole. All the minority applicants considered had P.F.Y.A.s that indicated passing grades in law school but only six had grades higher than DeFunis. Also given some weight among the minority applicants was their participation and progress in one of the Council on Legal Education (CLEO) summer schools. CLEO is a government-funded program, sponsored by the American Bar Association and other legal groups, which provides summer training schools and financial assistance to disadvantaged students seeking admission to law school.

By the time the admissions process was finished, 330 applicants had been offered admission to the University of Washington law school (including 44 minority students); and 150 of them had accepted (including 18 minority students). Of the 330 offered admission, 74 had lower P.F.Y.A.s than DeFunis (36 of these were minority students, 22 returning servicemen, and 16 applicants considered deserving of admission on the basis of other information in their files). But Marco DeFunis wasn't the only high-scoring white candidate rejected; 29 applicants with scores higher than his were also turned down.

DeFunis was not helped by a recommendation written by his college adviser which, while commending him for his goal orientation, worried that he demonstrated "the slight tendency of not caring upon whom he might step in the process...." To what degree this comment hurt him is not known. Moreover, it is possible (though not likely) that there were other factors against him that have not come out. He made law school's waiting list, but he was in the fourth quartile, and only students in the first two quartiles were eventually offered admission. Why the fourth quartile? Richard Roddis, dean of the law school, says, "It wasn't anything negative, but when you are down to shaving things so closely, it's just a matter of his not having pluses other people did." Other school authorities indicated such activities as work in political campaigns and community action programs were considered pluses.

The courts that have ruled on the case agree with DeFunis that some minority students were admitted with P.F.Y.A.s "so low that had they been white their applications would have been summarily denied." But what is pictured as a grand gulf between various P.F.Y.A.s turns out, upon analysis, to be narrow indeed. For example, take a hypothetical applicant who received the same L.S.A.T. score as DeFunis the first time he took it, but who did not retake the test, and who had college grades identical to DeFunis's except that he took four different and more difficult courses than DeFunis, earning Bs where DeFunis earned As; such a student would have had a P.F.Y.A. of 74.46, well below the cut-off point for most whites and almost two points lower than DeFunis's. Thus, the differences among applicants often were minuscule, and the fact that a student was black, or Chicano, or Indian was a big plus on his side. Women, and most Asian groups, were not included in the minority preference program, because they had achieved adequate representation in the student body without any special treatment. Women, for example, represented 25 percent of the applicants but 30 percent of those accepted.

Special treatment, however, is what the DeFunis case is all about. It is such a crucial and emotional issue that more than two dozen friend-of-the-court briefs were filed for and against DeFunis on behalf of more than one hundred organizations. Arrayed on his side are most of the big Jewish organizations, the National Chamber of Commerce, the A.F.L.-C.I.O., the National Association of Manufacturers, and several groups of Polish and Italian lawyers. Leading the pro-DeFunis forces is the B'nai B'rith Anti-Defamation League, which for the past two decades has fought alongside civil rights groups in race cases and now finds itself on the other side. The B'nai B'rith brief, written by constitutional scholars Philip Kurland and Alexander Bickel, socks its point home hard:

> If the Constitution prohibits exclusions of blacks and other minorities on racial grounds, it cannot permit exclusion of whites on racial grounds. For it must be the exclusion on racial grounds which offends the Constitution, and not the particular skin color of the person excluded.
>
> For at least a generation, the lesson of the great decisions of the [Supreme] Court and the lesson of contemporary history have been the same: Discrimination on the basis of race is illegal, immoral, and unconstitutional, inherently wrong and destructive of democratic society. Now this is to be unlearned and we are told that this is not a matter of fundamental principle but only a matter of whose ox is gored.

Kurland and Bickel argue that the University of Washington law school applicants are admitted through "separate, segregated admissions procedures," with the best students chosen out of each group, that the class that entered in 1971 "was in fact two classes... one of minority students and the other of majority students." The two professors go on to assert that "the only justification for use by a state of a racial classification is its use to cure or alleviate specific, illegal, racial discrimination," for example when an employer proved guilty of discriminating against blacks is forced to hire blacks preferentially. But Bickel and Kurland argued that there is no evidence of past discrimination at U.W. to be remedied.

These arguments have plenty of opponents, including most of the nation's law schools and the established bar. Arrayed against DeFunis are the American Bar Association; sixty law school deans; the Law School Admissions Council; the Association of American Law Schools; the Association of American Medical Colleges; dozens of civil rights groups, ranging from the old, established groups like the N.A.A.C.P. to the Chicano and women's rights groups of the nineteen-seventies, and the McGovern labor coalition (including the United Auto Workers, the United Farm Workers, the United Mine Workers, and the American Federation of State, County, and Municipal Employees).

Advocates of affirmative action like to compare the racial situation in America to two runners, one of whom has had his legs shackled for two hundred years. Suddenly, the shackles are removed, but, of course, one runner is still much faster than the other. Removing the shackles doesn't make the two instantly equal in ability to compete. The previously shackled runner has to be given some advantage in order to compete effectively until he gets his legs into condition.

The University of Washington argues that the key to past cases in which the Supreme Court has struck down racial classifications and presumed them unconstitutional is the element of inferior treatment or stigmatization of racial minorities by the majority. It asserts that no such stigmatization occurs in its system of selecting students. The university concedes that some white students may be excluded from law school because of the affirmative-action program, but it maintains that its program is "necessary" to achieve an "overriding purpose"—i.e., to increase the number of minority lawyers in the state and the nation, and to provide a diversified student body that will aid both minority and majority students in their preparations for dealing with a pluralistic society. And, the university notes, had it not been for the nation's history of racial discrimination, white students would have had far more students to compete with than they do now.

Tracing the history of the Fourteenth Amendment, attorney Marian Wright Edelman, on behalf of a coalition of labor and civil rights groups, argues that a racial classification can only be presumed unconstitutional if it disadvantages a group subject to a history of discrimination or held down by special disabilities. She contends that the Fourteenth Amendment was meant to help powerless, oppressed minorities, and that the white majority needs no such help. "One might hope that the work of the Fourteenth Amendment [guaranteeing equal protection of the laws] could be done simply by forbidding discrimination," she says. But "in the real world, the scars of past discrimination have gone too deep...color-blindness has come to represent the long-term goal. It is now well understood, however, that our society cannot be completely color-blind in the short term if we are to have a color-blind society in the long term."

She concludes:

> No doubt, it is tempting to some to believe that the job is over, that now we can relax. The nineteen-sixties are behind us, to be sure. But the task we set for ourselves then will not be accomplished quickly.... From the Congress to the Executive and down to smaller state institutions like the University of Washington Law School, Americans have grasped the tool of affirmative action and have been using it reasonably and effectively. The potential for real progress can now be seen. The question here is whether the Court will now take that tool from the hands of those who have been using it for almost a half decade now.

Also defending the University of Washington's policies is former Watergate Special Prosecutor Archibald Cox, who in his brief for Harvard University asserts that "if scholarly excellence were the sole or even predominant criterion, Harvard...would lose a great deal of its vitality and intellectual excellence, and the quality of its educational experience offered to all students would suffer." Cox asserts that there is no difference between admission programs that give some preference to minorities and others that give preference to athletes, musicians, farm dwellers, veterans, and children of alumni.

Former Solicitor General Erwin Griswold, in a brief for the Association of American Law Schools, notes that college grades and L.S.A.T. scores do not "pick up the factors of judgment, professionalism, or ethics" (a point that is certainly pertinent in the Watergate era). On the need for minorities in law school, Griswold says: "The color of a man's skin in our society still leads to the kinds of prior experience which result in differing perceptions of fact, for we can perceive 'fact' only through the lenses of our own experience." Thus, minority participation is "essential to the creation of a law-school class which can see and walk around and understand legal problems and solutions...."

The N.A.A.C.P. Legal Defense and Education Fund argues that minority lawyers are the most able to perform legal services for the minority communities they come from. DeFunis's lawyers dispute that. As Joe Diamond put it during his Supreme Court argument: "I'm not ready to subscribe to the theory that minority clients are looking for minority lawyers or doctors. I think they are looking for the best-qualified, and not one who matches their own skin color." But minority groups respond that a white or Anglo lawyer is far less likely than a lawyer from the ghetto or barrio to understand the background of a case in those communities, to be able to locate and interview witnesses (often in Spanish or street language), and to gather material evidence.

Indisputably, there exists in the United States today an incredible shortage of minority attorneys. Only 1 percent of the lawyers in America are black, although nearly 12 percent of the population is black. In specific areas of the country, the situation is worse—for example in South Carolina, where there is one black lawyer for every 75,000 black citizens.

As recently as 1965, only 1.5 percent of the law students in the country were black. For Chicanos and Indians, the statistics were even more stark. In California, where the Chicano population is over 2 million, there were only three Chicano graduates from California law schools in 1969. And as of 1969, no American Indian had ever been graduated from the Universities of Arizona, New Mexico, or Utah, despite large Indian populations in those states. (These figures are from the 1970 *Toledo Law Review*.)

Yet while almost everyone acknowledges the deplorable lack of minority lawyers, there is wide disagreement on the remedy. Many see the U.W. policy as raising the specter of quotas. As professors Kurland and Bickel put it in their B'nai B'rith brief: "The racial quota that is involved in this case is of particular concern to the Jewish minority in this country because of the long history of discrimination against Jews by the use of quotas.... After only thirty or forty years of open admissions, the universities, which for centuries set the style in excluding or restricting Jewish students, may again be able to do so."

The University of Washington insists that it has no quota system, that it merely seeks to attract a "reasonable representation" of minority students to its student body. Quota or not, just the mention of the word sends tremors throughout the Jewish community. However, one Jew who makes it clear his sympathies are not with the big Jewish organizations on this issue is Arthur Goldberg. "It is tragic that the two most persecuted minorities should fall apart on this issue," the former

Supreme Court justice says.

Arguments in the case are all very proper and legalistic. Yet, for whatever reason, the whole affirmative-action question seems to bring out the worst in Jews and blacks, and their feelings about each other. One brief filed by DeFunis's lawyers reads:

> The predominance of whites in the university law school may well be explained by a lack of inclination or aptitude on the part of blacks for such studies. Any observant person knows that certain races have certain bents or inclinations. The fact that the heavyweight-boxing field is dominated by blacks does not prove that whites are excluded by discrimination. Anyone who observes professional basketball will note an exceptionally high percentage of the professional players are black.... By the same logic that impels the preference of less qualified minorities to achieve racial balance in law, it might be argued that special treatment should be given to whites to achieve racial balance in athletics.

For an equally embarrassing slip on the other side, one has only to read black columnist William Raspberry in the *Washington Post:*

> The fight against affirmative action programs designed to help blacks and other minorities into the American mainstream is being led by Jews. ... The Jewish-led assaults... reached their current intensity when the equal-rights fight moved from the hiring halls and Government offices to the halls of academe. For a number of reasons, some cultural and some, no doubt, stemming indirectly from anti-Semitism, Jews are on America's campuses—as students and as faculty—out of all proportion to their numbers in general society. And it may be that attempts at making the campuses more representative of the country are seen by Jews as attacks on their special preserve.

With these feelings and facts in the background, it was clearly a special day at the United States Supreme Court when arguments were heard before a packed courtroom. The justices peppered the attorneys with questions, leaving almost no time for the prepared arguments both sides had planned to present. And at one point, some of the hostility obvious in the briefs flared into the open.

The incident arose when DeFunis's lawyer, Joe Diamond, was answering questions and chose to ignore one from Justice Thurgood Marshall, the first and only black justice ever to sit on the Court, who wanted to know what specific qualifications other than grades and test scores were considered by the admissions committee. When Diamond turned back to Marshall, he said, "Now, may I answer your question—I don't remember exactly what it was." Marshall snapped, "You have my permission to forget it."

The rest of the argument was less tense, but equally lively. Justice William H. Rehnquist said to Diamond: "You're not suggesting that a law-school admissions committee has to take the 150 brightest of the applicants, or the ones who demonstrate the highest scores on a test, are you?" Diamond replied: "No. . . . I am saying that they have got to treat everybody alike. . . not treat them as two separate classes as they did here. . . . If Mr. DeFunis had been black, he would have been in. He was kept out because he was white."

Washington Attorney General Slade Gorton, arguing for the university, put his case this way:

> Statistical scores. . . are not invariable and totally accurate predictors of success; nor do they solve the problem of ending the effects of racial discrimination. . . . We feel that in connection with these particular minorities, the fact of discrimination against them. . . over literally hundreds of years, has had a very real effect. It means that fewer of them actually graduate from college, by percentage, than other groups in our society. It means that those who do frequently have lower grade points, and certainly have shown up with lower law-school admissions test scores. So that if we used only these mathematical determinants of admission to law school, we would continue to exclude these same minorities.

Still, Gorton argued, "We didn't admit any of them who weren't qualified."

Justice Rehnquist observed: "When you say 'qualified,' Mr. Gorton, really by the time you've diluted that phrase as much as you have in your approach to admissions, it doesn't mean a whole lot. . . ."

Gorton was undaunted. Not only were all the minority students qualified, he asserted, but they would also "contribute more" to the class as a whole and to the bar, because of their race, than would DeFunis. Chief Justice Warren E. Burger wanted to know if the university had conducted any studies "to determine whether grades had a direct correlation with success and effectiveness in the practice of law." Gorton replied that P.F.Y.A.s "predict nothing about the contribution you will make to the bar," or "to the law school," or "how much income you will make in the bar," or "what kind of legal career you will seek."

Late in the argument, Justice Harry Blackmun asked Diamond a question that was particularly noteworthy because of Blackmun's well-known interest in medical matters. Blackmun wanted to know if Diamond thought it would be proper for a medical school to give preference to medical school applicants who wanted to practice in rural areas where there are few doctors. "At that level," replied Diamond, "I think an affirmative-action program...is good, valid, and I'm all for it...."

The argument continued, and over in the seats reserved for the solicitor general and other government lawyers, there was silence. Not suprisingly, the DeFunis case has also torn the government apart. Solicitor General Robert Bork wanted to file a government brief on behalf of DeFunis, according to administration sources, but was told by the White House that the case was too controversial and that he should keep hands off. Meanwhile, several other agencies were conducting their own little campaigns. According to some reports, the Civil Service Commission, which basically operates on a merit system, wanted a brief filed on behalf of DeFunis, while the Equal Employment Opportunity Commission (E.E.O.C.) wanted one filed on behalf of the University of Washington. The E.E.O.C. actually filed a brief with the Supreme Court, but Solicitor General Bork, in an extraordinary move, wrote the Court a letter asking that the brief not be accepted. His advice was accepted, and the brief was not.

Over at the Department of Health, Education, and Welfare, there also was considerable sentiment for filing a brief in behalf of the university. In fact, Washington Attorney General Gorton and his assistant Jim Wilson were furious that the government did not side with them.

Ironically, while the government was not supporting U.W. in its attempt to preserve affirmative action in admissions, H.E.W. was leaning hard on the university for alleged noncompliance with affirmative action in campus hiring. The university, like 2,500 other institutions of higher learning in the United States, holds government grants and contracts and thus is required by federal law to institute "goals and timetables" for hiring more women and minorities on its faculty. School authorities resent government pressure and are battling H.E.W. over the issue.

Whatever its problems with its faculty-hiring program, the University of Washington is convinced that its admissions program is working well. Out of the 18 minority students who began law school in 1971, 14 are still there. On the basis of their grades and test scores, all but one of the 14 was expected to be in the bottom quarter of the class. But at the end of their second year of law school, six were in the bottom quarter, five were in the third quarter, and three in the second quarter. Of those top three, two had among the highest predicted averages of the minority group, and one had among the lowest.

Thus the university believes that many of its judgments in the selection process have been borne out. Marco DeFunis, by the way, is about in the middle of his class, according to university officials. He plans to go into general law practice when he graduates. Asked if he is sorry he brought the case, DeFunis replied, "That's my secret." (Indeed, DeFunis has kept most of his feelings secret, refusing in recent months to be interviewed or photographed by the press.)

Whatever his feelings, the Supreme Court must now make a decision in the case that bears his name—a decision that the Court can live with, that the country can live with, and that will not offend the nation's sense of justice. Any ruling that would narrowly restrict affirmative-action programs would put an end to the civil rights revolution that began twenty years ago when the High Court for the first time declared school segregation illegal. A ruling permitting "benign" discrimination could eventually come back to haunt the Court, for a survey of the race cases of the past twenty years would show that many, if not most, acts of discrimination were alleged to be done benignly.

Many Court observers believe the justices might wait, declaring the DeFunis case moot, since the controversy will be resolved by the plaintiff's all-but-certain graduation. To moot the case, or in some other way duck the great issues posed by it, would give the nation more time to experiment at the state and local level. Nonetheless, a decision not to decide the great issues now, would, in its own way, be an affirmative action by the Supreme Court to let affirmative-action programs continue unhampered—at least for the time being.

Bibliographic Essay

The following essay seeks to provide students, general readers, and scholars with a synoptic view of the literature relating to the recent resurgence of ethnic awareness. It was not long ago that a listing of appropriate studies dealing with America's ethnic groups would have been relatively short. This situation has changed considerably over the past two decades. While there still are notable gaps in our knowledge of America's ethnic past, there has been an impressive outpouring of books, articles, and reports describing various aspects of group life in America.

This list can only be suggestive. It attempts to give some indication of the major scholarly works in the belief that an understanding of the historical backgrounds of the groups and trends discussed in this volume is necessary. It is from this foundation that recent developments become comprehensible. Where possible, there are suggestions for further reading into the ethnic resurgence, although the amount of writing available here is limited.

Everyone interested in the history of immigrant groups remains indebted to the early work of several scholars. Marcus Lee Hansen, for example, was perhaps the first historian to write with a sympathetic understanding of how the migration process fits into the broader panorama of American history. His *Atlantic Migration, 1607–1860* (1940) was important because it encompassed all the European immigrants arriving during these years and analyzed the full range of factors causing individuals to make the momentous decision to leave. This important volume also provided a very human look at the difficulties of the crossing to America and the problems of adjustment in such a new and different land.

Oscar Handlin narrowed his focus to a single city, Boston, but he covered the ethnic life of that urban area fully. His *Boston's Immigrants* (1941) noted that many different groups settled in Boston, but not all, underwent the same process of adjustment and assimilation. To be sure, each group faced opposition from the native residents, but the Irish came under special scrutiny and disfavor. They were criticized for their religion, their poverty, and their strong attachments to their own customs and traditions. Reacting to this hostility and to other urban problems, the Irish established their own ethnic community. Boston thus became a divided city with the natives on one side, possessing their churches and social groups, and the immigrant community on the other.

Handlin's Pulitzer Prize winning *The Uprooted* (1951) painted its own very special portrait of immigrant life. No other volume conveyed as effectively the sense of what it must have been like for an immigrant to leave the homeland and settle anew in a strange country. His generalized picture of the immigrant experience influenced the manner in which nearly a generation of scholars approached the immigrant question in American history. His view, however, has not remained unchallenged. Rudolph J. Vecoli, in particular, has contended in "*Contadini* in Chicago: A Critique of *The Uprooted*," *Journal of American History*, II (December, 1964) that the unique experiences encountered by each immigrant group must be examined and proper recognition given to the importance of Old World traditions in the new environment.

The reception that foreigners received in America has been critically examined in Ray Allen Billington's *The Protestant Crusade, 1800–1860* (1938) and John Higham's *Strangers in the Land* (1955). Billington focused his attention on the militant anti-Catholicism directed against the Germans and the Irish in particular. Higham casted a wider net to discuss the psychological development of nativism in American society and its gradual culmination in immigrant restriction legislation in the 1920s. He observed that "the kind of accusations which nativists leveled against foreign elements remained relatively constant. The big changes were not so much intellectual as emotional." Winthrop Jordan's widely acclaimed study *White over Black: American Attitudes toward the Negro, 1550–1812* (1968) discussed the formation of racial stereotypes and the impact these views had on African migration. Jordan claimed that from the beginning white Americans viewed and treated blacks as an inferior, backward race. Thomas Gossett's *Race: The History of an Idea in America* (1965) noted that racism affected in an important way the lives of not only blacks, but also non–Anglo-Saxon immigrants from southern and eastern Europe as well. These newcomers faced racial stereotypes that limited their access to the rewards of society.

The literature on assimilation is vast. Perhaps the most appropriate starting point for students is Milton Gordon's stimulating synthesis, *Assimilation in American Life* (1964). Gordon made the useful theoretical distinction between behavioral assimilation (acculturation) and structural assimilation (the deeper acceptance of a group by the host society). This volume also offered a handy review and critique of earlier theories of the assimilation process.

The role of ethnicity in American society after the closing of the nation's gates in the 1920s has been the subject of considerable debate. Scholars have been especially concerned with developments in the ethnic community once it was no longer refreshed by a constant supply of newcomers. Will Herberg's *Protestant, Catholic, Jew* (1955) contended that a "triple melting pot" had been created in America. Whereas the second generation had renounced the heritage of their parents to embrace American values, the third generation, secure in themselves and their place in American society, returned readily to the religious values of their grandparents.

Concentrating more closely on ethnic rather than religious identifications of subsequent generations, Nathan Glazer and Daniel P. Moynihan in *Beyond the Melting Pot* (1963) argued that ethnicity was still very much alive in New York City and that the melting pot simply "did not happen." Focusing on city politics, the authors noted that ethnic groups had in effect become interest groups that exerted considerable influence on political operations. Michael Novak developed the Glazer-Moynihan thesis more fully in his pathbreaking *The Rise of the Unmeltable Ethnics* (1972). Novak detailed the persistence of ethnicity in the social, cultural, and religious practices of America's white ethnics. His book remains today as perhaps the most effective statement supporting a continuation of the new ethnic awareness and calling for a recognition of these legitimate expressions of self-identity on the part of the American ethnic community. In common with Novak, Perry Weed, *The White Ethnic Movement and Ethnic Politics* (1973), found that the ethnic resurgence may have initially gained much of its momentum from a negative reaction to the black civil rights movement. He claimed, however, that it has since become a positive development in behalf of a retention and strengthening of individual heritages.

The vast majority of studies on the American ethnic past has examined individual groups and their historical record. America's largest minority group, Afro-Americans, has been the subject of considerable attention during the last twenty years. The stigma of slavery and the badge of color have created a barrier to a full acceptance of blacks into American society that has yet to be fully erased. Gunnar Myrdal's classic study *An American Dilemma: The Negro Problem and Modern Democracy* (2 vols., 1941) looked at America's racial situation through the eyes of a detached observer. Myrdal believed racial tensions are "in the heart of the American." Americans have been able to express the noble principles of democracy and Christianity on the one hand while they live their daily lives according to personal and local preferences. The historical development of these racial stereotypes and biases are presented in Jordan's *White over Black* and David B. Davis's *The Problem of Slavery in Western Civilization* (1966). John Hope Franklin's *From Slavery to Freedom: A History of Negro Americans* (1974) continues to offer the best overview of the Afro-American experience. The fourth edition of this work discussed the events of the recent black revolution. Nathan Huggins, "Afro-Americans: National Character and Community," *Commentary* (October, 1974), discussed the impact that the ethnic revival has had on the black community in the 1970s.

A view of black militancy in the 1960s through the eyes of a major participant is contained in *The Autobiography of Malcolm X* (1965). This book followed the stormy career of Malcolm X through a troublesome youth to his position as leading spokesman of the Black Muslims. *Soul on Ice* (1968) by Eldridge Cleaver also provided a powerful statement on black determination to rectify the inequities of the past through violence when necessary.

The Irish have received perhaps their most perceptive treatment at the hands of Oscar Handlin in his already mentioned *Boston's Immigrants*. Two very good chronological studies are those of William V. Shannon, *The American Irish* (1963), and John B. Duff, *The Irish in the United States* (1971). Each emphasized the causes for the Irish migration, the difficult period of adjustment, the anti-Catholic prejudice, the role of the Church in immigrant life, and the political wizardry of the Irish. Shannon also noted that the Irish maintained their wit and sense of humor despite the harshness of the American adjustment.

Students interested in the Italian immigrant experience will find that Robert Foerster's classic study *The Italian Emigration of Our Times* (1919) remains the best one-volume treatment. Foerster displayed a remarkable breadth of coverage and sensitivity to his subject, given the fact that his book was written at a time when immigration was such an emotional issue on the national scene. Much useful information that incorporates recent findings is available in L.J. Iorizzo and S. Mondello's *The Italian Americans* (1971) and Alexander DeConde's *Half Bitter, Half Sweet* (1971). Not to be overlooked are Rudolph Vecoli's incisive articles "Prelates and Peasants," *Journal of Social History* (1969), which examined religious accommodations, and "The Italian Americans," *The Center Magazine* (1974) which provided a provocative analysis of the twentieth-century Italian experience. Students should also be aware of two valuable studies of very recent developments among Italian Americans: Richard Gambino, "Twenty Million Italians Can't Be Wrong," the *New York Times Magazine* (April 30, 1972), and Joseph L. Vigilante, "Ethnic Affirmation, or Kiss Me, I'm Italian," *Social Work* (1972).

The Jewish ethnic group has benefited from a large number of excellent studies. Moses Rischin, *The Promised City: New York Jews, 1870-1914* (1970), for example, examined America's largest settlement of Jewish immigrants during the period of the great migration. Despite intense discrimination, Rischin noted that Jews did remarkably well in their adopted homeland. He attributed this to their ability to pull together as an ethnic community as well as to their optimism, diligence, and thrift. Arthur Goren's *The New York Jews and the Quest for Community* (1970) emphasized the drive by Jews to achieve a sense of community in polyglot New York.

Nathan Glazer, *American Judaism* (1972), and Henry L. Feingold, *Zion in America* (1974), are two useful general interpretations of the Jewish past, though the volume of Glazer has been largely concerned with the meaning of religion and religious history in Jewish history. Irving Howe has written a monumental study of the Jewish story from the European departure to modern times. *World of Our Fathers* (1976) embraces the economic, political, and particularly the cultural aspects of Jewish immigration. The liberal Jewish magazine *Commentary* often carries perceptive articles dealing with recent developments affecting the Jewish community.

The Slavic past has recently been the subject of active scholarly interest. William I. Thomas and Florian Znaniecki, *The Polish Peasant in Europe and America* (2 vols., 1918-1921), is a landmark study that still commands respect. Its age precludes any assessment of the second and third generations in America and it does not speak of the recent ethnic revival. This deficiency is somewhat rectified by Helena Z. Lopata's *Polish Americans: Status Competition in an Ethnic Community* (1976) which provided an historical overview of the Polish migration, and Theresita Polzin, *Polish Americans: Whence and*

Whither (1973).

Numerically, Oriental Americans have not been among the largest of the ethnic groups. Their impact, however, has been great, particularly on the West Coast, where the majority have traditionally resided. Two good general studies of the Japanese community are offered in Harry H.L. Kitano, *Japanese Americans: The Evolution of a Subculture* (1976), and William Petersen, *Japanese Americans: Oppression and Success* (1971). Both noted the intense racism encountered by Japanese that only began to abate after World War II. One very clear signal that an era had passed was the rejection by California voters in 1948 of a proposed alien land law which would have excluded Japanese from owning land. The Japanese have made dramatic economic success, especially since the war, but they have also put considerable emphasis on preserving their close family structure and their ethnic heritage. A dark page of America's ethnic past, the Japanese relocation of World War II, has been the subject of numerous studies, the most comprehensive being Roger Daniels, *Concentration Camps USA: Japanese Americans and World War II* (1971).

The recent Chinese American experience has received a sympathetic treatment in Victor G. and Brett DeBary Nee, *Longtime Californ': A Documentary Study of an American Chinatown* (1974). This book is particularly effective in recounting the tensions and frustrations that exist in a modern ethnic enclave. Its message is recounted largely through the use of oral history, and its stress is on the strength of family ties. Francis L.K. Hsu, *The Challenge of the American Dream: The Chinese in the United States* (1971), is a general survey of the Chinese American past. It noted not only the friction between Chinese and the native community, but also described tensions within the Chinese ethnic community. Another useful survey which includes very recent developments is Sanford Lyman, *Chinese Americans* (1974).

Mexican Americans and the Chicano movement have been the subject of an increasing number of studies over the past several years. Joan W. Moore's *Mexican Americans* (1970) with Harry Pachon, is a superior survey of the Mexican American past. She noted that the masses of Mexicans have been "politically inert." They have been reluctant to regard themselves as a minority and, despite pervasive discrimination, to seek redress for their grievances from the government. Only with the emergence of César Chávez and the Chicano movement has there been political mobilization by Mexicans. John Shockley in *Chicano Revolt in a Texas Town* (1974) described the gradual development of ethnic militancy among Mexican Americans in Crystal City, Texas. Crystal City has been unique in that the Mexicans used the political process to seize control of the town's government. Matthew S. Meier and Feliciano Rivera, *The Chicanos: A History of Mexican Americans* (1971), is a brief but informative history of major historical events in the Mexican American community since 1900.

The monumental work of Oscar Lewis, *La Vida* (1965), followed the story of a Puerto Rican family as its members move between the island and the mainland. Oscar Handlin has produced the most scholarly examination of Puerto Ricans in New York City in *The Newcomers: Negroes and Puerto Ricans in a Changing Metropolis* (1959). More recent events tying this group with the ethnic resurgence are recounted in Leonard Borman, "Melting Pot: Spanish-Americans and other Myths," *Library Trends* (1971). A brief survey of the Puerto Rican community from a sociological viewpoint is contained in Joseph P. Fitzpatrick, *Puerto Rican Americans* (1971).

Vine Deloria, Jr., a Standing Rock Sioux, has provided what is perhaps the best known expression of the contemporary "Red Power" movement in *Custer Died for Your Sins: An Indian Manifesto* (1969). This story is continued in Robert Burnette and John Koster, *The Road to Wounded Knee* (1974). The Indian point of view is also effectively outlined in Stan Steiner's *The New Indians* (1968) and Hazel W. Hertzberg's *The Search for an American Indian Identity: Modern Pan-Indian Movements* (1971).

While differing in important particulars from other groups involved in the ethnic resurgence, the women's liberation movement shares many of the goals, desires, and, indeed, frustrations, of the ethnics. At least one by-product of this heightened female awareness has been a body of scholarship aimed at revealing the significant role that women have played in shaping our society. The overall story of American feminist movements has been perhaps best told in Eleanor Flexner's *Century of Struggle* (1972). She discussed, among other things, the development of male attitudes toward women in American society and the impact these views had upon the suffrage movement, family life, and the economic activities of women. The full flavor of the early women's activism is contained in Elizabeth Cady Stanton's *Eighty Years and More* (1970) and, with regard to settlement house work, Jane Addams's classic *Twenty Years at Hull House* (1910). Anne Firor Scott's anthology *American Women: Who Was She?* (1971) is particularly effective in assessing the changing role of women in education, work, reform activities, and the domestic life.

Betty Friedan's *The Feminine Mystique* (1963) occupied an important place in the development of the women's liberation movement. She graphically outlined the yearning of women to move beyond the traditional roles of child rearer, homemaker, and sex object. There must be more to life, Friedan asserted, than the alleged joys of suburban life. Midge Decter, *The New Chastity, and Other Arguments against Women's Liberation* (1972), offered some strong critiques by a woman, against the current trends taking place among women's groups. Also to be consulted is Joan D. Mandel, "Women's Liberation: Humanizing Rather Than Polarizing," *The Annals* (1971).

Perhaps more than any other single scholar, Andrew Greeley of the National Opinion Research Center has attempted to measure and document the character of recent ethnic developments. Much of his research has consisted of opinion gathering, and he has offered in several publications a comprehensive, though at this stage still tentative, assessment of the nature of ethnicity in America. Readers should be aware of his *Why Can't They Be Like Us? America's White Ethnic Groups* (1971) and *Ethnicity in the United States: A Preliminary Reconnaissance* (1974).

The entire question of the impact of federal affirmative action guidelines and "quotas" on the character of ethnic group life is still very much in flux. A lucid and tightly argued statement on the entire matter is offered in Nathan Glazer's *Affirmative Discrimination* (1977). While agreeing that special deprivation in the past may require special considerations today for certain minorities, Glazer deplored the recent HEW trend of imposing quotas on the basis of race. There are many other ways of increasing the number of minority students in professional programs, he noted. In focusing on the up-coming Bakke case, Glazer contended that a ruling against the petitioner "reduces university freedom and leads to state imposition of quotas."

The role of ethnic groups in the American political arena has been ably covered in Mark R. Levy and Michael S. Kramer, *The Ethnic Factor: How America's Minorities Decide Elections* (1972), and Richard Krickus, *Pursuing the American Dream: White Ethnics and the New Populism* (1976). Krickus has explored the historic attachment of white ethnics to the Democratic Party, the current GOP ethnic strategy, the polarization of black-white ethnic conflict, and the reasons for ethnic dissatisfaction with George McGovern in 1972. The lifestyle of the average ethnic voter is examined in "The World of the Blue-Collar Worker," special issue, *Dissent* (1972). Robert D. Swierenga in "Ethnicity in Historical Perspective," *Social Science* (1972), examines the conflicting pressures of assimilation and pluralism through the major historical works of the last thirty years. A range of issues centering on recent ethnic developments are discussed, with varying degrees of sympathy, in "The Rediscovery of Diversity," *Antioch*

14.   As M. Elaine Burgess observed in 1965:

Neither the lower class nor the upper class could have mounted the resistance movement we are now witnessing throughout the South. The former does not possess the resources, either internal or external, essential for such a movement, and the latter is much too small and, very frequently, too far removed from the masses to do so. Such activity had to wait the development of an ample middle class that was motivated to push for validation of hard-won position, thus far denied by the white power structure. The question of unequal distribution of status and power between Negroes and whites would consequently appear as a special case of the more basic problems of order and change. By no means are we saying that all challenges to established social structures or power distributions are class oriented, or directly concerned with relative social position. Nevertheless, it is true that one of the major sources of tension and therefore of change and potential change in the South, as in the broader society, stems from the new middle-class Negro's disbelief in past rationales for inequality and the desire for substitution of new rationales. [M. Elaine Burgess, "Race Relations and Social Change," in *The South in Continuity and Change,* ed. John C. McKinney and Edgar T. Thompson (Durham, N.C.: Duke U.P., 1965), p. 352]

15.   As Martin Luther King, Jr., once observed, "What good is it to be allowed to eat in a restaurant if you can't afford a hamburger?"
16.   See, for example, William Brink and Louis Harris, *Black and White: A Study of U. S. Racial Attitudes Today* (New York: Simon & Schuster, 1966), p. 42; H. Cantrell, *The Pattern of Human Concerns* (New Brunswick, N. J.: Rutgers U.P., 1965), p. 43; and Pettigrew, chap. 7.
17.   See *Report of the National Advisory Commission on Civil Disorders* (New York: Bantam, 1968), and Nathan S. Caplan and Jeffrey Paige, "A Study of Ghetto Rioters," *Scientific American* 219:15-21 (Aug., 1968).
18.   Charles Silberman, *Crisis in the Classroom* (New York: Random House, 1970), pp. 19-20.
19.   John H. Bracey, August Meier, and Elliot Rudwick, eds., *Black Nationalism in America* (Indianapolis: Bobbs-Merrill, 1970), p. xxvi. It is true, as John Bracey has argued, that black nationalist philosophy has always existed among some segments of the black population (see "John Bracey Sketches His Interpretation of Black Nationalism," ibid., pp. lvi–lix), but what available research there is clearly establishes the fact that support for this philosophy increases and declines during certain periods in history.
20.   Killian, pp. 105–6.
21.   Harold Cruse, *Rebellion or Revolution* (New York: Apollo, 1968), chap. 13, and *The Crisis of the Negro Intellectual* (New York: Morrow, 1967), pp. 554–65.
22.   According to Bracey et al.:

The proliferation of nationalist ideologies and organizations that reached a climax during the 1920s was followed by a thirty-year period in which nationalism as a significant theme in black thought was virtually nonexistent. From the thirties until the sixties, with few exceptions, leading Negro organizations stressed interracial cooperation, civil rights, and racial integration. Among the chief reasons for the temporary demise of nationalism were the effects of the Depression and the consequent necessity of relying on the New Deal for survival, and the influx of trade unionists and Communists into the black community preaching and practicing racial equality and brotherhood. The principal ideological concerns of articulate blacks during the Depression decade focused on very practical aspects of the Negro's relationship to New Deal agencies and the Roosevelt Administration, on the role of industrial unions in the advancement of the race, and on the relevance of Marxist doctrines of the Negro's problem [Bracey et al., p. xiv]

23. Founded in the early 1930s, the Nation of Islam became a viable institution around 1950. It achieved its greatest popularity after the late Malcolm X became a convert to the Muslim sect and one of its most influential ministers until he resigned in 1964.

24. Cruse, *Rebellion or Revolution*, p. 211.

25. Bracey et al., p. xxviii. Also see *The Autobiography of Malcolm X* (New York: Grove, 1964).

26. For example, the Opinion Research Corporation survey in 1968 revealed that 86 percent of the blacks in their sample felt that black people should be taught subjects in school that added to their feeling of pride in being black. In their study of black attitudes in fifteen American cities, Angus Campbell and Howard Schuman have found that

> there is a strong trend in the data that is related to, but different from and much stronger than, "separation." It concerns the positive cultural identity and achievements of Negroes, rather than their political separation from whites. The finding appears most strikingly in the endorsement by 42 percent of the Negro sample of the statement "Negro school children should study an African Language." Two out of five Negroes thus subscribe to an emphasis on "black consciousness" that was almost unthought of a few years ago. [Angus Campbell and Howard Schuman, "Racial Attitudes in Fifteen American Cities," in *National Advisory Commission on Civil Disorders, Supplemental Studies* (Washington, D. C.: G. P. O., 1968), p. 6]

Despite the strong sentiment for cultural nationalism in the black community, institutional nationalism—i.e., the efforts of black citizens to gain control of the political, economic, and social institutions in their community and/or to establish separate institutions free of control by the dominant white society— although increasing in popularity, still receive support from only a minority of blacks. See, for example, Brink and Harris; *Report of the National Advisory Commission on Civil Disorders;* Campbell and Schuman; Caplan and Paige; and Gary T. Marx, *Protest and Prejudice: A Study of Belief in the Black Community,* rev. ed. (New York: Harper, 1970).

27. Robert Blauner, "Black Culture: Myth or Reality?" in *Americans from Africa: Old Memories, New Moods,* ed. Peter I. Rose (New York: Atherton, 1970), pp. 417–18.

28. Following Milton M. Gordon, "structural assimilation" is defined as "large scale entrance into cliques, clubs, and institutions of host society on primary group level." Milton M. Gordon, *Assimilation in American Life* (New York: Oxford U. P., 1964), p. 71.

29. As Robert A. Bone has noted, "Even at the peak of Renaissance nationalism the middle-class writers could never muster more than token enthusiasm for a distinctive Negro culture." Robert A. Bone, "The Negro Novel in America" in *America's Black Past,* ed. Eric Foner (New York: Harper, 1970), p. 385.

Moore: Mexican Americans

1. Armando Rendon, "La Raza: Today Not Mañana," in *Mexican Americans in the United States,* ed. John Burma (Cambridge: Schenkman Publishing Company, 1970), pp. 307–26.

2. A full and interesting account of *Chicanismo* of the late 1960s is given by Alfredo Cuellar in "Perspective on Politics" in the first edition of this book (1970).

3. Dial B. Torgerson, "'Brown Power' Unity Seen behind School Disorders," in *Mexican Americans,* ed. John Burma, pp. 279–88; and Carlos Muñoz, "The Politics of Educational Change in East Los Angeles," in *Mexican Americans and Educational Change* (collected papers from a symposium at the University of California, Riverside, May 21–22, 1971).

4.   Statement from F. C. García, assistant professor of political science, University of New Mexico, Albuquerque.
5.   "A Position Paper on the Status of La Raza Unida Party in Califas, Aztlan," August 21, 1972 (mimeographed).
6.   John Shockley, *Chicano Revolt in a Texas Town* (Notre Dame, Ind.: University of Notre Dame Press, 1974).
7.   Michael Lipsky, "Protest as a Political Resource," *American Political Science Review* 62 (December, 1968): 1144–58.

Coming to the Promised Land

1.   This figure may be misleading; it is instructive to note a 1971 Harris poll that showed that 12 percent of the United States population would emigrate if it were possible, or one in eight might leave given promises similar to those held out by the United States.
2.   Bulk of this list is from the *Congressional Record,* June 28, 1971, a speech by Sen. Abraham Ribicoff, pp. S20056–61.
3.   Edward S. Cooke, "Community Relations and the Miami Spanish Speaking Enclaves," an unpublished manuscript, September, 1969, p. 10.
4.   Ibid., p. 9.

Lopata: Polish Americans' Relations

1.   Stanislaw Piwowarski, "Conference Underscores the Difference between Polish Nation and Communist Regime," *Polish American Congress News Letter* 1 (July 20, 1970), 8.
2.   Ibid.
3.   Herbert Blumer, *Critiques of Research in the Social Sciences* (New York: Social Science Research Council, 1939), 104–5.
4.   Louis Gerson, *Woodrow Wilson and the Rebirth of Poland, 1914–20* (New Haven: Yale University Press, 1953), 55.
5.   Zwiazek Narodowy Polski, *60-ta Rocznica: Pamietnik Jubileuszowy, 1880–1940* (Chicago: Dziennik Zwiazkowy, 1940), 27.
6.   Alexander Janta, "Barriers into Bridges: Notes on the Problem of Polish Culture in America," *Polish Review* 2 (Spring-Summer, 1957), 94.
7.   Mieczyslaw Haiman, *Zjednoczenie Polskie Rzymsko-Katolickie (Polish Roman Catholic Union 1873-1948)* (Chicago: Polish Roman Catholic Union, 1948), 433.
8.   Zwiazek Narodowy Polski, 1940, 35.
9.   The assumption that other ethnic groups are better organized and united than are the Polish Americans, and that this contributes to their success in American society, is contained in pronouncements of the leaders of the 'Wisconsin Plan" asking readers of the Polish American ethnic press to support "a candidate of your own choice for a congressional or senatorial seat" (*Gwiazda Polarna* [February 16, 1974], 5.) Although indefinite as to the means by which the "Wisconsin Plan" will accomplish the goal of united action, the appeal for membership contains the following statements:

A more specific example [of united efforts which bring results] is the success story of the Jewish community in America. While small in members, they have become extremely effective through united action. . . . Americans of Polish heritage have built America, obeyed its laws, and contributed toward making it the great nation it is today, but they have been ignored. . . . Our brothers have labored long and hard to correct these injustices, but they have not been successful. Why? Part of the reason is that the average Congressman and Senator knows little about Poland and our problems, and probably cares even less.

10.   The persistence of the idea that there is a national character and that it prevents internal cooperation is evident over decades. Tomczak (1933) states that they are considered clannish by others but that "a queer paradox is observed in this respect. For clannish though they may be, they are still divided among themselves. While distinctions and policies are not very sharply drawn, there is nevertheless an intense rivalry and competition between organizations and between commercial houses" (p. 70). Tomczak continues: "It is said also that the Poles are unable to self-govern, that they are by nature independent and self-seeking, and that their achievements in sciences and the arts are merely accidental and not representative of the people as a whole" (p. 79).

The current president of the Polish American Congress and the Polish National Alliance referred to this "national character" in a speech (Alojzy Mazewski, "The Poles: A National Group Full of Dynamism and Individualism," *Dziennik Zwiazkowy* [October 17, 1973], 5) at a banquet following the unveiling of the Copernican Statue in Chicago: "It has been said and written many times in the past that Americans of Polish origin tend to weaken and fragmentize their strength and potential through internal discords." His argument was that although this "diversity and, at times, cross purposes, were the rule rather than the exception" in Poland's history, the presence of so many representatives of so many organizations and individually prominent Polish Americans in the audience is evidence of their ability to synthesize and reconcile.

11.   The Poles and Polish Americans most frequently mentioned include pianist Artur Rubenstein; conductors Leopold Stokowski and Artur Rodzinski; harpsicordist Wanda Landowska; singer Bobby Vinton; Pola Negri and Gilda Gray of films; Helena Modjewska of the theater; Henry Sienkiewicz, author of *Quo Vadis* and *Portrait of America;* Wieslaw Kuniczak, author of *The Thousand Hour Day;* sociologist Florian Znaniecki; political scientist Zbigniew Brzezinski; political leader Edmund Muskie; former Postmaster General John Gronouski; baseball stars Stan Musial and Carl Yastrzemski; and football players Ed Rutkowski, Larry Kaminski, and Bob Kowalkowski. A recent addition to the list is Jerzy Kosinski, author of *The Painted Bird* and *Steps.*

12.   T. Kostrzewski, "Polish Americans," *Polish Medical and Dental Bulletin* (November, 1938), 18.

13.   Ibid.

14.   *Dziennik Zwiazkowy,* "Poszukiwanie Danych o Stosunkach Polsko-Zydowskich" (October 13–14, 1973), 12.

15.   Thaddeus Kowalski, *Anti-Defamation Guide* (Chicago: Polish American Congress, n.d.) (October 13–14, 1973), 3.

16.   *Dziennik Zwiazkowy,* 7.

17.   *Dziennik Zwiazkowy* (June 29, 1974), 2.

Kitano: Japanese Americans

1.   Dr. C. C. O'Donnell, "The Japanese Must Go," quoted in the *Pacific Citizen,* December 20–27, 1968, p. 2a.

2.   James D. Phelan, "Why California Objects to the Japanese Invasion," *The Annals,* 93, pp. 16–17.

3.   Initial reference to the life of Makino was brought to attention by Paul Jacobs in Paul Jacobs and Saul Landau, *To Serve the Devil* (in process of publication).

4.   Edward Spicer, Asael Hansen, Katherine Luomala, and Marvin Opler, *Impounded People* (University of Arizona Press, 1969), p. 236.

5.   Jacobs and Landau.

6.   *Gidra,* vol. 1, no. 5 (August, 1969), p. 11.

7.   See Harry H. L. Kitano, *Japanese Americans: The Evolution of a Subculture* (Englewood Cliffs, N. J.: Prentice-Hall, 1969).

8.   See Roger Daniels and Harry H. L. Kitano, *American Racism* (Englewood Cliffs, N. J.: Prentice-Hall, 1969).

Index